200 best
ice pop
recipes

D1160524

200 best ice pop recipes

Andrew Chase

Robert ROSE

200 Best Ice Pop Recipes
Text copyright © 2013 Andrew Chase
Photographs copyright © 2013 Robert Rose Inc. *(except where noted below)*
Cover and text design copyright © 2013 Robert Rose Inc.

No part of this publication may be reproduced, stored in a retrieval system or transmitted, in any form or by any means, without the prior written consent of the publisher or a license from the Canadian Copyright Licensing Agency (Access Copyright). For an Access Copyright license, visit www.accesscopyright.ca or call toll-free: 1-800-893-5777.

For complete cataloguing information, see page 247.

Disclaimer

The recipes in this book have been carefully tested by our kitchen and our tasters. To the best of our knowledge, they are safe and nutritious for ordinary use and users. For those people with food or other allergies, or who have special food requirements or health issues, please read the suggested contents of each recipe carefully and determine whether or not they may create a problem for you. All recipes are used at the risk of the consumer.

We cannot be responsible for any hazards, loss or damage that may occur as a result of any recipe use.

For those with special needs, allergies, requirements or health problems, in the event of any doubt, please contact your medical adviser prior to the use of any recipe.

Design and production: Daniella Zanchetta/PageWave Graphics Inc.
Editor: Judith Finlayson
Proofreader: Gillian Watts
Indexer: Gillian Watts
Recipe tester: Audrey King-Wilson
Assorted Ice Pop Photos *(Front cover & photo pages 1, 5 & 8)*
    Photographer: Colin Erricson
    Associate photographer: Matt Johannsson
    Food stylist: Kathryn Robertson
    Prop stylist: Charlene Erricson

Cover image *(from top)*: Baked Plum with Rosemary Ice Pops (page 68), Pure Pineapple Ice Pops (page 79), Cherry Ice Pops (page 40), Red Currant Pink Lemonade Ice Pops (page 21), Kiwi Ginger Ice Pops (page 43) and Papaya Lime Ice Pops (page 85).

Other images:
Blueberry pops *(also on back cover)* © iStockphoto.com/Matka Wariatka; Orange pop © iStockphoto.com/Ryan Notch; GROUP 1: Kiwi pops © iStockphoto.com/Azurita; Coloured sticks © iStockphoto.com/McKevin Shaughnessy; Beach girl © iStockphoto.com/kali9; Girl eating orange pop © iStockphoto.com/Chris Bernard; Boy with striped shirt © iStockphoto.com/Courtney Weittenhiller; Fudge pop © iStockphoto.com/Neil Wysocki; Green, orange, yellow in bowl *(also on back cover)* © iStockphoto.com/Maris Zemgalietis; Kulfi pops © iStockphoto.com/Katherine_mor; GROUP 2: Girl with pink ice pop © iStockphoto.com/Irina Yun; Striped pop (blue sky) © iStockphoto.com/Sieto Verver; Striped pops (plate) © iStockphoto.com/Iuliia Malivanchuk; Blond girl (orange pop) © iStockphoto.com/Steven van Soldt; Young woman (orange pop) © iStockphoto.com/IGphotography; Frosty pops (handles) © iStockphoto.com/Moncherie; Boys (blue shorts) © iStockphoto.com/Clay Cartwright; Banana pops © iStockphoto.com/Matka Wariatka; Raspberry Meringue pops © iStockphoto.com/Lew Robertson; Coconut pop © iStockphoto.com/Lew Robertson; Fudge pops © iStockphoto.com/Lauri Patterson; Pomegranate Berry pops © iStockphoto.com/Azurita; Cranberry and Key Lime pops © iStockphoto.com/Maris Zemgalietis; GROUP 3: Girl with striped shirt © iStockphoto.com/Appletat; Sticky fingers © iStockphoto.com/Stephanie Kennedy; Girl with mint green shirt © iStockphoto.com/Kim Gunkel; Watermelon pops © iStockphoto.com/Matka Wariatka; Orange pop drip © iStockphoto.com/Lee Foster; Young man © iStockphoto.com/Cameron Pashak; Striped pops in glass bowl © iStockphoto.com/GMVozd; Strawberry & Vanilla pops © iStockphoto.com/Jack Puccio; Red, yellow, green pops © iStockphoto.com/Kadir Barcin; Mango-berry pops © iStockphoto.com/Azurita; GROUP 4: Purple pop boy © iStockphoto.com/Melissa Carroll; Three ladies © iStockphoto.com/Peter-John Freeman; Girl in pink dress © iStockphoto.com/AVAVA; Pops against grass © iStockphoto.com/Anthony Rosenberg; Three kids © iStockphoto.com/kali9; Toddler (orange pop) © iStockphoto.com/vitaphoto; Bucket of pops © iStockphoto.com/Olga Lyubkina; Margarita pops © iStockphoto.com/Lew Robertson; Strawberry Lassi pops © iStockphoto.com/Lew Robertson; Avocado pops © iStockphoto.com/Lew Robertson.

We acknowledge the financial support of the Government of Canada through the Book Publishing Industry Development Program (BPIDP) for our publishing activities.

Published by Robert Rose Inc.
120 Eglinton Avenue East, Suite 800, Toronto, Ontario, Canada M4P 1E2
Tel: (416) 322-6552 Fax: (416) 322-6936
www.robertrose.ca

Printed and bound in Canada

1 2 3 4 5 6 7 8 9 MP 21 20 19 18 17 16 15 14 13

Contents

Introduction

✳

What joy, what freedom, what fun and adventure! During my first school summer break, between kindergarten and first grade, my two sisters and I (ages six and a half, four and five and a half, respectively) were finally allowed to cross busy streets together without the supervision of adults. If we had behaved well enough — that meant essentially that we didn't fight too much for an entire day — we were sometimes rewarded with a quarter, in which case we would set off to the nearest corner store to buy Popsicles. In those days our favorite treat cost seven cents apiece (we used the change to buy penny candies). It was always orange or cherry for me, but I recall that my older sister sometimes had the yellow banana-flavored one or the root beer version, which seemed strange to me; I always felt she was wasting the opportunity to enjoy something better. On rare occasions we split the double Popsicles and shared different flavors while we walked up the hill to our home.

My memories of those childhood excursions are vivid. I can still feel the rush of independence and the indulgence that Popsicles represented to three rather mischievous kids. Those moments are frozen in time (forgive the pun) and often recalled some fifty years later. However, while I know that the first taste of a commercial ice pop might transport my soul to those carefree days, the second lick definitely brings me back to reality: my all-too-adult and more discriminating present. Nowadays I want to make better, tastier, more natural ice pops myself.

Fortunately, it's not hard to make your own ice pops. It's one of the quickest and easiest ways to satisfy your family and friends with real homemade treats. Years after our childhood trips to the corner store, our mother bought some simple ice pop molds and just froze orange juice on sticks. In those days it didn't occur to any of us to do more to brighten up the flavor — ice cold and fruity was enough to beat the summer heat. But now we tend to enjoy frozen treats year-round, and we are more demanding about everything we eat, especially things that fall into the category of indulgence. It's precisely because ice pops aren't essential that they should be fun and exciting, extremely flavorful and available in as many varieties as possible. From simple and straightforward to rich and luxurious, the one thing they should have in common is delicious, extravagant flavor.

In putting together this collection of recipes, I have strived to cover all the bases. I pursued delicious presentations of as many different kinds of fruit as was practically possible. I aspired to fully satisfy chocolate lovers and caramel fanatics, to give pleasure to those who love spices and to appease those whose main culinary concern is healthy eating. North American, East Asian, Southeast Asian, Latin American, Mediterranean and Indian flavors, among others, are explored. If you are feeding toddlers and small children, you can offer them healthy "less-drip" ice pops, while their relaxed parents can enjoy adult versions flavored like cocktails.

I am confident that everyone will find some favorite familiar flavors to enjoy. At the same time, I hope you will be enticed to try some of the more exotic offerings. That's the fun of food in our times: discovering new and exciting flavors from around the world while embracing our beloved local and seasonal foods.

In this book, including variations, I've created 250 recipes for ice pops — surely enough variety for everyone. In my opinion, each one is as tasty and fun as the next. So, relive your youth! Indulge yourself, your children, your friends and your family! In other words, enjoy making, serving and eating these ice pops.

– Andrew Chase

Acknowledgments

Once again I must thank my culinary and life partner, Camilo Costales, for all his help. Without his tireless shopping and kitchen assistance and, most important, his tasting and sound (albeit somewhat annoying!) criticisms, I would be unable to produce a book with such a broad scope of good, sound recipes.

I also must give thanks for the generous support of my many neighbors and friends, kids and adults, who helped to ensure that hundreds and hundreds of ice pops were duly consumed and who offered their valuable tasting notes too.

Thanks to my generous publisher, Bob Dees, who suggested this project, to my valuable editor, Judith Finlayson, and to a welcoming publishing staff. Also to the team at PageWave Graphics, especially designer Daniella Zanchetta. Photographer Colin Erricson, prop stylist Charlene Erricson and food stylist Kathryn Robertson also deserve a thank-you. I only wish I could have shared with all of you more of the bounty of ice pops produced during the writing of this cookbook.

I would like to particularly thank all the responsible fruit growers of the world for their fabulous and inspiring produce, without which well over half of this cookbook wouldn't exist. And finally, thanks to the inner child in all of us who still finds the idea of ice pops exciting and fun!

All About Ice Pops

*I**ce pops are** frozen treats on a stick.* This is the definition I have used to mark the boundaries of this book. They are not ice cream or ice cream bars, they are not sorbets or sherbets, and they are not mousses frozen on a stick. Yet this narrow definition allows for a huge variety of delicious frozen treats.

Ice pops can be icy and light or rich and smooth. Some are as sweet as candy, others are mouth-puckeringly tart, and some are even savory. There are many ice pops made from fruit, while others embrace chocolate and cream or nuts and seeds. Some find their inspiration in coffee or tea, others in cocktails or punches. There are even ice pops made from vegetables and legumes.

Ice pops are popular all over the world, anywhere where summers are hot and refrigeration is possible. But no matter what their origin or their ingredients, ice pops are first and foremost *treats*, and they are all made from liquid mixtures that are frozen solidly onto a stick.

Fruit

If you need one good reason to make ice pops, it's fruit. Using the ripest, freshest fruit, you can craft treats that are a frozen expression of a fruit's essence. Like other frozen fruit preparations or chilled desserts, ice pops can give a boost to the natural flavors of fruits, intensifying them through simple preparation methods and broadening them by adding complementary flavors. To develop a fruit ice pop recipe, I aim to get at the heart of the fruit — to enhance, not alter, its essence. Added sweetness, tartness and seasoning are there to highlight the original flavor.

And what an array of fruit there is! From the chilly fringes of its temperate zones to the hottest jungles of the tropics, the world is awash in fruit. That's good news for me, because I doubt there is a single palatable fruit that cannot be turned into a delicious ice pop.

Freshness and **ripeness** are essential. It is important that you find the best fruit you can to make ice pops. No matter how much you manipulate it, unripe or poor-quality fruit will give a disappointing result. Ice pops are a great way to use ripe fruit at its peak, especially in the summer and autumn months, when we tend to get overwhelmed by the quality and quantity of fruit available. Out of peak season, don't overlook **frozen fruit**, which is usually harvested at the peak of ripeness and then flash-frozen.

Lemons and **limes** are particularly important for making fruit-based ice pops. Besides being the base fruit for lemon- or lime-flavored ice pops, these fruits are essential flavoring agents in almost all fruit-based ice pops. The zest of both (as well as other citrus fruits) livens up syrups and fruit purées, and their tart juices balance the natural sugars in other fruits. Balancing sweetness in fruit mixtures with some natural acidity is necessary for good, well-rounded flavor. Always use **freshly squeezed** lemon juice or lime juice for your ice pops; bottled juice just doesn't compare. For other citrus juices, such as orange and grapefruit, freshly squeezed is of course the best, but fresh juice from cartons or from concentrate can also be used.

Citrus zest (rind) is used extensively in this cookbook as a flavoring for ice pops of all descriptions. For recipes that include citrus zest, I recommend using organic produce, which should have substantially fewer potentially harmful residues from agricultural sprays. All citrus fruit should be well rinsed and dried before use.

Citrus Zest

When a recipe calls for citrus zest, it means the colored part of the rind only. Avoid grating or cutting off any of the bitter white pith directly under the zest.

Dairy and Chocolate

After fruit pops, dairy and chocolate ice pops are the largest category in this book. They range from familiar fudge and orange cream ice pops to traditional Indian kulfi and Korean-style melon cream ice pops. Unlike ice creams, which are churned to achieve a smooth, soft texture, dairy ice pops must freeze solidly on their sticks. The texture is icier, with bigger crystals than ice cream. You can, of course, freeze ice cream on a stick, but that's an ice cream bar, not a proper ice pop. All the dairy ice pops in this book celebrate their "ice pop–ness" with their unique textures and flavors.

Sweeteners

Every ice pop needs a judicious amount of sweetening to be palatable. A great many sweeteners are used in the recipes. Plain white granulated **sugar** is perhaps the most common because it is the most neutral in flavor and often the best sugar for clear syrups. However, I have used many other kinds of sugar to take advantage of the wide range of flavors they offer, from moist, dark demerara to clear, light yellow rock sugar.

I recommend keeping several different varieties of **honey** in your pantry, because using different honeys is an easy way to vary the flavor of ice pops. Prepared **syrups** such as light agave, brown rice, malt or maple syrup can also make an important contribution; they improve the texture of ice pops, creating a softer and less icy mouth-feel. In addition, many contribute valuable flavors of their own.

Coatings

If you are so inclined, you can coat the outside of your ice pop, in whole or in part, with various toppings. Chopped nuts, flaked or shredded coconut, candy bits, sprinkles, cookie crumbs and sesame and other seeds are all appropriate coatings. Just dip or brush a solidly frozen ice pop with a little syrup, juice, liqueur or spirit to taste and sprinkle on the topping.

To coat an ice pop in chocolate, you must ensure that your ice pop is fully frozen, so let it freeze overnight. You will need about $1\frac{1}{2}$ ounces (45 g) chocolate per $\frac{1}{4}$ to $\frac{1}{3}$ cup (60 to 75 mL) ice pop mixture. Melt the chocolate in a heatproof bowl over barely simmering water. For a shinier coating that's just a touch softer, stir in $\frac{1}{2}$ tsp (2 mL) corn or agave syrup. After melting, remove the chocolate from the water bath and set aside to cool to room temperature. When the chocolate has cooled, dip in your frozen ice pop to coat. To set the chocolate, insert the ice pop stick in a Styrofoam block or flower-arranging foam and freeze upright until it is firm.

Flavoring Ice Pops

Freezing adds its own challenges to flavoring. Although every recipe in this book is well tested, the sweetness, ripeness and flavor levels of your fruit and other ingredients may vary slightly, so I always encourage tasting and adjusting to taste. However, don't judge the flavor of your mixtures while they are still warm. Wait until they reach room temperature or, better still, place them in the refrigerator to cool.

Here are a few guidelines for flavoring ice pops:

- Err on the sweet side. Freezing diminishes the level of sweetness in an ice pop mixture.
- Use a light hand with spices. They mysteriously gain strength after freezing, so take a subtle approach.
- Pique the flavor with a pinch of salt. If your fruit mixture seems a tad bland, try adding just a tiny pinch. The smallest amount is often enough to perfectly enhance the flavor of fruit.

Use the Best Ingredients

As with any kind of cooking, your ice pops will only be as good as your ingredients. Try to use the best ingredients you can find: the ripest and tastiest fruit, the finest chocolate, the richest dairy products, the freshest herbs and spices. You will be rewarded with standout ice pops — treats that are certainly worth the effort.

Alcohol and Ice Pops

Alcoholic beverages such as rum and brandy are used as flavoring in the occasional ice pop recipe. Because alcohol has a low freezing temperature, when it is used in an ice pop recipe, the texture is affected. I've added a small shot of neutral vodka to a few recipes to keep the ice pops from freezing too hard; if you wish, the alcohol can be left out. Rum extract can replace the flavor of real rum in some cases, as noted in the recipes.

Cocktail ice pops: Where alcohol is an integral component of an ice pop, it's important to keep the ratio down. Alcohol (40 percent/80 proof) should not comprise more than one part in five, or 20 percent of the volume. Otherwise the mixture will not freeze solidly. When making cocktail ice pops, it is best to let them freeze overnight to ensure that they set properly. All the cocktail ice pops will have a softer and smoother texture than those that don't contain alcohol, and you must take some care when unmolding them — the sticks are more likely to twist out and the ice pop will be more inclined to break in the mold.

Embellishing Ice Pops

Given all the recipes in this book, you might be wondering what else you could do with ice pops, but there is always room to gild the lily, so to speak. There are numerous ways of embellishing your ice pops for original presentation, for parties or just for fun.

Layered ice pops: Chapter 15, Holiday Ice Pops, includes a group of layered ice pops to represent certain holidays, but, naturally, you can make layered ice pops of your own invention too. Almost all the fruit mixtures would taste good layered with other flavors, and many of the dairy and chocolate recipes could also be layered successfully. Just pick two or three compatible recipes and halve or reduce the amounts proportionally, or plan on making a double (or triple) batch of pops. To layer ice pops, you don't need any special equipment or even any special skill. All you need is patience: each layer must be well frozen before another layer is added, and it will take at least 30 to 60 minutes to freeze hard enough. So make sure you have the time, and don't forget to add the stick after the first layer.

Added and suspended ingredients: Some people like to add bits of chopped or sliced fruit, whole small berries, candy bits, nuts, seeds and so on to their ice pops (for example, Tapioca Bubbles for Bubble Tea or Coffee Ice Pops, page 149). I'm a bit of a purist and not much of a fan of pieces of frozen fruit or seeds in my ice pops, so I have largely avoided these add-ins. However, ingredients suspended in ice are very attractive visually, so if you are looking for a wow factor in your ice pops, you may want to consider this option.

In general terms, when adding ingredients, stick to add-ins that are directly related to the ingredients in the recipe. For instance, a couple of slices of strawberry suspended in a strawberry ice pop makes sense and looks pretty, as does a slice or two of banana or pineapple in a tropical fruit punch ice pop.

Add-ins can be mixed directly into thicker ice pop mixtures. To suspend them properly in thin mixtures, you must first freeze a layer and then freeze the add-in ingredient(s) in subsequent layers.

Edible flowers and herbs are often added in styled photographs of ice pops, and they look very attractive when frozen. However, flowers may have a wilted mouth-feel when you eat the ice pop, so choose carefully.

Ice Pop Molds

Ice pop making is remarkably simple and straightforward. There are no "trade secrets" when it comes to making these treats.

There are many types of **ice pop molds** on the market. In most things I prefer the uncomplicated and traditional — in this case, nostalgic and familiar round-ended flat ice pop molds. The best are made of durable plastic set in a metal holder, with a metal cover that holds the sticks. Very inexpensive cone- and tube-shaped molds (largely made in China) are available in cheaper, less durable plastic and are easy to use too.

Cooking supply shops sell an array of **silicone ice pop molds**. These are extremely easy to unmold but are usually sold in fairly expensive sets that make just a few ice pops each. **Wax-lined paper cups** (often called "bathroom cups") make simple and useful throwaway molds. These are small cups that hold about 1/3 cup (75 mL), like the kind used in dentist's offices. Make sure they are actually wax-lined or you will have a horrible time unmolding the ice pops. You must ensure that you have a strong, flat base to rest your cups on in the freezer.

Pricey **ice pop makers** that you store in your freezer are also available. The advantage is that they make almost instant ice pops (in less than 10 minutes). However, they can make only a few at a time.

Sticks for Ice Pops

I prefer simple, traditional wooden sticks to all others. I like the rounded tips and the way they absorb liquid so that they expand and adhere securely to the frozen filling. They are cheap and plentiful, feel good to hold, are disposable and biodegradable, and don't have to be retrieved (which is especially important for picnics and for ice pops that will be served to children), unlike the special sticks that come with fancier molds.

Filling, Freezing and Unmolding Ice Pops

Filling the molds: Don't fill them all the way to the top. Leave a little bit of room — at least $\frac{1}{4}$ inch (0.5 cm) — for expansion from inserting the stick and the natural expansion from freezing.

Inserting sticks: The easiest method by far is to leave the molds uncovered and insert the sticks after the mixture has frozen to a slushy consistency (usually after about 90 minutes). Some people soak the sticks in water first to prevent them from floating, but I find that unnecessary, and any extra wet sticks will be susceptible to mold.

If you don't have time to pre-freeze the mixture, you may need a metal lid to hold the sticks securely in the molds, or you can cover the top of your molds with aluminum foil and make slits to hold the sticks in place. Make sure the sticks are straight and stay that way, especially when using a multiple mold with a metal lid; the stiff lid can be very difficult to remove if the sticks are wonky.

Freezing: Set your freezer thermostat for a cold temperature and make sure you have a clear, flat place to put the molds. Most freezers will take at least four hours to freeze non-alcoholic ice pops, but longer is always better.

Unmolding: Quickly run hot water over the outside of the mold and then pull out the ice pops without twisting (which can loosen the sticks).

Storing: Wrap individual ice pops tightly in plastic wrap and store in sealable freezer bags. They keep for several weeks or longer, provided that your freezer maintains a steady cold temperature.

Basic Tools for Making Ice Pops

Large Pyrex measuring cups with spouts are extremely convenient for making ice pops. Not only can you measure your ingredients, if you use a large measuring cup to hold the entire mixture you can quickly calculate exactly how many pops it will make. Also, the pouring spout makes it easy to pour directly into the molds. Most blender containers also have measurement markings and good spouts for pouring, so it isn't necessary to pour the mixture into a measuring cup if it is finished in the blender.

A good, strong **blender** is essential for making some of the recipes. Every brand of blender has a different power capacity, so the speeds vary greatly. Generally, to purée a mixture, start at a slow to medium speed and then move up to medium-high (with a powerful blender) or high speed (with a less powerful model). If the engine is very strong, too much air may be incorporated into a mixture at high speed. For blending mixtures that don't need to be entirely smooth or with small seeds that you don't want to break up, slow to medium speeds (or medium-high on a less powerful blender) are appropriate. Always start blending hot mixtures at the slowest speed and work your way up gradually.

You will also need a strong **fine-mesh sieve** to strain out unwanted solids (seeds, skins, spices and such) as well as to smooth out rougher mixtures. You can use a strong rubber or silicone **spatula**, a **wooden spoon** or a **soup ladle** to push mixtures through a fine sieve.

A good **silicone spatula** is immensely useful, and two are better. I like to use a narrow one for scraping down the blender and a wider one for scraping mixtures through a sieve or getting everything out of mixing bowls and measuring cups. Silicone spatulas are heatproof and nonstick too, so they are good for scraping hot syrup out of a saucepan.

One last bit of advice: **keep a separate cutting board for fruit only**, and rinse it right after use so other flavors will not contaminate your fruit flavors.

Citrus Fruits

Orangeade Ice Pops

**Makes about
2⅔ cups (650 mL)
8 to 10 ice pops**

Orange is the most popular flavor for commercially made ice pops. The good news is, it's a cinch to make your own all-natural orange ice pops, which have a more concentrated flavor and much less sugar. Using citrus zest in the syrup base intensifies the flavor, which is important for frozen treats.

Tip

Use this recipe to make ice pops from any variety of oranges. Valencia, Hamlin, pineapple or blood (moro), navel or pink-juiced cara cara oranges, as well as mandarin oranges and tangerines. Even orange-grapefruit hybrids such as tangelos (Orlando, Minneola or honeybell) work well.

- Fine-mesh sieve

½ cup	granulated sugar	125 mL
½ cup	water	125 mL
	Finely grated zest of 2 oranges (see Tips, page 17)	
2 cups	orange juice (see Tips, page 17)	500 mL

1. In a small saucepan, combine sugar, water and orange zest. Bring to a boil, stirring until sugar is dissolved; reduce heat and simmer for 1 minute. Remove from heat and cover; set aside to steep for 5 minutes. Strain through sieve into a large measuring cup. Stir in orange juice.

2. Pour into molds and freeze until slushy, then insert sticks and freeze until solid, for at least 4 hours. If you are using an ice pop kit, follow the manufacturer's instructions.

Bitter Orange Ice Pops

**Makes about
2⅔ cups (650 mL)
8 to 10 ice pops**

**Marmalade sweetens
and adds its distinctive
bitter-sweet flavor to
these rather sophisticated
orange ice pops.**

Tips

Whenever a recipe calls for
citrus zest (rind), it is best to
use organic produce to avoid
the residue from potentially
unhealthy agricultural sprays.
Citrus fruit should always be
well rinsed and dried before
use. Avoid including any of
the white pith directly under
the zest, as it is bitter. Don't
forget to zest citrus fruit
while it's still whole, before
juicing.

Angostura bitters, available
at all large grocery stores as
well as many liquor stores, is
a famous flavoring produced
in Trinidad. The original
recipe, which includes
gentian and other herbs, was
developed in the Venezuelan
town of Angostura. Orange
bitters are more difficult to
find. Their principal flavoring
is bitter (Seville) oranges, the
main ingredient in orange
marmalade. Both work
equally well in this recipe.

- Fine-mesh sieve

½ cup	water	125 mL
⅓ cup	granulated sugar	75 mL
¼ cup	orange marmalade	60 mL
	Finely grated zest of 1 orange (see Tips, left)	
2 cups	orange juice (see Tip, page 26)	500 mL
3 tbsp	freshly squeezed lemon juice	45 mL
2 dashes	angostura bitters or orange bitters (see Tips, left)	2 dashes

1. In a small saucepan, combine water, sugar, marmalade and orange zest. Bring to a boil, stirring until sugar is dissolved. Remove from heat and set aside to cool. Strain through sieve set over a large measuring cup. Discard solids. Stir in orange and lemon juices and bitters.

2. Pour into molds and freeze until slushy, then insert sticks and freeze until solid, for at least 4 hours. If you are using an ice pop kit, follow the manufacturer's instructions.

Sour Orange Ice Pops

**Makes about
3⅓ cups (825 mL)
10 to 13 ice pops**

If you love citrus fruit
and embrace its natural
tartness, then this
intense orange-lemon-
and-lime-flavored ice
pop is just for you.

- Fine-mesh sieve

⅔ cup	water	150 mL
½ cup	granulated sugar	125 mL
	Finely grated zest of 2 oranges	
	Finely grated zest and juice of 1 lime and 1 lemon	
2 cups	orange juice (see Tip, page 26)	500 mL

1. In a saucepan, combine water, sugar and orange, lime and lemon zests. Bring to a boil, stirring until sugar dissolves. Remove from heat and cover; set aside to steep for 5 minutes. Strain through sieve set over a large measuring cup. Discard solids. Stir in orange, lime and lemon juices.

2. Pour into molds and freeze until slushy, then insert sticks and freeze until solid, for at least 4 hours. If you are using an ice pop kit, follow the manufacturer's instructions.

Orange Cream Ice Pops

**Makes about
2½ cups (625 mL)
7 to 10 ice pops**

Intensely orange and
creamy at the same
time, these are for those
who crave the orange-
flavored cream pops
of their childhood but
prefer a more adult
flavor.

	Finely grated zest of 1 orange	
⅔ cup	orange juice	150 mL
⅓ cup + 1 tbsp	orange blossom or other light floral honey	90 mL
½ cup	frozen orange juice concentrate	125 mL
⅔ cup	heavy or whipping (35%) cream	150 mL
⅓ cup	evaporated milk	75 mL

1. In a small saucepan, combine orange zest and juice and honey. Bring to a boil, reduce heat and simmer for 4 minutes. Remove from heat and set aside to cool slightly. Whisk in concentrate. Pour into a large measuring cup and whisk in cream and milk.

2. Pour into molds and freeze until slushy, then insert sticks and freeze until solid, for at least 4 hours. If you are using an ice pop kit, follow the manufacturer's instructions.

Classic Lemonade Ice Pops

**Makes about
3¼ cups (800 mL)
9 to 13 ice pops**

If you can get your
hands on juicy
fresh lemons, make
lemonade, of course —
or even better, make
lemonade ice pops.
And if you are lucky
enough to get a bag of
Meyer lemons (see Tip,
below), you will end up
with the most delicious
lemonade ice pops ever!

Tip

Meyer lemons are thin-skinned lemons originally
from China. It is thought
they were bred from
crossing lemons with
mandarin or regular oranges.
They have a strong floral
perfume and slightly
sweeter juice than regular
lemons. During the winter
months they are exported
from Florida and California
to most North American
locations.

- Fine-mesh sieve

2½ cups	water, divided	625 mL
⅔ cup	granulated sugar	150 mL
1 tsp	finely grated lemon zest	5 mL
¾ cup	freshly squeezed lemon juice	175 mL

1. In a small saucepan over medium heat, combine
   ½ cup (125 mL) water, sugar and lemon zest.
   Bring to a boil, then reduce heat and simmer
   for 3 minutes. Set aside to cool. Strain resulting
   syrup through sieve placed over a large measuring
   cup, discarding solids. Whisk in lemon juice and
   remaining 2 cups (500 mL) water.

2. Pour into molds and freeze until slushy, then
   insert sticks and freeze until solid, for at least
   4 hours. If you are using an ice pop kit, follow the
   manufacturer's instructions.

Variation

Honey Lemonade Ice Pops: Reduce sugar to
¼ cup (60 mL). Proceed as above, whisking
⅓ cup (75 mL) liquid honey into syrup after
straining.

Grape Lemonade Ice Pops

**Makes about
3 cups (750 mL)
9 to 12 ice pops**

You can use this recipe as a template for other simple-to-make preserve-sweetened lemon ice pops. Try black currant or blackberry preserves or lighter-flavored rosehip jam or apricot conserve.

2 cups	water	500 mL
⅔ cup	freshly squeezed lemon juice	150 mL
½ cup	Concord grape or wild grape jam or jelly	125 mL

1. In a large measuring cup, whisk together water, lemon juice and jam until thoroughly combined.

2. Pour into molds and freeze until slushy, then insert sticks and freeze until solid, for at least 4 hours. If you are using an ice pop kit, follow the manufacturer's instructions.

Rhubarb Lemon Ice Pops

**Makes about
3½ cups (875 mL)
10 to 14 ice pops**

Rhubarb makes a great combination with equally tart lemon in these pretty pink ice pops. Use fresh or frozen rhubarb.

Tip

If your rhubarb is greenish, add a small handful of raspberries in Step 1 or a splash of grenadine syrup to the cooled mixture to give it an attractive pinkish hue.

- Fine-mesh sieve

3 cups	water, divided	750 mL
2 cups	chopped rhubarb	500 mL
½ cup	granulated sugar	125 mL
1½ tsp	finely grated lemon zest	7 mL
⅓ cup + 1 tbsp	freshly squeezed lemon juice	90 mL

1. In a saucepan, combine ⅔ cup (150 mL) water, rhubarb, sugar and lemon zest. Bring to a boil, stirring until sugar is dissolved. Reduce heat to medium-low and simmer, covered, until rhubarb is falling apart, about 10 minutes. Remove from heat and stir in lemon juice. Strain through sieve placed over a large measuring cup, pressing on solids to extract as much juice as possible. Discard solids. Stir in remaining water. Set aside to cool.

2. Pour into molds and freeze until slushy, then insert sticks and freeze until solid, for at least 4 hours. If you are using an ice pop kit, follow the manufacturer's instructions.

Red Currant Pink Lemonade Ice Pops

Makes about 3⅓ cups (825 mL) 10 to 13 ice pops

This is one of two fantastic berry-enhanced pink lemonade ice pops. Make this version when red currants are in season and available at farmers' markets or well-stocked supermarkets.

Tip

Always use freshly squeezed lemon juice or lime juice in your ice pops; bottled just doesn't compare.

● Fine-mesh sieve

3 cups	water, divided	750 mL
⅔ cup	stemmed red currants	150 mL
½ cup	granulated sugar	125 mL
1½ tsp	grated lemon zest	7 mL
½ cup	freshly squeezed lemon juice (see Tip, left)	125 mL

1. In a saucepan, combine ⅔ cup (150 mL) water, currants, sugar and lemon zest. Bring to a boil, stirring until sugar is dissolved, then reduce heat and simmer for 5 minutes. Remove from heat and stir in lemon juice. Strain through sieve placed over a large measuring cup, pressing on solids to extract as much juice as possible. Discard solids. Stir in remaining 2⅓ cups (600 mL) water. Set aside to cool.

2. Pour into molds and freeze until slushy, then insert sticks and freeze until solid, for at least 4 hours. If you are using an ice pop kit, follow the manufacturer's instructions.

Raspberry Pink Lemonade Ice Pops

Makes about 3⅓ cups (825 mL) 10 to 14 ice pops

Raspberries add flavor and color to these fine summertime ice pops.

- Fine-mesh sieve

3 cups	water, divided	750 mL
⅔ cup	fresh raspberries	150 mL
⅓ cup + 2 tbsp	granulated sugar	105 mL
1½ tsp	finely grated lemon zest	7 mL
½ cup	freshly squeezed lemon juice	125 mL

1. In a saucepan over medium heat, combine ⅔ cup (150 mL) water, raspberries, sugar and lemon zest. Bring to a boil, stirring until sugar is dissolved, then reduce heat and simmer for 5 minutes. Remove from heat and stir in lemon juice. Strain through sieve placed over a large measuring cup, pressing on solids to extract as much juice as possible. Discard solids. Stir in remaining 2⅓ cups (600 mL) water. Set aside to cool.

2. Pour into molds and freeze until slushy, then insert sticks and freeze until solid, for at least 4 hours. If you are using an ice pop kit, follow the manufacturer's instructions.

Classic Limeade Ice Pops

**Makes about
3 cups (750 mL)
9 to 12 ice pops**

**Use regular large
(Persian) limes, Key
limes or Mexican limes
for this classic.**

Tips

These ice pops are very
pale green; intensify the
green with a few drops of
food coloring, if you have
no concerns about potential
health issues.

Always use freshly squeezed
lemon juice or lime juice in
your ice pops; bottled just
doesn't compare.

- Fine-mesh sieve

2¼ cups	water, divided	550 mL
½ cup	granulated sugar	125 mL
¾ tsp	finely grated lime zest	3 mL
⅛ tsp	salt	0.5 mL
¾ cup	freshly squeezed lime juice	175 mL

1. In a saucepan over medium heat, combine ½ cup (125 mL) water, sugar, lime zest and salt. Bring to a boil, stirring until sugar dissolves, reduce heat and simmer for 3 minutes. Set aside to cool. Strain syrup through sieve into a large measuring cup. Whisk in lime juice and remaining 1¾ cups (425 mL) water.

2. Pour into molds and freeze until slushy, then insert sticks and freeze until solid, for at least 4 hours. If you are using an ice pop kit, follow the manufacturer's instructions.

Spicy Lime Ice Pops

**Makes about
2 cups (500 mL)
6 to 8 ice pops**

These ice pops are an intriguing mix of fruit and spice. Brown rice syrup or agave syrup adds a pleasant undertone of flavor but will slightly darken the mixture, while light corn syrup is clear and virtually tasteless. Choose the one that suits you best.

Tip

Ground roasted cumin is a useful ingredient to add to your spice cabinet. It has more flavor than unroasted cumin and it's easy to make: In a dry skillet over medium-low heat, cook cumin seeds until fragrant and lightly toasted, about 2 to 3 minutes. Pound or grind into a powder and store in an airtight container for up to one month.

- Fine-mesh sieve

2 tsp	finely grated lime zest	10 mL
2 tbsp	granulated sugar	30 mL
1½ cups	cold water	375 mL
½ cup	freshly squeezed lime juice	125 mL
⅓ cup	brown rice syrup or ¼ cup (60 mL) light agave or light corn syrup	75 mL
¼ tsp	salt	1 mL
¼ tsp	ground roasted cumin (see Tip, left)	1 mL
Pinch	cayenne pepper	Pinch
Pinch	black pepper	Pinch

1. In a bowl, mix together lime zest and sugar, pressing down with the back of a spoon to help release the oils in the zest. Stir in water until sugar is dissolved. Let sit for 5 minutes. Strain through sieve placed over a large measuring cup, pressing on solids to extract as much liquid as possible. Discard solids.

2. Stir in lime juice, syrup, salt, cumin, cayenne and black pepper until syrup is thoroughly incorporated.

3. Pour into molds and freeze until slushy, then, with sticks, stir to evenly redistribute spices. Insert sticks and freeze until solid, for at least 4 hours. If you are using an ice pop kit, follow the manufacturer's instructions.

Grapefruit Marmalade Ice Pops

**Makes about
2⅔ cups (650 mL)
8 to 10 ice pops**

Simply freezing
unsweetened or lightly
sweetened grapefruit
juice will make an
acceptable ice pop, but
sweetening and piquing
the natural bitterness
of the fruit with a little
marmalade makes for
a really different ice
pop with an intriguing
flavor. This is a sure bet
for grapefruit lovers.

Tip

Freshly squeezed grapefruit
juice is always best, but
you can also use juice from
cartons or from concentrate
to make these ice pops.

⅓ cup	grapefruit or orange marmalade	75 mL
½ cup	water	125 mL
2 cups	grapefruit juice (see Tip, left)	500 mL

1. In a small saucepan over low heat, combine
marmalade and water, stirring until marmalade
melts. Strain into a large measuring cup, reserving
rind. Chop rind finely and set aside. Add
grapefruit juice to liquid and mix well.

2. Pour liquid into molds, leaving a little extra
headspace, and freeze until slushy. Spoon a little
reserved rind into each mold, dividing equally, and
stir gently. Insert sticks and freeze until solid, for
at least 4 hours. If you are using an ice pop kit,
follow the manufacturer's instructions.

Kumquat Ice Pops

Makes about
3½ cups (875 mL)
10 to 14 ice pops

These ice pops are a bit more work to make than most of the recipes in this book, but the complex bitter/sour/sweet/floral taste is well worth the effort. Kumquats have a seriously imposing flavor that derives mostly from the rind. The inside pulp is full of pectin, which helps give these ice pops a nice consistency. Blanching helps remove most of the bitterness from the fruit.

Tip

Freshly squeezed juice is always best, but you can also use juice from cartons or from concentrate.

- Fine-mesh sieve
- Blender

8 oz	kumquats	250 g
	Water	
⅓ cup	granulated sugar	75 mL
⅓ cup	orange blossom or other light floral honey	75 mL
1½ cups	orange juice (see Tip, left)	375 mL
3 tbsp	freshly squeezed lemon juice	45 mL

1. Place kumquats in a saucepan with cold water to cover; bring to a boil. Drain. Repeat one more time. Add cold water and set aside to cool. Drain.

2. Cut kumquats in half lengthwise. With a demitasse or other small spoon, scoop out flesh into a large bowl. Set aside rinds. Add 2½ cups (625 mL) water to bowl and, using a potato masher, mash well. Strain mixture through sieve into saucepan, pushing down with the back of a spoon to extract as much liquid as possible. Discard pulp.

3. Add kumquat rinds and sugar to saucepan and bring to a boil over medium heat. Reduce heat and simmer, covered, for 20 minutes. Remove from heat and stir in honey. Set aside to cool.

4. Pour mixture into blender. Blend at medium-high speed until smooth, with tiny bits of rind visible. Add orange and lemon juices and pulse to blend.

5. Pour into molds and freeze until slushy, then insert sticks and freeze until solid, for at least 4 hours. If you are using an ice pop kit, follow the manufacturer's instructions.

Temperate-Climate Fruits

Apple Cider Ice Pops

¼ cup	water	60 mL
¼ cup	packed dark brown sugar	60 mL
2 tbsp	granulated sugar	30 mL
1 tbsp	cider vinegar	15 mL
Pinch	ground cinnamon	Pinch
Pinch	ground allspice	Pinch
3 cups	natural unsweetened apple cider	750 mL

**Makes about
3¼ cups (800 mL)
9 to 13 ice pops**

**All-natural unsweetened
apple cider makes
naturally delicious ice
pops without much
help. All that's needed
is a touch of additional
sweetness and flavor,
which is provided here
by brown sugar, a bit
of tartness for balance
from cider vinegar, and
a pinch or two of spice.**

Tip

Substitute 2 tbsp (30 mL)
lemon juice for the vinegar
and stir into the syrup after
cooking.

1. In a small saucepan, combine water, brown and granulated sugars, vinegar, a generous pinch of cinnamon and a scant pinch of allspice. Bring to a boil, stirring until sugar is dissolved, then reduce heat and simmer for 2 minutes. Remove from heat and set aside to cool.

2. Pour cider into a large measuring cup. Add cooled syrup and whisk well.

3. Pour into molds and freeze until slushy, then insert sticks and freeze until solid, for at least 4 hours. If you are using an ice pop kit, follow the manufacturer's instructions.

Rhubarb Apple Ice Pops

**Makes about
2⅓ cups (575 mL)
7 to 9 ice pops**

Strictly speaking,
rhubarb isn't a fruit but
a vegetable. However, it
is usually used as a fruit
or in combination with
other fruits, and, like
most tart fruits, it makes
an amazing ice pop.

Tip

The refreshing flavor of
rhubarb need not be enjoyed
only during its early-summer
growing season. Frozen
rhubarb, which makes
a perfectly acceptable
substitute, is available
year-round at most grocery
stores.

- Fine-mesh sieve

1½ lbs	chopped fresh or frozen rhubarb (about 3½ cups/875 mL)	750 g
1½ cups	apple cider or unsweetened apple juice	375 mL
¾ cup	granulated sugar	175 mL

1. In a saucepan, combine rhubarb, cider and sugar; bring to a boil, stirring until sugar is dissolved. Reduce heat, cover and simmer for 15 minutes. Strain through sieve placed over a large measuring cup, pushing down on solids to extract all the juices. Discard solids. Set aside to cool.

2. Pour into molds and freeze until slushy, then insert sticks and freeze until solid, for at least 4 hours. If you are using an ice pop kit, follow the manufacturer's instructions.

Variation

Gooseberry Apple Ice Pops: As with most rhubarb recipes, you can replace rhubarb with gooseberries for good results. Whether they're green or red, choose gooseberries that aren't too astringent. Simply substitute an equal quantity of stemmed gooseberries for the rhubarb. Add half a stick of cinnamon or a generous ¼ tsp (1 mL) ground cinnamon to the saucepan while simmering the fruit.

Red Wine–Poached Pear Ice Pops

**Makes about
2½ cups (625 mL)
7 to 10 ice pops**

In much of Europe,
pears poached in
sweetened red wine are
a standard autumn and
winter dessert. It is also
delightful year-round
in ice-pop form —
sweet, rich, fragrant
and refreshing.

Tips

The time the pears take to
cook will depend on their
variety and ripeness.

Choose a good-quality red
wine with a strong fruit
base. For a deep rich flavor,
merlot or shiraz is perfect;
for a lighter touch, try Gamay
(Beaujolais) or pinot noir.

- Blender

¾ cup	dry red wine	175 mL
¾ cup	granulated sugar	175 mL
2	strips (½ by 2 inches/1 by 5 cm) lemon zest	2
1½ lbs	ripe pears (about 4), peeled, cored and chopped	750 g
3 tbsp	freshly squeezed lemon juice	45 mL

1. In a saucepan, combine wine, sugar and lemon zest. Bring to a boil, stirring until sugar is dissolved; add pears and return to a boil. Reduce heat and simmer until pears are very soft, 10 to 20 minutes. Using a slotted spoon, transfer pears to a bowl. Return saucepan to high heat and reduce liquid to ⅔ cup (150 mL). Pour over pears and set aside to cool.

2. Discard lemon zest. In blender at medium-high speed, purée pear mixture with lemon juice.

3. Pour into molds and freeze until slushy, then insert sticks and freeze until solid, for at least 4 hours. If you are using an ice pop kit, follow the manufacturer's instructions.

Spiced Riesling–Poached Pear Ice Pops

**Makes about
2½ cups (625 mL)
7 to 10 ice pops**

Sweet ripe pears and
the distinctive taste of
Riesling wine have a
true affinity.

Tips

You can use either an off-dry
(semisweet) or dry Riesling
for these unusual spiced
ice pops.

Always use freshly squeezed
lemon juice or lime juice in
your ice pops; bottled just
doesn't compare.

● Blender

¾ cup	Riesling wine	175 mL
¾ cup	granulated sugar	175 mL
3	thin slices peeled gingerroot	3
10	black peppercorns	10
2	whole cloves	2
½	stick cinnamon (about 1½ inches/4 cm)	½
1½ lbs	ripe pears (about 4), peeled, cored and chopped	750 g
¼ cup	freshly squeezed lemon juice	60 mL

1. In a saucepan, combine wine, sugar, ginger, peppercorns, cloves and cinnamon. Bring to a boil, stirring until sugar is dissolved; add pears and return to a boil. Reduce heat and simmer until pears are very soft, 10 to 20 minutes, depending on variety and ripeness. Using a slotted spoon, transfer pears to a bowl (returning any spices sticking to pears to the saucepan). Set aside.

2. Return saucepan to high heat and reduce liquid to ⅔ cup (150 mL). Pour through a sieve over reserved pears, discarding spices. Set aside to cool.

3. In blender at medium-high speed, purée pear mixture and lemon juice.

4. Pour into molds and freeze until slushy, then insert sticks and freeze until solid, for at least 4 hours. If you are using an ice pop kit, follow the manufacturer's instructions.

Lemon Rosemary Pear Ice Pops

**Makes about
3 cups (750 mL)
9 to 12 ice pops**

The intrinsic pleasure of sweet ripe pears needs merely a boost of acidity and subtle flavoring to transform them into well-balanced and delicious ice pops. In this recipe lemon juice along with a rosemary-scented lemon syrup, does the trick.

- Blender

1⅓ cups	water	325 mL
½ cup	granulated sugar	125 mL
2	strips (½ by 2 inches/1 by 5 cm) lemon zest	2
⅓ cup	freshly squeezed lemon juice	75 mL
1	sprig fresh rosemary	1
1½ lbs	ripe pears (about 4), peeled, cored and chopped	750 g
3 tbsp	liquid honey	45 mL
¼ tsp	almond extract	1 mL

1. In a saucepan, combine water, sugar, lemon zest and juice and rosemary. Bring to a boil, stirring until sugar is dissolved; add pears and return to a boil. Reduce heat and simmer until pears are very soft, 10 to 20 minutes, depending on variety and ripeness. Stir in honey and almond extract. Set aside to cool.

2. Discard rosemary sprig and any loose rosemary leaves. Transfer pear mixture to blender and blend at medium-high speed until smooth.

3. Pour into molds and freeze until slushy, then insert sticks and freeze until solid, for at least 4 hours. If you are using an ice pop kit, follow the manufacturer's instructions.

Pure Crabapple Ice Pops

Makes about
2⅔ cups (650 mL)
8 to 11 ice pops

In apple-growing areas crabapples are often considered less edible poor cousins. In fact they have a remarkable, intense flavor that can be as good as any fruit. I love crabapples and pick them wherever I can find them (including public parks). They lend beautiful color, flavor and acidity when included in applesauce. By themselves, they have a strong apple-y, tannic tartness that, paired with the right amount of sweetening, can create a rewardingly refreshing and unexpected flavor for an ice pop.

Tip

The blossom end of a crabapple is the spiky part opposite the stem. For this recipe, cut out and discard these knobby bits.

- Fine-mesh sieve
- Cheesecloth

12 oz	crabapples	375 g
2⅓ cups	water	575 mL
½ cup	granulated sugar	125 mL

1. Remove stems from crabapples and, with tip of a paring knife, cut out blossom ends (see Tip, left). Cut into quarters. Place in a saucepan with water and sugar and bring to a boil over medium heat. Reduce heat, cover and simmer until fruit has completely fallen apart, at least 20 minutes. Remove from heat.

2. Line sieve with a double layer of cheesecloth. Over a large measuring cup, strain mixture through sieve, leaving it to drip through for 1 hour. Press down lightly on solids to extract remaining juice. Discard solids.

3. Pour liquid into molds and freeze until slushy, then insert sticks and freeze until solid, for at least 4 hours. If you are using an ice pop kit, follow the manufacturer's instructions.

Variation

Crabapple Mint Ice Pops: Add ⅓ cup (75 mL) more water and 1 tbsp (15 mL) more sugar to saucepan. After removing from heat, stir in ¾ cup (175 mL) loosely packed fresh mint leaves; cover and steep for 10 minutes before straining.

Spiced Crabapple Ice Pops

**Makes about
3 cups (750 mL)
9 to 12 ice pops**

**Dried orange peel —
or even fresh zest —
together with spices
adds a nice warm flavor
to the crabapple base.**

Tips

Dried orange peel is a traditional spice in Chinese as well as Provençal cooking. It is a wonderful flavoring to add to meat and poultry stews and braised dishes. You can buy dried tangerine or mandarin orange peel at Chinese grocery stores, or you can dry your own.

If making fresh orange zest, use mandarin or regular oranges.

- Fine-mesh sieve
- Cheesecloth

1	piece dried tangerine or mandarin orange peel or 2 strips (½ by 2 inches/1 by 5 cm) fresh orange zest	1
12 oz	crabapples	375 g
2⅔ cups	water	650 mL
⅓ cup	packed dark brown sugar	75 mL
3 tbsp	granulated sugar	45 mL
1	star anise	1
2	whole cloves	2
1	piece (1½ inches/4 cm) cinnamon stick	1

1. Cover dried peel in water and soak for 10 minutes; drain. (If using fresh zest, skip this step.)

2. Remove stems from crabapples and, with tip of a paring knife, cut out blossom ends. Cut into quarters. Place in a saucepan with water, brown and granulated sugars, star anise, cloves, cinnamon and drained dried orange peel or fresh zest, if using. Bring to a boil over medium heat, then reduce heat, cover and simmer until fruit has completely fallen apart, at least 20 minutes. Remove from heat.

3. Line sieve with a double layer of cheesecloth. Strain mixture through sieve placed over a large measuring cup, leaving to drip through for 1 hour. Press down lightly on solids to extract remaining juice. Discard solids.

4. Pour into molds and freeze until slushy, then insert sticks and freeze until solid, for at least 4 hours. If you are using an ice pop kit, follow the manufacturer's instructions.

Peaches and Cream Ice Pops

**Makes about
2½ cups (625 mL)
7 to 10 ice pops**

**Peaches and cream are
a classic combination.
Here I've added a few
raspberries to pique the
flavor and improve the
color of the ice pops.
Use the freshest and
ripest peaches you can
find. Out of season,
use thawed frozen ripe
peaches.**

Tip

Truly ripe peaches should
be easy to peel with the
side of a sharp knife blade.
If, however, the skin is a
bit tight, simply plunge the
peaches in boiling water for
about 10 seconds to loosen
the skins.

- Fine-mesh sieve
- Blender, immersion blender or potato masher

2 cups	chopped peeled peaches	500 mL
⅓ cup	water	75 mL
⅓ cup	packed dark brown sugar	75 mL
¼ cup	granulated sugar	60 mL
3 tbsp	fresh or frozen raspberries	45 mL
⅔ cup	heavy or whipping (35%) cream	150 mL
¼ tsp	vanilla extract	1 mL

1. In a saucepan, combine peaches, water and brown
   and granulated sugars. Bring to a boil, stirring
   until sugar is dissolved. Reduce heat and simmer
   until peaches are very tender, about 10 minutes.
   Meanwhile, place raspberries in sieve and
   immerse in simmering peaches until softened,
   about 2 minutes. Using a rubber spatula, scrape
   raspberry pulp and juice through sieve into peach
   mixture. Discard seeds. Remove from heat and set
   aside to cool.

2. Once cool, transfer to blender and blend at
   medium speed until smooth. Add cream and
   vanilla and pulse to blend.

3. Pour into molds and freeze until slushy, then
   insert sticks and freeze until solid, for at least
   4 hours. If you are using an ice pop kit, follow
   the manufacturer's instructions.

Roasted Peach Ice Pops

**Makes about
2 cups (500 mL)
6 to 8 ice pops**

Roasting peaches
concentrates their
flavor so you can make
an unembellished
peach ice pop with an
intensely peachy taste.

- Baking dish large enough to accommodate peaches in a single layer, buttered
- Preheat oven to 375°F (190°C)
- Fine-mesh sieve

1½ lbs	unpeeled ripe peaches (about 5), pitted and chopped	750 g
½ cup less 1 tbsp	granulated sugar	110 mL
½ cup	water	125 mL
1 tbsp	freshly squeezed lemon juice	15 mL

1. Place peaches in prepared baking dish in a single layer and sprinkle with sugar. Bake in preheated oven until fruit is completely soft, 25 to 40 minutes, depending on firmness of fruit. Remove from oven, let cool slightly and mash with a fork. Set aside to cool completely.

2. Strain peaches through sieve placed over a large measuring cup, pressing down and scraping solids with a rubber spatula to extract as much pulp and juice as possible. Pour water into sieve and work any remaining juices from solids into mixture. Discard solids. Whisk lemon juice into liquid.

3. Pour into molds and freeze until slushy, then insert sticks and freeze until solid, for at least 4 hours. If you are using an ice pop kit, follow the manufacturer's instructions.

Variation

Roasted Nectarine Ice Pops: Replace the peaches with an equal quantity of nectarines.

Red Plum Ice Pops

Makes about
2 cups (500 mL)
6 to 8 ice pops

When cooked in a light syrup, then frozen, red plums have an intense flavor that matches the deep red color of this ice pop.

- Fine-mesh sieve

1 lb	unpeeled red plums (5 large or 8 medium), pitted and chopped	500 g
½ cup	water	125 mL
⅓ cup + 1 tbsp	granulated sugar	90 mL
Pinch	salt	Pinch
2 tbsp	freshly squeezed lemon juice	30 mL

1. Place plums in a saucepan with water, sugar and a scant pinch of salt; bring to a boil. Reduce heat and simmer, covered, until fruit is soft, about 10 minutes. Stir in lemon juice.

2. Strain through sieve placed over a large measuring cup, pressing down and scraping solids with a rubber spatula to extract as much pulp and juice as possible. Discard solids. Set aside to cool.

3. Pour into molds and freeze until slushy, then insert sticks and freeze until solid, for at least 4 hours. If you are using an ice pop kit, follow the manufacturer's instructions.

Plum Cobbler Ice Pops

Makes about
2½ cups (625 mL)
7 to 10 ice pops

The flavor of freshly baked plum cobbler is incorporated into these treats. Use whatever plums are in season and at their best.

- Baking dish large enough to accommodate plums in a single layer, buttered
- Preheat oven to 375°F (190°C)
- Fine-mesh sieve

1¼ lbs	black, yellow, red or prune plums	625 g
3 tbsp	butter, melted	45 mL
½ cup	packed brown sugar	125 mL
½ tsp	finely grated lemon zest	2 mL
½ tsp	cinnamon (approx.)	2 mL
¼ tsp	ground ginger	1 mL
¼ tsp	ground nutmeg (approx.)	1 mL
Pinch	ground cloves	Pinch
Pinch	salt	Pinch
1 cup	water	250 mL
2 tbsp	freshly squeezed lemon juice	30 mL

1. Halve and pit plums (do not peel). Place cut side up in prepared baking dish. Drizzle with butter and sprinkle with sugar, lemon zest, a scant ½ tsp (2 mL) cinnamon, ginger, a scant ¼ tsp (1 mL) nutmeg, cloves and salt. Bake in preheated oven until fruit is completely soft, 25 to 35 minutes. Remove from oven, cool slightly and mash fruit with a fork. Set aside to cool.

2. Scrape fruit and accumulated juices into sieve placed over a large measuring cup. Strain through sieve, pressing down and scraping solids with a rubber spatula to extract as much pulp and juice as possible. Pour water into sieve and work any remaining juices from solids into mixture. Discard solids. Whisk lemon juice into liquid.

3. Pour into molds and freeze until slushy, then insert sticks and freeze until solid, for at least 4 hours. If you are using an ice pop kit, follow the manufacturer's instructions.

Persimmon Ice Pops

**Makes about
2¼ cups (550 mL)
6 to 10 ice pops**

Persimmons are often
overlooked as a cooking
fruit, although you
can make delicious
puddings and tarts with
them — and ice pops,
of course!

Tip

You can use any kind of
persimmon for this ice pop:
squat varieties such as
Sharon, Fuyu or Jiro, which
are ripe and sweet when still
fairly firm, or the elongated,
pointy-ended Hachiya or
Kaki varieties, which must
be very soft — almost
mushy — before being
eaten. Just make sure that,
whatever persimmons you
are using, they are very ripe
and not astringent.

- Blender
- Fine-mesh sieve

⅓ cup	granulated sugar	75 mL
⅓ cup	water	75 mL
4	cardamom pods, crushed, or ¼ tsp (1 mL) ground cardamom	4
2	strips (each ½ by 2 inches/1 by 5 cm) lemon zest	2
1	whole clove	1
2 cups	chopped peeled, seeded ripe persimmons	500 mL
½ cup	orange juice	125 mL
1 tbsp	freshly squeezed lemon juice	15 mL

1. In a small saucepan, combine sugar, water, cardamom, lemon zest and clove. Bring to a boil, stirring until sugar is dissolved, then reduce heat and simmer for 1 minute. Remove from heat and cover; set aside to steep for 5 minutes. Strain into blender, discarding solids.

2. Add persimmons, orange juice and lemon juice to blender. Blend at medium-high speed until smooth.

3. Strain through sieve placed over a large measuring cup, pressing down and scraping solids with a rubber spatula or wooden spoon to extract as much pulp and juice as possible. Discard skins.

4. Pour into molds and freeze until slushy, then insert sticks and freeze until solid, for at least 4 hours. If you are using an ice pop kit, follow the manufacturer's instructions.

Cherry Ice Pops

**Makes about
2¼ cups (550 mL)
6 to 9 ice pops**

Unlike artificially
flavored commercial ice
pops, these ones taste
of real cherries — a
beautiful summer treat.

- Fine-mesh sieve

3 cups	whole sweet cherries (generous 1 lb/500 g), pitted	750 mL
1 cup + 2 tbsp	water	280 mL
½ cup	granulated sugar	125 ml
4 tsp	freshly squeezed lemon juice	20 mL

1. In a saucepan, combine cherries, water and sugar. Bring to a boil, stirring until sugar is dissolved, then reduce heat, cover and simmer until cherries are soft, about 20 minutes.

2. Strain through sieve placed over a large measuring cup, pressing down and scraping solids with a rubber spatula or wooden spoon to extract as much pulp and juice as possible. Discard skins. Whisk in lemon juice and set aside to cool.

3. Pour into molds and freeze until slushy, then insert sticks and freeze until solid, for at least 4 hours. If you are using an ice pop kit, follow the manufacturer's instructions.

Variations

Rainier Cherry Ice Pops: Use Rainier cherries and increase lemon juice to 5 tsp (25 mL). Rainier cherries are pale yellow, red-splotched cherries that have a more delicate flavor and are slightly sweeter than black cherries.

Sour Cherry Ice Pops: Use pie or sour (tart red) cherries such as Montmorency or Morello. Increase sugar to ⅔ cup (150 mL) for pleasantly tart ice pops or ¾ to 1 cup (175 to 250 mL), to taste, for sweet ones.

Sweet Cherry and Currant Ice Pops

**Makes about
2 cups (500 mL)
6 to 8 ice pops**

Sweet cherries share the same season as white and red currants, and the tartness of currants adds considerable depth to the sweet cherry flavor.

Tips

White currants are sweeter than the red variety but have a bit less flavor; both, however, are excellent for this ice pop.

Because the cherries are uncooked, make sure they are perfectly ripe and tasty.

- Fine-mesh sieve
- Blender

1 cup	white or red currants, stemmed	250 mL
1 cup	water	250 mL
½ cup	granulated sugar	125 mL
2 cups	pitted ripe sweet cherries	500 mL

1. In a small saucepan over high heat, bring currants, water and sugar to a boil, stirring until sugar is dissolved. Reduce heat to medium and boil for 5 minutes. Strain through sieve placed over a large measuring cup, pressing down and scraping solids with a rubber spatula to extract as much pulp and juice as possible. Discard solids. Set aside to cool.

2. In blender at medium-high speed, purée cherries with currant syrup. Over a large measuring cup, strain through sieve, pressing down and scraping solids with rubber spatula to extract as much pulp and juice as possible. Discard skins.

3. Pour into molds and freeze until slushy, then insert sticks and freeze until solid, for at least 4 hours. If you are using an ice pop kit, follow the manufacturer's instructions.

Tart Cherry Ice Pops

**Makes about
2½ cups (625 mL)
7 to 10 ice pops**

During their fleeting
season in midsummer,
you can make these ice
pops with fresh ripe
tart cherries. During
the rest of the year, you
can make them from
frozen fruit or preserved
cherries imported from
Eastern Europe.

Tip

If you are using unpitted
frozen sour cherries, they
will be too soft after thawing
to pit easily. Simmer them
whole (no need to thaw) in
Step 1 until they are falling
apart. Strain in two or three
batches through a fine-mesh
sieve, pressing through
as much pulp and juice as
possible and discarding pits.

- Blender

3 cups	pitted fresh or frozen sour cherries (see Tip, left)	750 mL
1 cup	water	250 mL
⅓ cup	granulated sugar	75 mL
3 tbsp	dark liquid honey, such as buckwheat, chestnut or manuka	45 mL
2 tsp	freshly squeezed lemon juice	10 mL
¼ tsp	almond extract	1 mL

1. In a saucepan, combine cherries, water and sugar. Bring to a boil, stirring until sugar is dissolved, then reduce heat and simmer until cherries are soft, 5 to 10 minutes. Remove from heat and set aside to cool.

2. In blender at medium-high speed, purée cherry mixture with honey, lemon juice and almond extract.

3. Pour into molds and freeze until slushy, then insert sticks and freeze until solid, for at least 4 hours. If you are using an ice pop kit, follow the manufacturer's instructions.

Variation

Preserved Sour Cherry Ice Pops: Substitute
1 bottle (796 mL) preserved sour cherries
for the fresh cherries. Reserving syrup, drain
cherries to make about 3 cups (750 mL) and
check them carefully for pits. Place in blender
with 1½ cups (375 mL) reserved syrup and
set aside. Reduce granulated sugar to 3 tbsp
(45 mL) and bring to a boil with 3 tbsp (45 mL)
water; reduce heat and simmer for 2 minutes.
When cool, add to blender with honey, lemon
juice and almond extract. Purée at medium-
high speed and then continue with Step 3.

Kiwi Ginger Ice Pops

**Makes about
2½ cups (625 mL)
7 to 10 ice pops**

**A ginger syrup
highlights the exotic
taste of New Zealand's
signature fruit.**

Tip

Green kiwifruit give these
ice pops a really fabulous
look, but for a sweeter and
milder taste you can use
golden kiwis, which make
an attractive yellow ice
pop flecked with tiny black
seeds.

- Blender
- Fine-mesh sieve

½ cup	granulated sugar	125 mL
1½ tbsp	finely grated gingerroot	22 mL
Pinch	salt	Pinch
¾ cup	water	175 mL
5 or 6	kiwifruit	5 or 6

1. In a small saucepan, combine sugar, ginger and a
scant pinch of salt. Cook over medium heat until
sugar has melted into a completely clear liquid
and large bubbles have subsided, 4 to 5 minutes.
Stir in water and bring to a boil. Remove from heat
and set aside to cool.

2. Peel and halve kiwis lengthwise and cut out any
hard cores. Chop enough fruit to make 2 cups
(500 mL). Place in blender, then strain ginger
syrup through sieve into blender. Discard ginger.
Purée mixture at medium-high speed.

3. Pour into molds and freeze until slushy, then
insert sticks and freeze until solid, for at least
4 hours. If you are using an ice pop kit, follow
the manufacturer's instructions.

Concord Grape Ice Pops

**Makes about
2⅓ cups (575 mL)
7 to 9 ice pops**

**Native North American
grapes are full of
rich sweet-and-sour
fruity flavors that
are considered too
"foxy" for fine wine.
Fortunately they make
wonderful desserts,
jams and jellies, as this
ice pop proves.**

Tip

Concord grapes and
Coronation grapes have
very similar flavor profiles,
but Coronation grapes are
seedless.

- Fine-mesh sieve

1 lb	Concord or Coronation grapes (about 3 cups/750 mL)	500 g
1 cup	water	250 mL
⅓ cup	granulated sugar	75 mL

1. In a saucepan, combine grapes, water and sugar. Bring to a boil, stirring until sugar is dissolved. Reduce heat and simmer, covered, until grapes are falling apart, about 10 minutes. Over a large measuring cup, strain through sieve, pressing down and scraping solids with a rubber spatula to extract as much pulp and juice as possible. Discard skins and seeds. Set aside to cool.

2. Pour into molds and freeze until slushy, then insert sticks and freeze until solid, for at least 4 hours. If you are using an ice pop kit, follow the manufacturer's instructions.

Prickly Pear and White Grape Ice Pops

Makes about
2½ cups (625 mL)
7 to 10 ice pops

Prickly pears, the fruit of a desert cactus native to North America, pair beautifully with grapes, especially native North American (*labrusca*) grapes. Like Concord grapes and other native North American varieties, white Niagara grapes often get short shrift, even though they are bursting with fruity flavor and an almost floral fragrance. In the early autumn you can buy these wonderfully tasty grapes to make these ice pops from scratch, or you can use Old World Muscat (muscatel) grapes.

Tip

Use a glove to hold the prickly pears to protect your hand from the sharp spines.

- Fine-mesh sieve

1 lb	white Concord, Niagara or Muscat or other white grapes	500 g
½ cup	water	125 mL
¼ cup	granulated sugar	60 mL
1 lb	prickly pears (about 4)	500 g

1. In a saucepan, combine grapes, water and sugar. Bring to a boil, stirring until sugar is dissolved. Reduce heat, cover and simmer until grapes are falling apart, 15 to 25 minutes.

2. Slice prickly pears in half lengthwise and scoop out flesh. Add to grape mixture and return to a simmer; simmer for 2 minutes. Using a fork or potato masher, mash fruit.

3. Strain through sieve placed over a large measuring cup, pressing down and scraping solids with a rubber spatula to extract as much pulp and juice as possible. Discard skins and seeds. Set aside to cool.

4. Whisk mixture to even out any settling and to oxygenate it a bit. Pour into molds and freeze until slushy, then insert sticks and freeze until solid, for at least 4 hours. If you are using an ice pop kit, follow the manufacturer's instructions.

Variation

"Instant" Prickly Pear and Grape Ice Pops: You can make these ice pops using bottled grape juice, which has a less intense grape flavor. In a blender, combine prickly pear flesh (Step 2) with 2 cups (500 mL) unsweetened white grape juice (bottled or from concentrate) and 3 tbsp (45 mL) extra-fine (fruit) sugar or liquid honey. Blend at low speed until seeds are separated from pulp (do not break up seeds). Force through a sieve and freeze as above.

Watermelon Punch Ice Pops

Makes about 2 cups (500 mL) 6 to 8 ice pops

Incredibly simple to make and very refreshing, these ice pops score high with both children and adults.

Tips

Grenadine syrup is a clear red syrup originally made from pomegranates (*grenades* in French) and now often from a combination of red fruit flavorings. It's what gives this ice pop its "punch" and its beautiful red color. Look for it in well-stocked supermarkets or liquor stores.

If your watermelon has soft white immature seeds embedded in the flesh, then strain mixture through a fine sieve before pouring into molds.

- Blender

4 cups	chopped seedless (or seeded) watermelon	1 L
3 tbsp	grenadine syrup (see Tip, left)	45 mL
2 tbsp	freshly squeezed lemon juice	30 mL

1. In blender at medium-high speed, purée watermelon, grenadine syrup and lemon juice.

2. Pour into molds and freeze until slushy, then insert sticks and freeze until solid, for at least 4 hours. If you are using an ice pop kit, follow the manufacturer's instructions.

Minty Honeydew Ice Pops

**Makes about
3⅓ cups (825 mL)
10 to 13 ice pops**

Ripe honeydew pairs
with fresh mint syrup
to make a lovely green,
fragrant ice pop. This
is a great way to use up
abundant mint from
your summer garden,
just when honeydew
melons are also at
their best.

Tips

Rock (yellow crystal) sugar is
a clear, light yellow sugar in
large crystals used primarily
in Chinese cooking. It is
slightly less sweet than
granulated sugar and makes
a clear, shiny syrup. You
can purchase it at Asian
markets and some large
supermarkets. It comes in
either large, irregular natural
crystals or regular smaller
ones, which are obviously
easier to measure. If using
large crystals, break them up
before measuring.

If you can't find rock sugar,
in this recipe substitute
½ cup less 1 tbsp (110 mL)
granulated sugar.

- Blender
- Fine-mesh sieve

½ cup	rock (yellow crystal) sugar (see Tips, left)	125 mL
½ cup	water	125 mL
1 cup	lightly packed mint leaves	250 mL
4 cups	chopped ripe honeydew melon	1 L
2 tbsp	freshly squeezed lemon juice	30 mL

1. In a small saucepan, bring sugar and water to a boil. Reduce heat to medium and simmer, stirring, until sugar is dissolved, about 5 minutes (if using granulated sugar, simmer for 2 minutes). Stir in mint. Cover and set aside to steep for 5 minutes.

2. Transfer to blender and purée at medium-high speed. Strain through sieve without pressing down on solids. Discard solids and set liquid aside.

3. In blender at medium-high speed, purée melon and lemon juice. Strain through sieve placed over a large measuring cup; do not press down on solids, but shake sieve to strain out as much liquid as possible. Discard solids. Whisk reserved mint syrup into melon mixture.

4. Pour into molds and freeze until slushy, then insert sticks and freeze until solid, for at least 4 hours. If you are using an ice pop kit, follow the manufacturer's instructions.

Cantaloupe Fennel Ice Pops

Makes about 2½ cups (625 mL) 7 to 10 ice pops

These cantaloupe ice pops have a whisper of fennel seed and a touch of lime — all that's needed if you have a truly ripe melon.

Tip

A good ripe melon should give slightly to the touch (particularly at the blossom end) and be heavy with juice. If you put your nose close to the blossom end, the melon should smell as sweet as a tropical flower. A melon without a strong fragrance will have little flavor.

- Blender

1 tsp	fennel seeds	5 mL
½ cup	water	125 mL
⅓ cup + 1 tbsp	granulated sugar	90 mL
2	strips (each about ½ by 1½ inches/1 by 4 cm) lime zest	2
3 cups	chopped ripe cantaloupe or musk melon	750 mL
1½ tbsp	freshly squeezed lime juice	22 mL

1. In a small saucepan over medium heat, toast fennel seeds until slightly darkened and fragrant, 2 to 3 minutes. Add water, sugar and lime zest. Bring to a boil, then simmer over medium heat for 3 minutes. Remove from heat and set aside to cool.

2. Strain syrup into blender, discarding seeds and zest. Add melon and purée at medium-high speed.

3. Pour into molds and freeze until slushy, then insert sticks and freeze until solid, for at least 4 hours. If you are using an ice pop kit, follow the manufacturer's instructions.

Berries

Raspberry Meringue Ice Pops

**Makes about
2⅔ cups (650 mL)
8 to 10 ice pops**

Italian meringue is
a cooked meringue,
which has a thick, silky
texture. It is often used
as a base for European-
style sorbets, but here
I have used it in sweet
and smooth ice pops.

Tip

You can replace the frozen
raspberries with 2½ cups
(625 mL) fresh berries.
Place in a saucepan over
medium heat with 2 tbsp
(30 mL) water and 1 tbsp
(15 mL) granulated sugar.
Cook until berries are soft,
about 3 to 5 minutes. Set
aside to cool.

- Electric mixer
- Fine-mesh sieve

2	egg whites	2
Pinch	cream of tartar	Pinch
⅔ cup	granulated sugar	150 mL
¼ cup	water	60 mL
2 cups	thawed frozen raspberries (see Tip, left)	500 mL

1. In a large bowl, using electric mixer at high speed, beat egg whites and cream of tartar until stiff but not dry. Set aside.

2. In a small saucepan over high heat, cook sugar and water until it reaches the large-ball (hard-ball) stage: 250° to 255°F (121° to 124°C) on a candy thermometer or when it forms a hard ball when a little is dropped from a spoon into cold water. Beating constantly, pour syrup in a thin stream into reserved egg whites. Beat at low speed until meringue is cool, about 2 to 3 minutes. Set aside.

3. Place sieve over a large measuring cup and strain raspberries, pressing down and scraping solids with a rubber spatula to extract as much pulp and juice as possible. Discard solids. Fold in meringue until thoroughly combined.

4. Pour into molds and freeze until slushy, then insert sticks and freeze until solid, for at least 4 hours. If you are using an ice pop kit, follow the manufacturer's instructions.

Raspberry Ice Pops

**Makes about
2⅔ cups (650 mL)
8 to 10 ice pops**

**An intensely flavored
apple juice made from
frozen concentrate
sweetens naturally tart
raspberries without
sugar or syrup.**

- Fine-mesh sieve

3 cups	fresh or frozen raspberries	750 mL
1 cup	water	250 mL
½ cup	frozen unsweetened apple juice concentrate	125 mL

1. In a saucepan, combine raspberries, water and concentrate. Bring to a simmer and cook until fruit is very soft, 2 to 5 minutes. Strain through sieve placed over a large measuring cup, pressing down on solids to extract as much pulp and juice as possible. Discard solids. Set aside to cool.

2. Pour into molds and freeze until slushy, then insert sticks and freeze until solid, for at least 4 hours. If you are using an ice pop kit, follow the manufacturer's instructions.

Strawberry Ice Pops

**Makes about
3 cups (750 mL)
9 to 12 ice pops**

**Strawberries are
versatile fruits that
readily embrace many
added flavors, but when
fresh berries are at
their peak, they need
little help to shine. You
can use thawed frozen
strawberries here.**

Tip

I prefer to strain the fine seeds out of the mix before freezing.

- Blender

4 cups	chopped hulled strawberries	1 L
½ cup	water	125 mL
¼ cup	brown rice syrup or 3 tbsp (45 mL) agave or corn syrup	60 mL
3 tbsp	extra-fine (fruit) sugar or granulated sugar	45 mL
2 tbsp	freshly squeezed lemon juice	30 mL

1. In blender at medium speed, purée strawberries, water, syrup, sugar and lemon juice, ensuring that sugar is fully dissolved. Pass through a fine-mesh sieve, if desired (see Tip, left).

2. Pour into molds and freeze until slushy, then insert sticks and freeze until solid, for at least 4 hours. If you are using an ice pop kit, follow the manufacturer's instructions.

Strawberry Banana Ice Pops

**Makes about
2¼ cups (550 mL)
6 to 9 ice pops**

Cooler climates meet
the tropics in this fruit
combo — although
there actually are
adjacent temperate
and subtropical zones,
such as Florida, where
both strawberries and
bananas can be grown
quite successfully.
Whether your bananas
and strawberries are
imported or grown
locally, you'll love this
ice pop.

- Blender

⅓ cup	water	75 mL
¼ cup	packed dark brown sugar	60 mL
2 cups	halved hulled ripe strawberries	500 mL
1 cup	sliced ripe banana (1 large)	250 mL
2 tbsp	freshly squeezed lime juice	30 mL
1 tbsp	dark rum or scant ½ tsp (2 mL) rum extract	15 mL

1. In a small saucepan, bring water and sugar to a boil, stirring until sugar is dissolved. Add strawberries and return to a boil, then remove from heat. Set aside to cool.

2. In blender at medium speed, purée strawberry mixture, banana, lime juice and rum.

3. Pour into molds and freeze until slushy, then insert sticks and freeze until solid, for at least 4 hours. If you are using an ice pop kit, follow the manufacturer's instructions.

Wild Blueberry Ice Pops

**Makes about
3 cups (750 mL)
9 to 12 ice pops**

Wild blueberries are smaller and have a more intense flavor than cultivated varieties. If you don't pick your own or live in a place where fresh wild blueberries are common, frozen ones are easy to find. They are just as good as fresh for these ice pops.

Tip

If you have access to blueberry honey, which can be difficult to find, use it to replace the syrup. Blueberry honey has medium body, full flavor and a subtle blueberry aftertaste.

- Fine-mesh sieve

3 cups	wild blueberries	750 mL
1 cup	water	250 mL
1/3 cup	apple juice concentrate	75 mL
1/4 cup	light agave, corn syrup or honey, or 1/3 cup (75 mL) brown rice syrup (see Tip, left)	60 mL
2 tbsp	freshly squeezed lemon juice	30 mL

1. In a saucepan, combine blueberries, water, apple juice concentrate, syrup and lemon juice. Bring to a boil, then reduce heat and simmer, stirring often, until fruit is falling apart, about 3 minutes for frozen fruit or up to 8 minutes for fresh. Strain through sieve placed over a large measuring cup, pressing down on solids with a rubber spatula to extract as much pulp and juice as possible. Discard solids. Set aside to cool.

2. Pour into molds and freeze until slushy, then insert sticks and freeze until solid, for at least 4 hours. If you are using an ice pop kit, follow the manufacturer's instructions.

Blueberry Lemon Yogurt Swirl Ice Pops

**Makes about
2⅔ cups (650 mL)
8 to 10 ice pops**

White swirls of honey-sweetened yogurt dance around a lively blueberry and lemon mixture — simple and pretty. Blueberry honey is naturally the perfect honey to use for these ice pops.

Tip

Blueberry honey is fairly rare, but it is perfect in these ice pops. It has medium body, full flavor and a subtle blueberry aftertaste. If unavailable, any medium- to light-bodied honey will suffice.

- Blender

⅓ cup	granulated sugar	75 mL
⅓ cup	water	75 mL
	Finely grated zest of 1 lemon	
2 cups	blueberries, thawed if frozen	500 mL
¼ cup	freshly squeezed lemon juice	60 mL
¾ cup	Greek- or Balkan-style yogurt or drained plain yogurt	175 mL
¼ cup	blueberry honey or other liquid honey (see Tip, left)	60 mL

1. In a small saucepan, bring sugar, water and lemon zest to a boil, stirring until sugar is dissolved; reduce heat and simmer for 2 minutes. Set aside to cool. Pour into blender and add blueberries and lemon juice. Blend at medium to medium-high speed until smooth.

2. In a measuring cup, whisk together yogurt and honey.

3. Fill molds to two-thirds full with blueberry mixture. Top each with yogurt mixture. Using a stick or narrow knife, carefully swirl yogurt mixture into blueberry mixture, leaving it streaky. Freeze until solid, for at least 4 hours. If you are using an ice pop kit, follow the manufacturer's instructions.

Blackberry Ice Pops

**Makes about
2⅓ cups (575 mL)
7 to 9 ice pops**

Blackberries are one of
the real pleasures of late
summer. Their intensity
has always made them
popular for sweets,
and ice pops are no
exception.

- Blender
- Fine-mesh sieve

1 lb	blackberries (4 cups/1 L)	500 g
1⅓ cups	unsweetened apple juice	325 mL
⅓ cup	granulated sugar	75 mL
1 tbsp	freshly squeezed lemon juice	15 mL

1. In blender at medium speed, blend blackberries and apple juice until mostly liquid and berries are completely broken up. Scrape into a saucepan and add sugar; stir until dissolved. Bring to a boil and immediately remove from heat. Set aside to cool slightly.

2. Over a large measuring cup, strain blackberry mixture through sieve, pressing down and scraping solids with a rubber spatula to extract as much pulp and juice as possible. Discard seeds. Stir in lemon juice.

3. Pour into molds and freeze until slushy, then insert sticks and freeze until solid, for at least 4 hours. If you are using an ice pop kit, follow the manufacturer's instructions.

Red Berry Ice Pops

**Makes about
2 cups (500 mL)
6 to 8 ice pops**

Raspberries and red
currants share the
limelight in these red
and fruity, satisfyingly
tart ice pops.

- Fine-mesh sieve
- Blender

1 cup	red currants, stemmed	250 mL
1 cup	water	250 mL
½ cup	granulated sugar	125 mL
2 cups	raspberries	500 mL

1. In a small saucepan over high heat, combine currants, water and sugar. Bring to a boil, stirring until sugar is dissolved, then reduce heat to medium and boil for 5 minutes. Strain through sieve, pressing down and scraping solids with a rubber spatula to extract as much pulp and juice as possible. Discard seeds and skins.

2. In blender at medium speed, purée raspberries and red currant syrup. Over a large measuring cup, strain through sieve, pressing down and scraping solids to extract as much pulp and juice as possible. Discard seeds.

3. Pour into molds and freeze until slushy, then insert sticks and freeze until solid, for at least 4 hours. If you are using an ice pop kit, follow the manufacturer's instructions.

Variation

Blueberry and Currant Ice Pops: Use either red or white currants and replace the raspberries with blueberries. After puréeing the blueberries with the strained currant syrup, you do not need to strain the mixture again — just pour it directly into the molds.

Pink Gooseberry Ice Pops

**Makes 2 cups
(500 mL)
6 to 8 ice pops**

**Ripe red gooseberries,
with their irresistibly
fresh, tart-sweet flavor,
make a really fantastic
ice pop with a very
pretty pink hue.**

Tip

You can also make this
ice pop with green
gooseberries, which are a bit
more tart; just add an extra
tablespoon (15 mL) of sugar.

- Fine-mesh sieve

2 cups	ripe red gooseberries (12 oz/375 g)	500 mL
1 cup	water	250 mL
1/3 cup	granulated sugar	75 mL
1	cinnamon stick (about 3 inches/8 cm)	1
2 tbsp	grenadine syrup	30 mL

1. In a saucepan, combine gooseberries, water, sugar and cinnamon. Bring to a boil, stirring until sugar is dissolved. Reduce heat, cover and simmer until berries are falling apart, about 5 minutes. Set aside to cool.

2. Over a large measuring cup, strain gooseberry mixture through sieve, pressing down and scraping solids with a rubber spatula to extract as much pulp and juice as possible. Discard skins and seeds. Stir in grenadine syrup.

3. Pour into molds and freeze until slushy, then insert sticks and freeze until solid, for at least 4 hours. If you are using an ice pop kit, follow the manufacturer's instructions.

Blackcurrant Ice Pops

**Makes about
2½ cups (625 mL)
7 to 10 ice pops**

Raw black currants have
a deep, rich purple color
and an intense fruity
flavor with a strong dose
of acidity. Their taste
also has a characteristic
"foxy" note that some
people find a bit off-
putting, but a quick
cooking removes that
flavor without losing
any freshness.

Tip

Always use freshly squeezed
lemon juice or lime juice in
your ice pops; bottled just
doesn't compare.

- Blender or immersion blender
- Fine-mesh sieve

2 cups	black currants	500 mL
1½ cups	water	375 mL
½ cup + 1 tbsp	granulated sugar	140 mL
3 tbsp	freshly squeezed lemon juice	45 mL

1. In a saucepan, bring blackcurrants, water and
   sugar just to a boil, stirring until sugar is dissolved.
   Immediately remove from heat and set aside to
   cool.

2. Blend mixture at medium to medium-high speed
   until smooth. Strain through sieve placed over a
   large measuring cup, pressing down on solids with
   a rubber spatula to extract as much pulp and juice
   as possible. Discard seeds and other solids. Stir in
   lemon juice.

3. Pour into molds and freeze until slushy, then
   insert sticks and freeze until solid, for at least
   4 hours. If you are using an ice pop kit, follow
   the manufacturer's instructions.

Red Currant Ice Pops

**Makes about
2¼ cups (550 mL)
6 to 9 ice pops**

I love red currants.
Many people overlook
them in favor of sweeter
fruits or use them only
in combination with
other fruits, but fresh
red currants have such
a deliciously distinctive
and unashamedly tart
flavor — and their
midsummer season is
so fleeting — that I don't
think you should miss
them in their purest
form. With that in
mind, here is a brilliant
red and refreshingly
sweet-tart ice pop that
proudly proclaims
its unadulterated
"redcurrantness"!

- Fine-mesh sieve

2 cups	stemmed red currants	500 mL
1½ cups	water	375 mL
⅔ cup	granulated sugar	150 mL
¼ cup	light corn or light agave syrup	60 mL

1. In a saucepan, bring red currants, water and sugar to a boil, stirring until sugar is dissolved. Reduce heat and simmer until fruit is completely soft, about 5 minutes.

2. Strain through sieve placed over a large measuring cup, pressing down on solids with a rubber spatula to extract as much pulp and juice as possible. Discard solids. Stir in syrup and set aside to cool.

3. Pour into molds and freeze until slushy, then insert sticks and freeze until solid, for at least 4 hours. If you are using an ice pop kit, follow the manufacturer's instructions.

White Currant and Strawberry Ice Pops

Makes about
2½ cups (625 mL)
7 to 9 ice pops

White currants and strawberries come to perfect ripeness at the same time in midsummer, and they make a beautiful couple. Look for sweet local varieties of strawberries for the best pairing with the jewel-like white currants.

Tip

In many ice pops that include solid ingredients or combine liquids of different viscosities, there is a bit of layering after freezing, which is normal. However, if you want a seamless result, give the mixture a stir after it has reached the slushy stage to ensure the ingredients remain integrated.

- Fine-mesh sieve
- Blender

1½ cups	stemmed white currants	375 mL
1 cup	water	250 mL
¾ cup	granulated sugar	175 mL
3 cups	halved hulled strawberries	750 mL

1. In a saucepan, bring white currants, water and sugar to a boil, stirring until sugar is dissolved. Reduce heat and simmer until fruit is completely soft, about 5 minutes.

2. Strain through sieve placed over a large measuring cup, pressing down on solids with a rubber spatula to extract as much pulp and juice as possible. Discard solids. Set aside to cool.

3. In blender at medium to medium-high speed, purée strawberries and white currant syrup.

4. Pour into molds and freeze until slushy, then insert sticks and freeze until solid, for at least 4 hours. If you are using an ice pop kit, follow the manufacturer's instructions.

Cranberry Ice Pops

Makes about 2⅔ cups (650 mL) 8 to 10 ice pops

This is an ice pop for true cranberry lovers.

Tip

This deep red pop is pleasantly but decidedly on the tart side. If you prefer a sweet ice pop, increase the sugar to ½ cup (125 mL).

- Fine-mesh sieve

3 cups	fresh or frozen cranberries	750 mL
2 cups	apple juice or apple cider	500 mL
⅓ cup	granulated sugar	75 mL
1 tsp	finely grated orange zest	5 mL

1. In a saucepan, combine cranberries, apple juice, sugar and orange zest. Bring to a boil, stirring until sugar is dissolved. Reduce heat and simmer, covered, until berries are falling apart, about 15 minutes for fresh berries and 10 minutes for frozen.

2. Strain through sieve placed over a large measuring cup, pressing down on solids with a rubber spatula to extract as much pulp and juice as possible. Discard solids. Set aside to cool.

3. Pour into molds and freeze until slushy, then insert sticks and freeze until solid, for at least 4 hours. If you are using an ice pop kit, follow the manufacturer's instructions.

Spiced Cranberry Orange Ice Pops

Makes about 2½ cups (625 mL)
7 to 10 ice pops

These ice pops are like a frozen cranberry chutney, rich with fruit flavors and warm spices.

Tip

The spiced flavor of these cranberry ice pops improves after freezing for a day, so plan ahead.

- Fine-mesh sieve

2 cups	fresh or frozen cranberries	500 mL
1 cup	apple juice or apple cider	250 mL
1 cup	orange juice	250 mL
3 tbsp	packed dark brown sugar	45 mL
2 tbsp	granulated sugar	30 mL
¼ tsp	ground cinnamon	1 mL
¼ tsp	fenugreek seeds	1 mL
¼ tsp	ground ginger	1 mL
Pinch	nutmeg	Pinch
Pinch	cayenne pepper	Pinch
Pinch	cloves	Pinch
Pinch	salt	Pinch

1. In a saucepan, combine cranberries, apple juice, orange juice, brown and granulated sugars, a generous ¼ tsp (1 mL) cinnamon, fenugreek, ginger, a generous pinch nutmeg, cayenne, cloves and salt. Bring to a boil, stirring until sugar is dissolved. Reduce heat and simmer, covered, until fruit is mushy and falling apart, about 15 minutes for fresh berries and 10 minutes for frozen.

2. Strain through sieve placed over a large measuring cup, pressing down on solids with a rubber spatula to extract as much pulp and juice as possible. Discard solids. Set aside to cool.

3. Pour into molds and freeze until slushy, then insert sticks and freeze until solid, for at least 4 hours. If you are using an ice pop kit, follow the manufacturer's instructions.

Mediterranean Flavors

Clementine and Rose Ice Pops

Makes about 2¾ cups (675 mL) 8 to 11 ice pops

Tangy-sweet clementines and fragrant rose blend harmoniously in these ice pops. If you prefer, make them with mandarin oranges or tangerines.

Tip

Rose water (and orange flower water) are traditional Middle Eastern and southern Mediterranean flavorings. Look for them in well-stocked supermarkets or specialty stores.

½ cup	granulated sugar	125 mL
½ cup	water	125 mL
1½ tsp	finely grated clementine zest	7 mL
2 cups	freshly-squeezed clementine juice	500 mL
1 tsp	rose water	5 mL

1. In a small saucepan, bring sugar, water and clementine zest to a boil. Remove from heat and set aside to cool. Add clementine juice and rose water and stir well.

2. Pour into molds and freeze until slushy, then insert sticks and freeze until solid, for at least 4 hours. If you are using an ice pop kit, follow the manufacturer's instructions.

From top: Pure Pineapple Ice Pops (page 79),
Red Currant Pink Lemonade Ice Pops (page 21),
Papaya Lime Ice Pops (page 85), Kiwi Ginger Ice Pops
(page 43) and Red Plum Ice Pops (page 37)

Blueberry and Currant Ice Pops
(variation, page 56)

Orange Carrot Less-Drip Ice Pops (page 204)

Classic Lemonade Ice Pops (page 19),
Sour Orange Ice Pops (page 18) and Classic Limeade Ice Pops (page 23)

Traditional Kulfi Ice Pops (page 192)

Banana Ice Pops (page 87)

Raspberry Meringue Ice Pops (page 50)

Coconut Ice Pops (page 82)

Blood Orange Ice Pops

Makes about
2⅔ cups (650 mL)
8 to 10 ice pops

A touch of grenadine syrup intensifies the red juice of blood oranges (also known as moro oranges), while a couple of dashes of bitters lends a subtle layer of flavor — as in many a traditional Italian aperitif.

Tip

Angostura bitters are available at large grocery stores as well as many liquor stores. It is a famous flavoring produced in Trinidad. The original recipe, which includes gentian and other herbs, was developed in the Venezuelan town of Angostura.

- Fine-mesh sieve

½ cup	water	125 mL
⅓ cup	granulated sugar	75 mL
	Grated zest of 1 blood orange	
2 cups	freshly squeezed blood orange juice	500 mL
2 tbsp	grenadine syrup	30 mL
2 dashes	angostura or other bitters	2 dashes

1. In a small saucepan, bring water, sugar and orange zest to a boil, stirring until sugar is dissolved. Reduce heat and simmer for 1 minute. Remove from heat, cover and set aside to steep for 5 minutes.

2. Strain through sieve placed over a large measuring cup. Discard solids. Stir in orange juice, grenadine syrup and bitters.

3. Pour into molds and freeze until slushy, then insert sticks and freeze until solid, for at least 4 hours. If you are using an ice pop kit, follow the manufacturer's instructions.

Nectarine and Aniseed Ice Pops

**Makes about
2⅓ cups (575 mL)
7 to 9 ice pops**

Here nectarines are
graced with the bright
flavors of anise seed and
lemon. When making
these pops, it is essential
that the nectarines be
fully ripe, sweet and
fragrant; otherwise
the anise flavor will
overwhelm the fruit.

Tip

A good silicone spatula is
immensely useful, and two
are better. I like to use a
narrow one for scraping the
blender and a wider one for
pressing mixtures through
a sieve or scraping clean
mixing bowls and measuring
cups. The silicone ones are
heatproof and nonstick too,
so they are good for scraping
hot syrup out of saucepans.
If you don't have a silicone
spatula, you can always use
a wooden spoon or soup
ladle for pushing mixtures
through a fine-mesh sieve.

- Blender
- Fine-mesh sieve

½ tsp	anise seeds	2 mL
⅓ cup	granulated sugar	75 mL
⅓ cup + ¼ cup	water, divided	135 mL
½ tsp	finely grated lemon zest	2 mL
1 lb	ripe nectarines (about 4 medium), halved and pitted	500 g
1½ tbsp	freshly squeezed lemon juice	22 mL
¼ cup	water	60 mL

1. In a small saucepan over medium heat, toast anise seeds until fragrant, about 2 minutes. Add sugar, ⅓ cup (75 mL) water and lemon zest; bring to a boil, stirring until sugar is dissolved. Reduce heat and simmer for 2 minutes. Remove from heat and set aside to cool.

2. Place nectarines in blender with lemon juice and ¼ cup (60 mL) water. Blend at medium speed until smooth. Strain through sieve placed over a large measuring cup, pressing down and scraping solids with rubber spatula to extract as much pulp and juice as possible. Discard skins. Stir in aniseed syrup.

3. Pour into molds and freeze until slushy, then insert sticks and freeze until solid, for at least 4 hours. If you are using an ice pop kit, follow the manufacturer's instructions.

Apricot Saffron Ice Pops

**Makes about
2⅔ cups (650 mL)
8 to 10 ice pops**

Besides sharing the
same color, apricots
and saffron also share
a fondness for hot, dry
climates. In eastern
Mediterranean and
Persian cuisines they are
sometimes combined in
savory dishes. Apricots
and saffron make a
delicious sweet pairing
too, as proven by this
wonderful ice pop.

Tips

Use only the sweetest ripe
apricots you can find. If
unavailable, use preserved
apricots, which will make a
sweeter but very tasty ice
pop (see Variation, right).

These ice pops are slightly
tart. If you prefer a sweeter
treat, increase the honey to
⅓ cup (75 mL). Use a light,
fragrant Mediterranean-
style honey such as orange
blossom, wild thyme or
acacia, or a North American–
style wildflower or clover
honey.

- Blender or immersion blender

1 lb	ripe apricots (about 10 medium or 16 small)	500 g
1 cup	water	250 mL
Pinch	saffron threads	Pinch
¼ cup	liquid honey	60 mL

1. Plunge apricots in boiling water for 15 seconds to loosen skins, then peel, halve and pit. Place in a saucepan with water, a small pinch saffron and honey; bring to a boil. Reduce heat and poach at a low simmer for 5 minutes. Remove from heat and set aside to cool.

2. In blender at medium-high speed, purée cooled apricot mixture.

3. Pour into molds and freeze until slushy, then insert sticks and freeze until solid, for at least 4 hours. If you are using an ice pop kit, follow the manufacturer's instructions.

Variation

Omit the fresh apricots from the syrup.
Add 2 cups (500 mL) drained preserved
apricots to the blender along with the saffron
syrup. Adjust the sweetness to taste, using
1 to 2 tbsp (15 to 30 mL) freshly squeezed
lemon juice.

Baked Plum with Rosemary Ice Pops

**Makes about
2 cups (500 mL)
6 to 8 ice pops**

The rich, full flavor of
ripe black plums can
easily handle added
herbs or spices. Baking
further concentrates the
taste of the fruit.

- 8- or 9-inch (20 or 23 cm) square baking dish
- Preheat oven to 375°F (190°C)
- Fine-mesh sieve

1 lb	unpeeled black plums (about 8 medium) or prune plums (about 14), halved and pitted	500 g
2 tbsp	butter, melted	30 mL
⅓ cup + 1 tbsp	granulated sugar	90 mL
1 tsp	fresh rosemary leaves	5 mL
Pinch	salt	Pinch
¾ cup	water	175 mL
2 tbsp	freshly squeezed lemon juice	30 mL
1 tbsp	liquid honey	15 mL

1. Place plums, cut side up, in baking dish in a single layer. Drizzle with butter and sprinkle with sugar, rosemary and a tiny pinch of salt. Bake in preheated oven until fruit is completely soft, 25 to 35 minutes. Remove from oven and mash fruit with a fork. Set aside to cool.

2. Scrape plums and accumulated juices into sieve placed over a large measuring cup. Strain, pressing down and scraping solids with a rubber spatula to extract as much pulp and juice as possible. Add water to sieve and work any remaining juices from solids into mixture. Discard solids. Whisk in lemon juice and honey.

3. Pour into molds and freeze until slushy, then insert sticks and freeze until solid, for at least 4 hours. If you are using an ice pop kit, follow the manufacturer's instructions.

Pomegranate Ice Pops

2 cups	unsweetened pomegranate juice, divided	500 mL
3 tbsp	corn, agave or brown rice syrup or liquid honey	45 mL

Makes about 2¼ cups (550 mL) 6 to 9 ice pops

Natural pomegranate juice makes a nice ice pop all by itself, but it is more palatable if slightly sweetened. Because the pomegranate flavor is so special, I prefer to use light corn syrup, which has a neutral taste, as a sweetener, but you can experiment with honey or other syrups.

Tips

It is more economical — and definitely more convenient — to use bottled 100% pomegranate juice.

If you are making juice from fresh pomegranates, cut the fruit in half and use a grapefruit or orange juicer to extract the juice; one large pomegranate yields about ½ cup (125 mL) juice. Otherwise, remove the seeds, discarding skin and pulp, and put the seeds through a food mill. You can also put them in a blender and blend briefly, trying not to break up the seed kernels, and strain.

1. In a microwavable container, mix ¼ cup (60 mL) juice with syrup. Heat until mixture is thin, about 10 to 20 seconds on High. (You can also do this on the stovetop, in a small saucepan over medium heat, heating for about 1 minute.) Stir into remaining juice, mixing well.

2. Pour into molds and freeze until slushy, then insert sticks and freeze until solid, for at least 4 hours. If you are using an ice pop kit, follow the manufacturer's instructions.

Variations

Pomegranate Watermelon Ice Pops: After mixing pomegranate juice and syrup (Step 1), place in a blender. Add 3 cups (750 mL) chopped seedless watermelon and purée until smooth. Strain through a fine-mesh sieve and complete Step 2. Makes about 4 cups (1 L) or 12 to 16 ice pops.

Pomegranate Apple Ice Pops: Replace syrup with ½ cup (125 mL) frozen unsweetened apple juice concentrate and ⅓ cup (75 mL) water. Makes about 2¾ cups (675 mL) or 8 to 11 ice pops.

Pomegranate Berry Ice Pops

**Makes about
3 cups (750 mL)
9 to 12 ice pops**

Pomegranate juice makes a wonderful base for strong-flavored berries such as wild blueberries or raspberries. The result is an intensely fruity, pleasantly tart and undoubtedly healthy ice pop. You can use frozen berries year-round for convenience.

Tip

Because every brand of blender has a different power capacity, speeds vary greatly. Generally, to purée a mixture, start at slow to medium speed and move up to medium-high speed on a powerful blender, or high speed on a less powerful model. If the engine is very strong, too much air may be incorporated into the mixture at high speed.

- Blender
- Fine-mesh sieve

2 cups	unsweetened pomegranate juice, divided	500 mL
3 tbsp	agave or corn syrup, or ¼ cup (60 mL) brown rice syrup	45 mL
2 cups	wild blueberries, raspberries or blackberries, thawed if frozen	500 mL

1. In a glass measuring cup, mix ¼ cup (60 mL) pomegranate juice with syrup. Heat in a microwave oven until mixture is thin, about 10 to 20 seconds on High. (You can also do this on the stovetop, in a small saucepan over medium heat, heating for about 1 minute.) Add to blender with remaining juice and berries; purée at medium speed (see Tip, left).

2. Strain through sieve placed over a large measuring cup, pressing down and scraping solids with a rubber spatula to extract as much pulp and juice as possible. Discard solids.

3. Pour into molds and freeze until slushy, then insert sticks and freeze until solid, for at least 4 hours. If you are using an ice pop kit, follow the manufacturer's instructions.

Pomegranate Yogurt Swirl Ice Pops

**Makes about 2¾ cups (675 mL)
8 to 11 ice pops**

This is a quick, pretty and very easy ice pop to make. The sweet-and-sour flavor of natural pomegranate juice mimics the tartness and sweetness of the yogurt-honey mixture.

Tips

It is more economical — and definitely more convenient — to use bottled 100% pomegranate juice.

To make fresh pomegranate juice, see page 69.

3 tbsp	liquid honey	45 mL
¼ tsp	ground cardamom	1 mL
¾ cup	Greek- or Balkan-style yogurt or drained plain yogurt	175 mL
1¾ cups	unsweetened pomegranate juice (see Tips, left)	425 mL
2 tbsp	agave, brown rice or corn syrup or granulated sugar	30 mL

1. Place honey and cardamom in a glass measuring cup. Heat in a microwave oven on High until honey is liquid and beginning to bubble at the edges, about 30 seconds. (You can also do this on the stovetop, in a small saucepan over medium heat.) Set aside until just warm. Whisk in yogurt and chill.

2. In another measuring cup, stir together pomegranate juice and syrup until thoroughly incorporated. (If using sugar, stir until sugar is dissolved.)

3. Fill molds two-thirds full with pomegranate juice mixture. Top with yogurt mixture. Using a chopstick or narrow knife, carefully swirl yogurt mixture into pomegranate mixture, leaving it streaky. Freeze until slushy; if desired, gently swirl once more, being careful to keep mixtures streaky. Freeze until solid, for at least 4 hours. If you are using an ice pop kit, follow the manufacturer's instructions.

Strawberry Sherry Cream Ice Pops

**Makes about
3¼ cups (800 mL)
9 to 13 ice pops**

**Strawberries and cream
is a combination that
can only be improved
by a generous splash of
sweet sherry or Madeira
wine and a touch of
light floral honey.**

Tip

Extra-fine sugar (fruit sugar)
is just granulated sugar with
extremely small crystals
which dissolve quickly in
cold or thick liquids. It's
useful for sweetening fruit
purées and mixtures that are
uncooked or cold. You can
make your own by grinding
regular granulated sugar in
a blender.

• Blender

4 cups	halved hulled fresh strawberries or whole frozen strawberries, thawed	1 L
⅓ cup	extra-fine (fruit) sugar or granulated sugar	75 mL
⅓ cup	sweet (cream) sherry or sweet Madeira wine	75 mL
2 tbsp	light liquid honey, such as orange blossom, acacia or wildflower	30 mL
2 tsp	freshly squeezed lemon juice	10 mL
¾ cup	heavy or whipping (35%) cream	175 mL

1. In blender, combine strawberries, sugar, sherry, honey and lemon juice. Purée at medium speed, ensuring that sugar is completely dissolved. Add cream and pulse to blend.

2. Pour into molds and freeze until slushy, then insert sticks and freeze until solid, for at least 4 hours. If you are using an ice pop kit, follow the manufacturer's instructions.

Muscat Grape Ice Pops

Makes about
3 cups (750 mL)
9 to 12 ice pops

Muscat grapes have a floral fragrance and fruity taste that make them particularly good as table and cooking grapes. They are also full of sweet juice, so turning them into ice pops is a natural.

Tip

In many ice pops that include solid ingredients or combine liquids of different viscosities, there is a bit of layering after freezing, which is normal. However, if you want a seamless result, give the mixture a stir after it has reached the slushy stage to ensure that the ingredients remain integrated.

- Fine-mesh sieve

1 lb, 6 oz	Muscat grapes (3 cups/750 mL)	650 g
½ cup	water	125 mL
⅓ cup	granulated sugar	75 mL
2 tbsp	freshly squeezed lemon juice	30 mL

1. In a saucepan, combine grapes, water and sugar and bring to a boil over high heat. Reduce heat to medium and simmer, covered, until grapes are falling apart, 15 to 25 minutes. With a potato masher or fork, mash grapes.

2. Strain through sieve placed over a large measuring cup, pressing down and scraping solids with a rubber spatula to extract as much pulp and juice as possible. Discard solids. Stir lemon juice into liquid and set aside to cool.

3. Pour into molds and freeze until slushy, then insert sticks and freeze until solid, for at least 4 hours. If you are using an ice pop kit, follow the manufacturer's instructions.

Black Fig Ice Pops

Makes about
2¾ cups (675 mL)
8 to 11 ice pops

Ripe black figs are a specialty of the Mediterranean region, from Spain to Greece and from Lebanon to Morocco. You may be surprised to learn how good they are for making ice pops. Make sure your figs are fully ripe, fragrant and supple to the touch.

Tip

Because every brand of blender has a different power capacity, speeds vary greatly. Generally, to purée a mixture, start at slow to medium speed and move up to medium-high speed, on a powerful blender, or high speed, on a less powerful model. If the engine is very strong, too much air may be incorporated into the mixture at high speed.

- Blender

⅓ cup	dry red wine	75 mL
¼ cup	granulated sugar	60 mL
1	strip (½ by 2 inches/1 by 5 cm) lemon zest	1
5	black peppercorns, crushed	5
1 lb	fresh black figs, stemmed and quartered (9 to 12)	500 g
½ cup	water	125 mL
2 tbsp	liquid honey	30 mL
2 tbsp	freshly squeezed lemon juice	30 mL

1. In a small saucepan, combine wine, sugar, lemon zest and peppercorns. Bring to a boil, then reduce heat and simmer for 2 minutes. Remove from heat and set aside to cool.

2. Strain into blender, discarding solids. Add figs, water, honey and lemon juice; purée at medium-high speed (see Tip, left).

3. Pour into molds and freeze until slushy, then insert sticks and freeze until solid, for at least 4 hours. If you are using an ice pop kit, follow the manufacturer's instructions.

Fig and Orange Ice Pops

Makes about
2¾ cups (675 mL)
8 to 11 ice pops

In this recipe, sweet ripe white or green figs make the most visually attractive ice pops, but fully ripe black figs can also be used.

Tips

Freshly squeezed juice is always best, but you can also use juice from cartons or from concentrate. In this recipe, if you do not have enough juice after zesting and juicing one orange, top off the quantity with prepared juice.

I prefer the pleasant bit of texture in these ice pops that results from not straining the mixture.

Rose water (and orange flower water) are traditional Middle Eastern and southern Mediterranean flavorings. Look for them in well-stocked supermarkets or specialty stores.

• Blender

⅓ cup	dry white wine	75 mL
3 tbsp	granulated sugar	45 mL
½ tsp	finely grated orange zest	2 mL
1 lb	ripe white or green figs (9 to 14), stemmed and quartered	500 g
½ cup	orange juice	125 mL
2 tbsp	orange blossom or other floral honey	30 mL
2 tbsp	freshly squeezed lemon juice	30 mL
1 tsp	orange-flower water, optional	5 mL

1. In a small saucepan, combine wine, sugar and orange zest. Bring to a boil, then reduce heat and simmer for 2 minutes. Remove from heat and set aside to cool.

2. Transfer cooled syrup to blender. Add figs, orange juice, honey, lemon juice and orange-flower water, if using, and purée at medium-high speed.

3. Pour into molds and freeze until slushy, then insert sticks and freeze until solid, for at least 4 hours. If you are using an ice pop kit, follow the manufacturer's instructions.

Honey, Yogurt and Pistachio Ice Pops

Makes about
3 cups (750 mL)
9 to 12 ice pops

Inspired by eastern Mediterranean and Middle Eastern flavors, these ice pops are a refreshing combination of sweet honey, tart yogurt and nutty pistachios. Rose water or orange-flower water adds a light floral note.

Tip

Because of the large volume of honey used here, its flavor will come through quite strongly. That means your choice of honey will change the taste of the ice pop. If you are using orange-flower water, orange blossom honey is a natural choice to further emphasize the citrus flavor. Other honeys have their own characteristics, which makes it satisfying and fun to vary your choices when cooking.

4 tsp	butter	20 mL
½ cup	coarsely chopped raw (unsalted) pistachios	125 mL
2 tbsp	granulated sugar	30 mL
2 cups	plain yogurt (2% to full-fat)	500 mL
½ cup	liquid honey	125 mL
½ tsp	rose water or orange-flower water (see Tip, page 64)	2 mL

1. In a small skillet over medium heat, melt butter. Add pistachios and stir to coat. Sprinkle with sugar; continue cooking and stirring until sugar is melted, no longer granular and lightly caramelized. Scrape onto a plate and set aside to cool.

2. In a large measuring cup, whisk together yogurt, honey and rose water. Fold in reserved pistachios.

3. Pour into molds and freeze until slushy, then insert sticks and freeze until solid, for at least 4 hours. If you are using an ice pop kit, follow the manufacturer's instructions.

Tropical Fruits

Mango Ice Pops

**Makes about
3 cups (750 mL)
9 to 12 ice pops**

Using a combination of cooked and fresh mango makes these ice pops an exceptionally flavorful and honest expression of the fruit. Make sure you use only fully ripe mangoes.

Tip

A ripe mango should be fragrant, and soft but not mushy to the touch. If you see sap oozing from the stem end, it's a good sign that the mango is sweet and ripe.

- Blender

2 cups	chopped fresh ripe mango, divided	500 mL
1¼ cups	water, divided	300 mL
⅓ cup	granulated sugar	75 mL
2 tbsp	freshly squeezed lime juice	30 mL

1. In a saucepan, combine ⅔ cup (150 mL) mango, ¾ cup (175 mL) water and sugar. Bring to a boil, stirring until sugar is dissolved. Reduce heat and simmer, uncovered, for 5 minutes. Set aside to cool.

2. In blender, at medium-high speed, purée cooked mango mixture, remaining 1⅓ cups (325 mL) mango, ½ cup (125 mL) water and lime juice.

3. Pour into molds and freeze until slushy, then insert sticks and freeze until solid, for at least 4 hours. If you are using an ice pop kit, follow the manufacturer's instructions.

Pure Pineapple Ice Pops

Makes about
3½ cups (875 mL)
10 to 14 ice pops

Choose a perfectly ripe pineapple for these delicious ice pops. They are made from cooked pineapple, which gives them a mellow yet full flavor.

Tip

To mince pineapple: Peel pineapple, removing eyes. Cut in half lengthwise, then cut each half lengthwise into 4 pieces. Cut out core. Thinly slice each piece lengthwise, then stack pieces and slice crosswise into a thin julienne. Cut across julienne to mince. Save the juices on the cutting board for use in the recipe.

1	pineapple, peeled, cored and minced (see Tip, left)	1
2½ cups	water	625 mL
Pinch	salt	Pinch
⅔ cup	granulated sugar	150 mL

1. In a saucepan over high heat, bring pineapple, with juices, water and salt to a boil. Reduce heat to medium and boil for 10 minutes. Add sugar and stir until dissolved, then reduce heat and simmer for 5 minutes. Remove from heat and set aside to cool.

2. Pour into molds and freeze until slushy, then insert sticks and freeze until solid, for at least 4 hours. If you are using an ice pop kit, follow the manufacturer's instructions.

Pineapple Sage Ice Pops

**Makes about
3⅓ cups (825 mL)
10 to 13 ice pops**

**Sweet ripe, fresh
pineapple plus a subtle
undertone of sage
makes a fantastic flavor
combination.**

Tip

Because every brand of
blender has a different
power capacity, speeds vary
greatly. Generally, to purée
a mixture, start at slow to
medium speed and move up
to medium-high speed, on
a powerful blender, or high
speed, on a less powerful
model. If the engine is very
strong, too much air may be
incorporated into the mixture
at high speed.

● Blender or food processor

1⅓ cups	water	325 mL
¾ cup	granulated sugar	175 mL
12	fresh sage leaves	12
¼ tsp	salt	1 mL
1	pineapple, peeled	1

1. In a saucepan, combine water, sugar, sage
and salt. Bring to a boil, stirring until sugar is
dissolved, then reduce heat and simmer for
1 minute. Remove from heat and set aside to
cool. Remove and discard sage leaves.

2. Cut pineapple lengthwise into quarters and cut
out and discard core. Roughly chop two of the
quarters and place in blender with sage syrup.
Purée. Chop remaining pineapple, add to mixture
and pulse just until pineapple is crushed (finer
than minced but not puréed).

3. Pour into molds and freeze until slushy, then
insert sticks and freeze until solid, for at least
4 hours. If you are using an ice pop kit, follow
the manufacturer's instructions.

Lichee Ice Pops

**Makes about
3 cups (750 mL)
9 to 12 ice pops**

For lichee ice pops,
readily available canned
lichees, surprisingly,
give just as good results
as fresh lichees, which
have a short season
and are much more
expensive and fussier
to prepare.

Tip

Always use freshly squeezed
lemon juice or lime juice in
your ice pops; bottled just
doesn't compare.

- Blender
- Fine-mesh sieve

2	cans (each 20 oz/565 g) lichees, drained, syrup reserved	2
1 tsp	grated lime zest	5 mL
1/3 cup + 1 tbsp	freshly squeezed lime juice	90 mL

1. In blender, at medium-high speed, purée lichees, 1⅓ cups (325 mL) reserved lichee syrup, and lime zest and juice. Discard remaining lichee syrup. Strain purée through sieve placed over a large measuring cup, pushing down on solids with a rubber spatula to extract as much pulp and juice as possible. Discard solids.

2. Pour into molds and freeze until slushy, then insert sticks and freeze until solid, for at least 4 hours. If you are using an ice pop kit, follow the manufacturer's instructions.

Variation

Lichee Rose Ice Pops: Add 2 tsp (10 mL) rose water to the lichee mixture before puréeing.

Coconut Ice Pops

Makes about
2¼ cups (550 mL)
6 to 9 ice pops

Coconut milk — the
juice extracted from
grated mature coconut
flesh mixed with
water — has a natural
affinity with palm sugar,
which is made from the
sweet sap of various
palm trees. These two
ingredients are all you
need to make a perfect
tropical ice pop.

Tips

Palm sugar is used
extensively in Asian cooking
and is generally available at
Asian markets. It is usually
sold in solid tablets or cakes
measuring about ¼ cup
(60 mL) each; chop or grate
the cakes into loose sugar
before measuring. "Coconut
sugar," which is palm sugar
made from coconut sap,
is sold in granulated form
at bulk and natural foods
stores.

You can substitute an equal
quantity of light brown
(golden yellow) sugar or
raw cane sugar for the palm
sugar.

½ cup	palm sugar (see Tips, left)	125 mL
3 tbsp	water	45 mL
2 cups	coconut milk (see Tips, left)	500 mL

1. In a saucepan over medium-low heat, melt sugar
   in water, stirring until smooth. Stir in coconut
   milk; increase heat to high and bring to a boil,
   stirring. Reduce heat to medium-low and simmer
   for 1 minute. Set aside to cool.

2. Pour into molds and freeze until slushy, then
   insert sticks and freeze until solid, for at least
   4 hours. If you are using an ice pop kit, follow
   the manufacturer's instructions.

Variations

Cardamom-Scented Coconut Ice Pops:
After the sugar is melted, stir in 4 crushed
cardamom pods or ¼ tsp (1 mL) ground
cardamom before adding the coconut milk.
When cool, strain out the spice.

Spiced Coconut Ice Pops: After the sugar is
melted and before adding the coconut milk,
stir in 4 crushed cardamom pods or ¼ tsp
(1 mL) ground cardamom; 3 whole cloves;
and 1 whole star anise or ½ stick cinnamon
or a generous ¼ tsp (1 mL) ground cinnamon.
When cool, strain out the spices.

Vanilla Coconut Ice Pops: Stir ½ tsp (2 mL)
vanilla extract to cooled coconut mixture.

Pandan Leaf–Scented Coconut Ice Pops:
Add 1 pandan (pandanus) leaf to the coconut
mixture before bringing it to a boil (double leaf
over lengthwise and tie it in a knot). Simmer
and let steep, covered, for 10 minutes.
Remove leaf and set aside to cool.

Toasted Coconut Ice Pops

Makes about 2½ cups (625 mL) 7 to 10 ice pops

½ cup	grated fresh coconut or flaked or shredded dried coconut	125 mL
½ cup	palm sugar (see Tips, page 82)	125 mL
3 tbsp	water	45 mL
2 cups	coconut milk	500 mL

Gently toasting grated coconut until it is golden brown considerably changes its flavor profile. Freshly grated coconut (also available frozen) is preferable, but you can toast dried coconut too.

Tips

Canned coconut milk is widely available. If you are shopping at an Asian market, look for frozen coconut milk (often exported from the Philippines). The taste is superior — practically identical to that of freshly prepared coconut milk. Don't bother making your own grated coconut meat unless you live in a place where you can get freshly picked coconuts.

Tropical pandan leaves are long, spear-like green leaves used for flavoring, particularly in rice and sweet dishes. They are available frozen and occasionally fresh at Asian markets.

1. In a dry skillet over medium-low heat, toast coconut, stirring often, until golden brown. Set aside.

2. In a saucepan over medium-low heat, melt sugar in water, stirring until smooth. Stir in coconut milk and toasted coconut; increase heat and bring to a boil. Reduce heat to medium-low and simmer for 1 minute. Remove from heat and set aside to cool.

3. Pour into molds and freeze until slushy, then insert sticks and freeze until solid, for at least 4 hours. If you are using an ice pop kit, follow the manufacturer's instructions.

Variations

Spiced Toasted Coconut Ice Pops: After sugar is melted (Step 2), add 4 crushed cardamom pods or ¼ tsp (1 mL) ground cardamom or ½ stick cinnamon or a generous ¼ tsp (1 mL) ground cinnamon. Stir in coconut milk and bring to a boil; reduce heat and simmer, covered, for 5 minutes. Strain into a clean saucepan, stir in toasted coconut and complete recipe.

Vanilla Toasted Coconut Ice Pops: Add ½ tsp (2 mL) vanilla extract to cooled coconut mixture.

Pandan Leaf–Scented Toasted Coconut Ice Pops: In Step 2, add 1 pandan (pandanus) leaf to coconut milk before it comes to a boil (double leaf over lengthwise and tie it in a knot). Simmer and let steep, covered, for 10 minutes. Remove leaf, shaking any toasted coconut back into the mixture, and set aside to cool.

Young Coconut Ice Pops

> **Makes about 2 cups (500 mL) 6 to 8 ice pops**

Young coconut ice pops are extremely popular throughout Southeast Asia. Young coconut is also used for iced treats in Central America and other warm regions where coconuts are plentiful.

Tips

Unripe young (green) coconuts have a thin layer of soft, gelatinous flesh and an abundance of refreshing clear juice, which is as nutritious as it is delicious. The flavor is entirely different from that of ripe mature coconut: it is less rich and has a touch of acidity, and its light, watery consistency makes it more refreshing.

You can buy young coconuts in some larger supermarkets and in most Asian and Caribbean markets.

- Blender

1	young coconut	1
⅓ cup	brown rice syrup or ¼ cup (60 mL) light agave or light corn syrup	75 mL
¼ cup	evaporated milk	60 mL

1. With a cleaver or large chef's knife, cut top off coconut to make a hole large enough for a soup spoon. Pour juice into blender. With spoon, scrape out the soft white flesh. Chop enough of the flesh to make 2 tbsp (30 mL) fine julienne; set aside. Place remainder in blender with juice and purée at medium-high speed. Add syrup and evaporated milk and blend at low speed until combined.

2. Divide reserved julienned coconut evenly among molds. Pour liquid into molds and freeze until slushy, then insert sticks and freeze until solid, for at least 4 hours. If you are using an ice pop kit, follow the manufacturer's instructions.

Variation

Young Coconut and Rum Ice Pops: Stir in ¼ cup (60 mL) amber rum along with the syrup and evaporated milk. Freeze for at least 4 hours or, preferably, overnight.

Papaya Lime Ice Pops

**Makes about
3¾ cups (925 mL)
11 to 15 ice pops**

**Papaya is a native of
the Americas but is
cultivated throughout
the tropical world. There
it is a favorite fruit for
both its nutritional and
digestive value and
its distinctive flavor.**

Tips

If you are using the sweet
and delicious small, red-
fleshed papayas from
the West Indies, you will
probably need two, weighing
a total of about 3 lbs (1.5 kg).

A ripe papaya should be
fairly soft and give when
gently pressed, but it
shouldn't be mushy. Halve
the papaya and spoon out
the seeds, then use the
spoon to scoop out its
tender flesh. Avoid spooning
out any of the harder, less
ripe flesh closer to the skin.

- Blender

⅔ cup	water	150 mL
⅓ cup	granulated sugar	75 mL
	Zest of 1 lime, cut into strips	
1	ripe papaya (about 3 lbs/1.5 kg)	1
¼ cup	freshly squeezed lime juice	60 mL

1. In a small saucepan, combine water, sugar and
lime zest. Bring to a boil, stirring until sugar is
dissolved. Remove from heat, cover and let steep
for 5 minutes. Uncover and set aside to cool.
Strain into blender, discarding lime zest.

2. Halve and seed papaya. Spoon out flesh and add
to blender with lime juice. Purée at medium-high
speed.

3. Pour into molds and freeze until slushy, then
insert sticks and freeze until solid, for at least
4 hours. If you are using an ice pop kit, follow
the manufacturer's instructions.

Papaya Milkshake Ice Pops

**Makes about
2¾ cups (675 mL)
8 to 11 ice pops**

Papaya milkshakes
are extremely popular
throughout tropical
Asia, and they make
great ice pops too. Even
better, they are simple
to make.

Tips

A ripe papaya should be
fairly soft and give when
gently pressed, but it
shouldn't be mushy. Halve
the papaya and spoon out
the seeds, then use the
spoon to scoop out its
tender flesh. Avoid spooning
out any of the harder, less
ripe flesh closer to the skin.

Extra-fine sugar (fruit sugar)
is just granulated sugar with
extremely small crystals,
which dissolve quickly in
cold or thick liquids. It's
useful for sweetening fruit
purées or mixtures that are
uncooked or cold. You can
make your own by grinding
regular granulated sugar in
a blender.

- Blender

1½ cups	chopped fresh papaya	375 mL
1 cup	milk	250 mL
2 tbsp	extra-fine (fruit) sugar or granulated sugar	30 mL
2 tbsp	liquid honey	30 mL

1. In blender at medium-high speed, purée papaya, milk, sugar and honey, ensuring that sugar is fully dissolved.

2. Pour into molds and freeze until slushy, then insert sticks and freeze until solid, for at least 4 hours. If you are using an ice pop kit, follow the manufacturer's instructions.

Banana Ice Pops

Makes about
3 cups (750 mL)
9 to 12 ice pops

Use ripe, sweet bananas for these ice pops, which can be made in the blink of an eye. The touch of molasses adds a lot to these treats — use whatever type you have on hand.

Tip

You can vary the flavor by using different varieties of bananas. Red-skinned bananas and mini-bananas are particularly good for sweet preparations such as these pops.

- Blender

2½ cups	sliced ripe bananas (3 medium-large)	625 mL
⅔ cup	5% (light) cream, whole milk or evaporated milk	150 mL
½ cup	water	125 mL
3 tbsp	brown rice, agave or corn syrup	45 mL
1 tsp	molasses	5 mL

1. In blender at medium-high speed, purée bananas, cream, water, syrup and molasses.

2. Pour into molds and freeze until slushy, then insert sticks and freeze until solid, for at least 4 hours. If you are using an ice pop kit, follow the manufacturer's instructions.

Variation

Banana and Honey Ice Pops: Replace the syrup with the same amount of buckwheat honey or other rich, dark liquid honey (such as manuka or avocado). Omit the molasses.

Creamy Spiced Banana Ice Pops

**Makes about
3½ cups (875 mL)
10 to 14 ice pops**

It's your choice:
cardamom- or
cinnamon-scented
banana ice pops.
**Fully ripe bananas are
required for these pops,
no matter which flavor
you choose.**

Tips

If you prefer, substitute a
scant ½ tsp (2 mL) ground
cardamom or ground
cinnamon for the whole
spice.

Along with the cardamom or
cinnamon, further spice up
the syrup with 2 whole star
anise and 3 whole cloves.
Simmer the syrup for 3
minutes before steeping.

- Blender

⅔ cup	water	150 mL
⅓ cup	granulated sugar	75 mL
8	cardamom pods, crushed, or 1 stick (about 3 inches/8 cm) cinnamon (see Tips, left)	8
2 cups	sliced ripe bananas	500 mL
1 cup	evaporated milk	250 mL

1. In a small saucepan, combine water, sugar and cardamom. Bring to boil, stirring until sugar is dissolved; remove from heat. (If using cinnamon stick, simmer for an additional 2 minutes before removing from heat.) Cover and set aside to steep for 5 minutes. Strain into blender, discarding spice, then add bananas and evaporated milk. Blend until smooth.

2. Pour into molds and freeze until slushy, then insert sticks and freeze until solid, for at least 4 hours. If you are using an ice pop kit, follow the manufacturer's instructions.

Variations

Creamy Banana Chocolate Chip Ice Pops:
Leave a little headspace when pouring banana mixture into molds. Divide ⅓ cup (75 mL) mini semisweet chocolate chips or chopped chocolate pieces evenly among the molds, stirring to distribute evenly.

Chunky Creamy Banana Ice Pops: Before adding banana mixture to molds, stir in 1 diced small banana. Or leave a little headspace and add a few thin slices of banana to each mold after pouring in the mixture.

Jackfruit Ice Pops

Makes about
3 cups (750 mL)
9 to 12 ice pops

Jackfruit is a blimp-shaped tropical fruit. It is the largest tree-borne fruit, weighing up to 80 pounds (36 kg), though the usual market offerings are about the same size and weight as watermelons. The yellow flesh is moist but only slightly juicy, wonderfully tasty, sweet and intensely fragrant.

Tips

Make this ice pop with 1 lb (450 to 500 g) peeled and seeded fresh or thawed frozen jackfruit; you should have about 3½ cups (825 mL). Simmer in the sugar syrup until it is tender, 3 to 5 minutes; complete the recipe.

Jackfruit is sometimes imported fresh and is also available frozen in Asian markets, but it is usually found canned in light syrup. The canned fruit is perfect for making ice pops.

- Blender

1⅓ cups	water	325 mL
⅔ cup	granulated sugar	150 mL
2	cans (each 8 oz/250 g) jackfruit in syrup, drained	2
⅓ cup + 1 tbsp	freshly squeezed lime juice	90 mL

1. In a small saucepan, bring water and sugar to a boil, stirring until sugar is dissolved. Remove from heat and set aside to cool. Place cooled syrup in blender with jackfruit and lime juice; purée at medium-high speed.

2. Pour into molds and freeze until slushy, then insert sticks and freeze until solid, for at least 4 hours. If you are using an ice pop kit, follow the manufacturer's instructions.

Durian Ice Pops

**Makes about
2¾ cups (675 mL)
8 to 11 ice pops**

Durian is a fruit unlike
any other. Its thick,
viciously spiked husk
cracks open when ripe,
releasing an aroma so
strong that animals
can apparently detect
it up to half a mile
away. To aficionados
the fruit smells rich
and sweet, with
appealingly sulfurous
and heady floral notes,
but detractors think
it smells like rotting
onions — or even worse.
The flavor of the fruit
pulp is sweet yet savory,
almost like a sweet
natural cheese. Most
Southeast Asians are
wild about durian. It has
its worldwide fans too.

Tip

Look for durian, fresh or
frozen, whole or in pieces,
in Asian markets. The frozen
fruit is more economical and
just as good as fresh for
ice pops.

- Blender
- Fine-mesh sieve

½ cup	palm sugar, raw cane sugar or light brown sugar	125 mL
3 tbsp	water	45 mL
Pinch	salt	Pinch
1⅔ cups	coconut milk	400 mL
1 lb	seedless durian (about 2⅓ cups/575 mL)	500 g

1. In a saucepan over medium heat, combine sugar, water and a scant pinch of salt, stirring until sugar is dissolved. Stir in coconut milk and heat just until it comes to a boil. Remove from heat and set aside to cool.

2. In blender at medium-high speed, purée durian with coconut milk mixture. Strain through sieve placed over a large measuring cup, pushing down on solids to extract as much pulp and juice as possible. Discard solids.

3. Pour into molds and freeze until slushy, then insert sticks and freeze until solid, for at least 4 hours. If you are using an ice pop kit, follow the manufacturer's instructions.

Passion Fruit Ice Pops

**Makes about
2½ cups (625 mL)
7 to 10 ice pops**

The pulp and juice
surrounding the many
seeds inside the passion
fruit (also known by
its Spanish name,
granadilla) make an ice
pop with an intriguing
tropical flavor. It's
reminiscent of guava,
only with a brilliant
touch of tartness and
a hint of well-ripened
pineapple. Passion fruit
juice is often used to
enhance punches, fruit
salads and the like,
but it has a wonderful
flavor all by itself, as
demonstrated by these
ice pops.

Tip

Commercially sold passion
fruits are generally one
of two varieties, purple-
skinned and yellow-skinned.
The yellow fruits are usually
larger than the purple ones;
both have orange seeds
and juice. The fruits vary
considerably in size, from
about 1 oz (30 g) to 2 oz
(60 g) each, so you will need
anywhere from 16 to 32
fruits for this recipe.

- Fine-mesh sieve

2 lbs	passion fruit (see Tip, left)	1 kg
3/4 cup	water	175 mL
1/3 cup + 1 tbsp	granulated sugar	90 mL
1/3 cup	freshly squeezed lime juice	75 mL

1. Split open passion fruit husks by hand and spoon out seeds, surrounding pulp and any juices; you should have about 2 cups (500 mL). Place in a bowl and set aside.

2. In a small saucepan, bring water and sugar to a boil, stirring until sugar is dissolved; reduce heat and simmer for 2 minutes. Remove from heat and stir in lime juice. Pour over passion fruit. With a fork, mash fruit and mix until seeds are loosened from pulp.

3. Place sieve over a large measuring cup and strain mixture, pushing down on solids to extract as much pulp and juice as possible. Discard solids.

4. Pour into molds and freeze until slushy, then insert sticks and freeze until solid, for at least 4 hours. If you are using an ice pop kit, follow the manufacturer's instructions.

Cape Gooseberry Ice Pops

**Makes about
2 cups (500 mL)
6 to 8 ice pops**

Cape gooseberries are also known as ground cherries, Colombian golden berries or physalis. A tropical/ subtropical vine or shrub, it bears orange berries enclosed in a papery brown husk. (The plant is in no way related to real gooseberries.) They make a delicious ice pop and terrific jam.

Tip

Cape gooseberries are usually sold in tiny baskets in supermarkets and are a bit expensive because they are generally imported. The plants can be grown as a summer annual in temperate climates, so sometimes in the fall you can find them economically priced in farmers' markets.

- Fine-mesh sieve

1½ cups	water	375 mL
½ cup	granulated sugar	125 mL
2 cups	husked, stemmed cape gooseberries (10 oz/300 g)	500 mL

1. In a saucepan, bring water, sugar and berries to a boil, stirring until sugar is dissolved. Reduce heat, cover and simmer until fruit is very soft, about 10 minutes. Remove from heat, uncover and smash with a potato masher until mixture reaches a jam-like consistency. Set aside to cool.

2. Strain through sieve placed over a large measuring cup, pushing down on solids to extract as much pulp and juice as possible. Discard solids.

3. Pour into molds and freeze until slushy, then insert sticks and freeze until solid, for at least 4 hours. If you are using an ice pop kit, follow the manufacturer's instructions.

Chocolate, Fudge, Caramel and Cream

Fudge Ice Pops

Makes about
3 cups (750 mL)
9 to 12 ice pops

These ice pops are rich and chocolate-fudgy, definitely a step up from the commercial treat, but they still retain the youthful spirit of a fun indulgence.

Tip

Tapioca flour is often called tapioca starch. They are identical products.

2¼ cups	milk	550 mL
1 tbsp	tapioca flour (see Tips, left)	15 mL
½ cup	unsweetened cocoa powder	125 mL
2 oz	semisweet chocolate, chopped	60 g
¾ cup	sweetened condensed milk	175 mL
¾ tsp	vanilla extract	3 mL

1. In a saucepan, whisk together milk and tapioca flour, then whisk in cocoa. Whisking constantly, bring to a boil; reduce heat and simmer, stirring often, for 5 minutes. Remove from heat and whisk in chocolate, until melted, thoroughly incorporated and smooth. Stir in condensed milk and vanilla. Set aside to cool.

2. Pour into molds and freeze until slushy, then insert sticks and freeze until solid, for at least 4 hours. If you are using an ice pop kit, follow the manufacturer's instructions.

Chocolate Ginger Ice Pops

**Makes about
2 cups (500 mL)
6 to 8 ice pops**

Rich and dark, these
sophisticated ice pops
pair dark chocolate with
stem ginger in syrup, a
terrific combination. The
ginger adds sweetness
and piquancy to the
slightly bitter chocolate.

Tips

The quantity of ginger should
be varied according to taste.
Add as much as 5 tbsp
(1/3 cup) but only if you are a
confirmed ginger-lover.

Look for stem ginger in
syrup in supermarkets and
bulk food stores, usually
alongside the dried and
candied fruit sold for baking.
It is also sold at gourmet
shops and some Chinese
grocers. If you wish,
substitute crystallized ginger,
which is harder than ginger
in syrup and has a bit more
bite. Rinse off the granular
sugar coating before dicing.

1¼ cups	water	300 mL
⅓ cup + 1 tbsp	agave or corn syrup	90 mL
¼ cup	unsweetened cocoa powder	60 mL
4 oz	bittersweet or semisweet chocolate, chopped	125 g
1½ oz	milk chocolate	45 g
3 tbsp	drained ginger in syrup, finely diced (see Tips, left)	45 mL

1. In a saucepan, whisk together water, syrup and cocoa; bring to a boil over high heat. Reduce heat to medium and cook, stirring often, for 5 minutes. Remove from heat and whisk in bittersweet and milk chocolates until thoroughly incorporated and smooth. Pour into a measuring cup. Chill in refrigerator until thick but still pourable, about 1 hour.

2. Pour mixture into molds, leaving headspace for the ginger. Add ginger to molds, dividing equally; stir into chocolate mixture to distribute evenly. Insert sticks and freeze until solid, at least 4 hours in total.

Malted Chocolate Ice Pops

**Makes about
2¾ cups (675 mL)
8 to 11 ice pops**

I find that a combination
of soy milk and malt
tastes even better than
traditional malted milk.

Tip

Barley malt syrup has a more
intense flavor than regular
malt syrup, but both are good
options for this recipe.

2⅓ cups	soy milk or almond milk (see page 105)	575 mL
½ cup	malt syrup (see Tip, left)	125 mL
1½ oz	bittersweet chocolate, chopped	45 g

1. In a saucepan, combine soy milk and malt syrup; bring to a simmer, stirring until syrup is incorporated. Remove from heat and whisk in chocolate, until thoroughly incorporated and smooth. Set aside to cool.

2. Whisk mixture. Pour into molds and freeze until slushy, then insert sticks and freeze until solid, for at least 4 hours. If you are using an ice pop kit, follow the manufacturer's instructions.

Berry Chocolate Ice Pops

**Makes about
3¼ cups (800 mL)
9 to 13 ice pops**

Strawberries dipped
in chocolate are a very
popular summertime
dessert, but I like these
ice pops even better.

Tip

Substitute an equal quantity
of mini semisweet chocolate
chips for the finely chopped
chocolate.

⅓ cup	heavy or whipping (35%) cream	75 mL
⅓ cup	granulated sugar	75 mL
½ cup	milk	125 mL
3 cups	halved hulled strawberries or whole frozen strawberries, thawed	750 mL
¼ cup	finely chopped semisweet chocolate (see Tip, left)	60 mL

1. In a small saucepan, combine cream and sugar. Heat, stirring, until sugar is dissolved; when bubbles form around edges, remove from heat and stir in milk. Pour into blender. Add strawberries and purée at medium speed.

2. Pour into molds, leaving a little headspace for the chocolate. Divide chocolate equally among molds; stir gently to distribute evenly. Freeze until slushy, then insert sticks and freeze until solid, for at least 4 hours. If you are using an ice pop kit, follow the manufacturer's instructions.

Creamy Mint Chocolate Swirl Ice Pops

**Makes about
2¾ cups (675 mL)
8 to 11 ice pops**

Look for natural
peppermint essence or
flavoring made from
peppermint oil to flavor
these luxurious, sweet
and creamy ice pops.
For the chocolate swirl,
no commercial sauce
will compare to one you
make yourself (if you
use my Rich Chocolate
Sauce), but a good-
quality commercial
version is convenient
and will do the trick.

1½ cups	milk	375 mL
⅔ cup	heavy or whipping (35%) cream	150 mL
½ cup	sweetened condensed milk	125 mL
¾ tsp	finely grated orange zest	3 mL
1	bar (3½ oz/100 g) white chocolate, chopped	1
1½ tsp	peppermint essence	7 mL
¼ cup	Rich Chocolate Sauce (page 143) or dark chocolate sauce	60 mL

1. In a saucepan, combine milk, cream, condensed milk and orange zest; whisk together and bring to a boil. Remove from heat and whisk in white chocolate, until thoroughly incorporated and smooth. Pour into a large measuring cup and set aside to cool. Whisk in peppermint essence.

2. Pour into molds, filling two-thirds full. Divide chocolate sauce evenly among molds, pouring over white chocolate mixture (if sauce is too thick to pour, warm it slightly). Using a chopstick or narrow knife blade, swirl chocolate sauce into mixture. Freeze until slushy, then insert sticks and freeze until solid, for at least 4 hours. If you are using an ice pop kit, follow the manufacturer's instructions.

Vanilla Custard Ice Pops

Makes about
3 cups (750 mL)
9 to 12 ice pops

Both children and adults love these creamy vanilla-flavored treats.

Tips

Tapioca flour is often called tapioca starch. They are identical products.

If desired, use one vanilla bean instead of the extract. Split vanilla pod lengthwise and, using the tip of a knife, scrape out the seeds. Whisk seeds into mixture with tapioca flour. (Put the scraped pod in a jar of sugar to make vanilla sugar.)

● Fine-mesh sieve

3	egg yolks	3
1/3 cup + 1 1/2 tbsp	granulated sugar	100 mL
3 tbsp	tapioca flour (see Tips, left)	45 mL
2 1/2 cups	whole milk	625 mL
1/2 cup	heavy or whipping (35%) cream	125 mL
1 1/2 tsp	vanilla extract (see Tips, left)	7 mL

1. In a saucepan, whisk egg yolks with sugar until smooth; whisk in tapioca flour. Gradually whisk in milk and cream. Place over medium-high heat and, stirring constantly, heat just until mixture starts to boil. Reduce heat to low and stir barely simmering mixture until it thickly coats a spoon, 2 to 3 minutes.

2. Strain through sieve placed over a large measuring cup (do not push solids through, but shake sieve to strain out as much smooth mixture as possible). Discard solids. Whisk in vanilla. Cover with plastic wrap, pressing it down directly onto surface to prevent a skin forming. Set aside to cool.

3. Pour into molds and freeze until slushy, then insert sticks and freeze until solid, for at least 4 hours. If you are using an ice pop kit, follow the manufacturer's instructions.

French Vanilla Ice Pops

Makes about
3 cups (750 mL)
9 to 12 ice pops

These are richer than Vanilla Custard Ice Pops (page 98) because they contain more cream and egg yolks. The combination of thyme and vanilla gives these ice pops an intriguing fragrance and flavor.

Tips

Rinse and dry the used vanilla bean pod and add to a jar of sugar to make vanilla sugar.

Instead of using a combination of milk and heavy cream, make these with 3 cups (750 mL) half-and-half (10%) cream for a slightly less rich ice pop. If you prefer a richer pop, use all table (18%) cream.

● Fine-mesh sieve

1	vanilla bean	1
2	sprigs fresh thyme	2
2 cups	whole milk	500 mL
1 cup	heavy or whipping (35%) cream	250 mL
4	egg yolks	4
1/3 cup + 1 1/2 tbsp	granulated sugar	100 mL
3 tbsp	tapioca flour (see Tips, page 98)	45 mL

1. Split vanilla bean in half lengthwise and, using the tip of a knife, scrape out the seeds. Place seeds and pod in a saucepan with thyme, milk and cream. Heat over medium-high heat until mixture is bubbling at the edges. Cover, remove from heat and set aside to steep for 10 minutes.

2. Discard thyme and reserve vanilla pod for another use (see Tips, left).

3. In a bowl, whisk egg yolks with sugar until smooth. Whisk in tapioca flour. Gradually whisk in milk mixture. Place over medium-high heat and cook, stirring constantly, just until it starts to boil. Reduce heat to low and stir barely simmering mixture until it thickly coats a spoon, 2 to 3 minutes (do not boil).

4. Place sieve over a large measuring cup and strain mixture (do not push solids through, but shake sieve to strain out as much smooth mixture as possible). Discard any solids. Cover with plastic wrap, pressing it down directly onto surface to prevent a skin forming. Set aside to cool.

5. Pour into molds and freeze until slushy, then insert sticks and freeze until solid, for at least 4 hours. If you are using an ice pop kit, follow the manufacturer's instructions.

Chocolate Pudding Ice Pops

**Makes about
3¼ cups (800 mL)
9 to 14 ice pops**

**Smooth, rich and
chocolaty, these ice pops
are a chocolate dessert–
lover's dream.**

Tips

Tapioca flour is often called
tapioca starch. They are
identical products.

For a slightly less rich and
less sweet ice pop, replace
the bittersweet and milk
chocolates with 6 oz (175 g)
semisweet chocolate.

- Fine-mesh sieve

3	egg yolks	3
⅓ cup + 1 tbsp	granulated sugar	90 mL
3 tbsp	tapioca flour (see Tips, left)	45 mL
3 cups	whole milk	750 mL
4 oz	bittersweet chocolate, chopped	125 g
2 oz	milk chocolate, chopped	60 g
½ tsp	vanilla extract	2 mL

1. In a saucepan, whisk egg yolks with sugar until smooth; whisk in tapioca flour. Gradually whisk in milk. Place over medium-high heat and heat, stirring constantly, just until mixture starts to boil. Reduce heat to low; stir barely simmering mixture until it thickly coats a spoon, 2 to 3 minutes (do not boil). Remove from heat and whisk in bittersweet and milk chocolates until melted. Whisk in vanilla and continue whisking until chocolate is thoroughly incorporated and mixture is smooth.

2. Place sieve over a large measuring cup and strain (do not push solids through, but shake sieve to strain out as much smooth mixture as possible). Discard any solids. Cover with plastic wrap, pressing it down directly onto surface to prevent a skin forming. Set aside to cool.

3. Pour into molds and freeze until slushy, then insert sticks and freeze until solid, for at least 4 hours. If you are using an ice pop kit, follow the manufacturer's instructions.

Caramel Ice Pops

Makes about
3⅔ cups (900 mL)
11 to 14 ice pops

1 cup	granulated sugar	250 mL
Pinch	sea salt	Pinch
2 cups	water, divided	500 mL
2 tbsp	butter	30 mL
¾ cup	evaporated milk	175 mL

These ice pops are sweet and creamy, with a strong caramel flavor. The high sugar content prevents them from freezing hard, but they are certainly stable enough to enjoy if you let them freeze overnight. Just don't keep them out of the freezer for too long before serving (definitely not the ice pop for a picnic on a hot summer day!).

Tip

If sugar crystallizes on the side of the saucepan while you are caramelizing it (Step 1), soak a pastry brush in water and use it to brush down any crystals.

1. In a heavy-bottomed saucepan, combine sugar, salt and ½ cup (125 mL) water. Over high heat, bring to a boil and cook, without stirring, until sugar is melted and turns a warm, deep, nutty brown.

2. Remove from heat. Turning head away and standing well back (mixture will sputter), stir in butter and remaining 1½ cups (375 mL) water. Return to medium heat and cook, stirring, until mixture is smooth and no longer bubbling. Remove from heat and stir in evaporated milk. Set aside to cool.

3. Pour into molds and freeze until slushy, then insert sticks and freeze until solid, for at least 12 hours. If you are using an ice pop kit, follow the manufacturer's instructions.

Ginger Caramel Ice Pops

**Makes about
3⅔ cups (900 mL)
11 to 14 ice pops**

A good dose of ginger complements the strong caramel flavor of these ice pops. The caramel prevents them from freezing hard, but they are solid enough to enjoy if you let them freeze overnight. As with Caramel Ice Pops (page 101), you shouldn't leave them out too long on a hot day.

Tip

If sugar crystallizes on the side of the saucepan while you are caramelizing it (Step 1), soak a pastry brush in water and use it to brush down any crystals.

- Fine-mesh sieve

1 cup	granulated sugar	250 mL
Pinch	sea salt	Pinch
2 cups	water, divided	500 mL
2 tbsp	finely grated gingerroot	30 mL
1 tbsp	lemon juice	15 mL
¾ cup	evaporated milk	175 mL

1. In a heavy-bottomed saucepan, combine sugar, salt and ½ cup (125 mL) water. Over high heat, bring to a boil and cook, without stirring, until sugar is melted and a warm, deep, nutty brown.

2. Remove from heat. Turning head away and standing well back (mixture will sputter), stir in ginger. When bubbling subsides, stir in lemon juice and remaining 1½ cups (375 mL) water. Return to medium heat and cook, stirring, until mixture no longer bubbles. Place sieve over a large measuring cup and strain, discarding solids. Stir in evaporated milk. Set aside to cool.

3. Pour into molds and freeze until slushy, then insert sticks and freeze until solid, for at least 12 hours. If you are using an ice pop kit, follow the manufacturer's instructions.

Cherry Cheesecake Ice Pops

Makes about
2¾ cups (675 mL)
8 to 11 ice pops

Fresh cherries enhance this frozen cream cheese–enriched dairy ice pop. It really tastes like cheesecake!

Tip

In many ice pops that include solid ingredients or combine liquids of different viscosities, there is a bit of layering after freezing, which is normal. However, if you want a seamless result, give the mixture a stir after it has reached the slushy stage to ensure that the ingredients remain integrated.

- Electric mixer

½ cup	granulated sugar	125 mL
½ cup	water	125 mL
2	strips (each ½ by 2 inches/ 1 by 5 cm) lemon zest	2
2 cups	chopped pitted cherries (about 12 oz/375 g whole cherries)	500 mL
¾ cup	cream cheese, softened	175 mL
¼ cup	light or regular sour cream	60 mL
⅓ cup	heavy or whipping (35%) cream	75 mL
½ tsp	vanilla extract	2 mL

1. In a saucepan, bring sugar, water and lemon zest to a boil, stirring until sugar is dissolved; reduce heat and simmer for 2 minutes. Add cherries, increase heat and bring to a boil. Remove from heat and set aside to cool.

2. When cherry mixture has cooled, strain, setting aside syrup and cherries separately. Remove and discard lemon zest. Place cherries in refrigerator to chill.

3. In a large measuring cup, using electric mixer at medium speed, beat cream cheese and sour cream until smooth and fluffy. Beat in cream and vanilla. Add reserved cherry syrup and beat until thoroughly blended.

4. Pour cream cheese mixture into molds, filling three-quarters full. Freeze until slushy. Divide reserved cherries evenly among molds and stir into half-frozen mixture to distribute evenly. Insert sticks and freeze until solid, at least 4 hours in total. If you are using an ice pop kit, follow the manufacturer's instructions.

Toasted Almond Ice Pops

Makes about
2⅓ cups (575 mL)
7 to 9 ice pops

**Almond milk makes a
naturally good base for
almond ice pops such as
these sweet and nutty
ones.**

Tip

You can buy plain almond
milk at most supermarkets
or make your own (see
page 105).

½ cup	sliced almonds	125 mL
½ cup	packed dark brown sugar	125 mL
2 tbsp	butter or almond oil	30 mL
Pinch	salt	Pinch
2 cups	plain almond milk (see Tip, left)	500 mL
¼ tsp	almond extract	1 mL

1. In a dry skillet over medium heat, toast almonds, stirring frequently, until fragrant and lightly toasted, 3 to 5 minutes. Remove from heat and set aside.

2. In a saucepan over medium heat, combine brown sugar and butter. Cook, stirring, until sugar is no longer granular but fudgy and forms a loose mass when stirred, 5 to 7 minutes. Stir in reserved toasted almonds and cook for 1 minute. Stir in almond milk and bring to a boil. Remove from heat and set aside to cool. Stir in almond extract.

3. Pour into molds and freeze until slushy, then insert sticks and freeze until solid, for at least 4 hours. If you are using an ice pop kit, follow the manufacturer's instructions.

Homemade Almond Milk

Makes about 4 cups (1 L)

Tip

You can sweeten homemade almond milk to taste with your sweetener of choice. I like to add about 1½ tbsp (22 mL) sugar or brown rice syrup, as I find honey adds a little too much flavor. The milk definitely requires some sweetening, so at first add 1 tbsp (15 mL) of whatever sweetener you choose and then taste to see if you prefer more.

- Blender
- Fine-mesh sieve
- Cheesecloth

1⅓ cups	blanched or natural whole almonds	325 mL
4 cups	water, divided	1 L
Pinch	salt, optional	Pinch
1 tbsp	granulated sugar, brown rice syrup, agave syrup or liquid honey (approx. see Tip, left)	15 mL

1. Soak almonds in water to cover for at least 4 hours or, preferably, overnight. Drain.

2. Place in blender with 1½ cups (375 mL) water and blend at medium to medium-high speed until a smooth paste forms. Add remaining 2½ cups (625 mL) water and salt, if using. Blend at high speed for a few minutes, stopping blender partway through to let motor cool down, if necessary, until liquid is as smooth as possible.

3. Strain through sieve lined with a double layer of cheesecloth, pressing down on solids to extract as much liquid as possible. Discard solids. Sweeten liquid to taste. Cover and refrigerate for up to 4 days.

Rich Almond Ice Pops

2 cups	plain almond milk (see Tips, left)	500 mL
½ cup	almond butter	125 mL
⅓ cup	agave, brown rice or corn syrup	75 mL
2 tsp	tapioca flour (see Tips, left)	10 mL
Pinch	nutmeg	Pinch
Pinch	salt	Pinch

Makes about 2¾ cups (675 mL) 8 to 11 ice pops

These pops are as rich as a good almond truffle filling and can easily be served as a dessert course. To gild the lily, try coating these with chocolate (see Coatings, page 10).

Tips

If you want to use homemade almond milk, see the recipe on page 105.

Tapioca flour is often called tapioca starch. They are identical products.

1. In a saucepan, whisk together almond milk, almond butter, syrup, tapioca flour, nutmeg and salt. Whisking constantly, bring to a boil over medium-high heat. Reduce heat and simmer, whisking constantly, for 3 minutes. Remove from heat and set aside to cool.

2. Pour into molds and freeze until slushy, then insert sticks and freeze until solid, for at least 4 hours. If you are using an ice pop kit, follow the manufacturer's instructions.

Variation

Toasted Almond Toffee Ice Pops: Reduce syrup to 3 tbsp (45 mL). After mixture has cooled, chill in refrigerator. When cold, stir in ¼ cup (60 mL) toffee bits, then pour into molds and freeze.

Hazelnut Chocolate Ice Pops

Makes about
2½ cups (625 mL)
7 to 10 ice pops

If you love truffles and other chocolates with nut and nut cream fillings, you'll be a fan of these ice pops, which are nutty and chocolaty without being overwhelmingly rich.

Tip

You can buy already roasted hazelnuts (rub as much skin off the nuts as possible) or you can make your own. Roast in a 350°F (180°C) oven for about 10 minutes (check after 8 minutes) or toast in a dry skillet over medium heat, stirring occasionally, for about 7 minutes. Remove most of the skins by rubbing hot nuts in a kitchen towel.

- Blender
- Fine-mesh sieve

1 cup	roasted hazelnuts (see Tip, left)	250 mL
1¾ cups	water	425 mL
⅓ cup + 2 tbsp	granulated sugar	105 mL
⅔ cup	evaporated milk	150 mL
1¾ oz	bittersweet or semisweet chocolate, chopped	50 g

1. In a saucepan over medium heat, combine hazelnuts, water and sugar; bring to a simmer. Cover, reduce heat to low and simmer for 1 hour. Remove from heat and set aside to cool.

2. Transfer to blender and blend at medium speed until mixture forms a paste. Add evaporated milk and blend at medium speed for 1 minute, then at high speed for 1 or 2 minutes, until mixture is as smooth as possible. Strain through sieve into a saucepan, discarding solids. Bring to a simmer over low heat; simmer, stirring constantly, for 2 minutes. Remove from heat and whisk in chocolate, until thoroughly incorporated and smooth. Set aside to cool.

3. Pour into molds and freeze until slushy, then insert sticks and freeze until solid, for at least 4 hours. If you are using an ice pop kit, follow the manufacturer's instructions.

Creamy Molasses Pecan Ice Pops

**Makes about
3 cups (750 mL)
9 to 12 ice pops**

**A touch of molasses
adds a lot of taste to the
buttermilk base of these
nutty ice pops, which
are inspired by the
flavors of the American
South.**

1 tbsp	butter	15 mL
½ cup	chopped pecans	125 mL
3 tbsp	dark brown sugar	45 mL
¼ tsp	nutmeg	1 mL
Pinch	cayenne pepper	Pinch
1½ cups	buttermilk	375 mL
⅓ cup + 1 tbsp	heavy or whipping (35%) cream	90 mL
⅓ cup + 1 tbsp	sweetened condensed milk	90 mL
3 tbsp	light (fancy) molasses	45 mL

1. In a skillet over medium heat, melt butter; add pecans and stir to coat. Sprinkle with brown sugar, nutmeg and cayenne; continue cooking and stirring until sugar is melted, no longer granular and lightly caramelized. Scrape onto a plate and set aside to cool.

2. Whisk together buttermilk, cream, condensed milk and molasses. Pour into molds, filling three-quarters full. Freeze until slushy. Divide sugared pecans evenly among molds and stir into half-frozen mixture to distribute evenly. Insert sticks and freeze until solid, at least 4 hours in total. If you are using an ice pop kit, follow the manufacturer's instructions.

Soda Fountain Ice Pops

Cream Soda Ice Pops

Makes about
2½ cups (625 mL)
7 to 10 ice pops

Cream soda, like ginger beer (page 114), was originally a homemade preparation. It was simply lightly fermented sweet vanilla-flavored water. Ice cream or cream was usually added to round out the taste. Go back to the basics with these old-fashioned soda ice pops. Don't be surprised by the soda's unusually sharp smell right after fermenting — the flavor is actually very mellow.

Tip

If you prefer, you can make a more vanilla-intense version of these ice pops by using a vanilla bean. Instead of adding the vanilla extract, split one vanilla bean lengthwise and scrape the seeds into the bottle along with the other ingredients; then add the scraped pod. Remove the pod along with the lemon zest.

- 4-cup (1 L) plastic soda pop bottle, with cap

¼ cup	warm water	60 mL
½ cup + 2 tbsp	granulated sugar, divided	155 mL
Pinch	dry active yeast	Pinch
2 tsp	vanilla extract	10 mL
Pinch	cream of tartar	Pinch
1	strip (2 by ½ inches/5 by 1 cm) lemon zest	1
2 cups	water	500 mL
½ cup	heavy or whipping (35%) cream	125 mL

1. In a small bowl, stir together warm water and 2 tbsp (30 mL) sugar until sugar is dissolved. Sprinkle yeast evenly over surface. Set aside until foamy, about 10 minutes.

2. In soda pop bottle, shake together remaining ½ cup (125 mL) sugar, vanilla, cream of tartar, lemon zest and water until sugar is dissolved. Pour in yeast mixture and shake to mix. Seal bottle with original screw top and set aside in a warm place for at least 24 hours or up to 36 hours. Open bottle slowly to allow built-up air pressure to escape. Pour into a large measuring cup. Remove and discard lemon zest; stir in cream.

3. Pour into molds and freeze until slushy, then insert sticks and freeze until solid, for at least 4 hours. If you are using an ice pop kit, follow the manufacturer's instructions.

Root Beer Float Ice Pops

**Makes about
2½ cups (625 mL)
7 to 10 ice pops**

**This is the essence of a
perennial favorite, root
beer topped with vanilla
ice cream. You can also
make it with birch beer,
sarsaparilla or cola.**

Tip

Many of the root beers made
by smaller, craft-style soda
pop manufacturers have a
much richer flavor than the
more common international
brands. They are often
all-natural or organic.

½ cup	heavy or whipping (35%) cream	125 mL
2 tbsp	sweetened condensed milk	30 mL
½ tsp	vanilla extract	2 mL
1½ cups	root beer (see Tip, left)	375 mL

1. In a large measuring cup, whisk together cream, condensed milk and vanilla. Stir in root beer. After bubbles subside, stir again.

2. Pour into molds, leaving a generous ¾-inch (2 cm) headspace for bubbling up, and freeze until slushy, then insert sticks and freeze until solid, for at least 4 hours. If you are using an ice pop kit, follow the manufacturer's instructions.

Lemon Cola Ice Pops

**Makes about
2½ cups (625 mL)
7 to 10 ice pops**

**In Hong Kong's hot,
steamy summer weather,
"lemon cola" — iced
cola enriched with a
generous amount of
lemon juice — is a
favorite beverage.**

2	cans (12 oz/355 mL each) cola	2
	Zest of ½ lemon, cut into strips	
⅓ cup	freshly squeezed lemon juice	75 mL

1. In a saucepan, bring cola and lemon zest to a boil. Boil over medium-high heat until reduced by about one-quarter, about 10 minutes. Remove from heat and set aside to cool. Remove and discard zest. Stir in lemon juice.

2. Pour into molds and freeze until slushy, then insert sticks and freeze until solid, for at least 4 hours. If you are using an ice pop kit, follow the manufacturer's instructions.

Cherry Soda Ice Pops

**Makes about
3 cups (750 mL)
9 to 12 ice pops**

**Real cherry syrup makes
a genuine cherry soda,
which is not easy to find
in the commercial soda
pop world. Fortunately,
it's easy to make at home.**

Tip

Some cherry sodas have a
bit of vanilla flavoring. If you
are a fan of that type, add
½ tsp (2 mL) vanilla extract
to the cooled cherry syrup.

• Fine-mesh sieve

1 lb	cherries, pitted	500 g
½ cup	granulated sugar	125 mL
¼ cup	water	60 mL
⅓ cup	light agave syrup or corn syrup	75 mL
2 cups	soda water or seltzer water	500 mL

1. Place cherries in a saucepan and sprinkle with
   sugar and water. Bring to a boil over high heat.
   Reduce heat to medium-low and simmer, covered,
   until cherries are mushy, 15 to 20 minutes.

2. Scrape mixture into sieve placed over a measuring
   cup or bowl. Strain out as much liquid as possible,
   lightly pressing down on solids to extract liquid
   but not pushing them through. Discard solids. Stir
   in agave syrup and chill in refrigerator for at least
   2 hours.

3. Pour soda water into a large measuring cup. Slowly
   add chilled cherry syrup, stirring to mix well.

4. When bubbles have subsided, pour into molds,
   leaving a little headspace for bubbles, and freeze
   until slushy, then insert sticks and freeze until
   solid, for at least 4 hours. If you are using an ice
   pop kit, follow the manufacturer's instructions.

Lemon-Lime Soda Ice Pops

**Makes about
3½ cups (875 mL)
10 to 14 ice pops**

This homemade version
of lemon-lime soda pop
has much more citrus
flavor and tartness but is
as sweet as a commercial
pop. In my opinion,
this gives it a much
better sweet-tart profile,
producing a particularly
delicious ice pop.

Tips

Always use freshly squeezed
lemon juice or lime juice in
your ice pops; bottled just
doesn't compare.

If using water rather than
soda water, add a scant
pinch of salt.

½ cup	granulated sugar	125 mL
⅓ cup + 1 tbsp	water	90 mL
1 tsp	finely grated lime zest	5 mL
1 tsp	finely grated lemon zest	5 mL
½ cup	freshly squeezed lime juice	125 mL
¼ cup	freshly squeezed lemon juice	60 mL
3 tbsp	unsweetened apple juice concentrate	45 mL
2 cups	soda water, or plain water (see Tips, left)	500 mL

1. In a small saucepan, combine sugar, water and lime and lemon zests; bring to a boil, stirring until sugar is dissolved. Remove from heat and set aside for 5 minutes.

2. In a large measuring cup, mix together reserved syrup, lime and lemon juices and apple juice concentrate. Add soda water and stir to mix well.

3. Pour into molds (if using soda water, leave a little headspace for bubbles) and freeze until slushy, then insert sticks and freeze until solid, for at least 4 hours. If you are using an ice pop kit, follow the manufacturer's instructions.

Ginger Beer Ice Pops

Makes about
4½ cups (1.125 L)
13 to 18 ice pops

Homemade Caribbean-style ginger beer, with its strong ginger bite and slight yeastiness, has a special appeal. You can easily double all of the ingredients except for the yeast, providing enough to make the ice pops and extra to enjoy as a drink (see Tips, below).

Tips

Use the coarse holes of a box grater to grate the gingerroot.

For extra ginger beer to enjoy as a drink: After straining mixture in Step 3, pour into plastic soda pop bottles, leaving 2 to 3 inches (5 to 8 cm) headspace. Seal bottle with original screw top and set aside in a warm place for 24 hours. Unseal to release gas. Seal again and refrigerate. Drink within 4 or 5 days, before carbonation weakens.

- Fine-mesh sieve

1½ cups	granulated sugar	375 mL
⅓ cup	grated gingerroot (see Tips, left)	75 mL
	Zest from ½ lemon, cut into wide strips	
2 tbsp	freshly squeezed lemon juice	30 mL
1½ tsp	ground ginger	7 mL
½ tsp	cream of tartar	2 mL
2	whole cloves	2
4½ cups	boiling water	1.125 L
½ tsp	active dry yeast	2 mL

1. In a non-metallic heatproof bowl, mix together sugar, grated ginger, lemon zest and juice, ground ginger, cream of tartar and cloves. Add boiling water and stir until sugar is dissolved. Set aside to cool to about body temperature.

2. Sprinkle a scant ½ tsp (2 mL) yeast over surface of ginger mixture. When yeast begins to foam, stir mixture well. Cover with plastic. Set aside in a warm place for at least 24 or up to 36 hours.

3. Open the bottle slowly to allow the built-up air pressure to escape. Strain mixture through sieve placed over a large measuring cup. Set aside strained mixture for 15 minutes to allow yeast particles to settle to the bottom. Pour into molds, discarding any sediment. Freeze until slushy, then insert sticks and freeze until solid, for at least 4 hours. If you are using an ice pop kit, follow the manufacturer's instructions.

Variation

Moscow Mule Cocktail Ice Pops: Use some of your ginger beer to make these boozy ice pops. After final straining (Step 3), stir 3 tbsp (45 mL) vodka and 2 tbsp (30 mL) lime juice into 2 cups (500 mL) ginger beer. Pour into molds and freeze until solid, at least 4 hours or preferably overnight.

Homemade Chocolate Syrup

Makes about 2⅔ cups (650 mL)

This chocolate syrup will keep, refrigerated, for months. You can use it for ice pops, of course, but also to make fabulous chocolate milk, to drizzle over waffles or cake, or as an ice cream or frozen yogurt topping. It's definitely more intensely chocolate-flavored than commercial versions.

- Fine-mesh sieve

1 cup + 2 tbsp	granulated sugar	280 mL
⅔ cup	unsweetened cocoa powder	150 mL
1½ cups	water	375 mL
⅓ cup	agave or corn syrup	75 mL
Pinch	salt	Pinch
1	bar (3½ ounces/100 g) fine bittersweet (85%) or semisweet (70%) chocolate, chopped or grated	1
¾ tsp	vanilla extract	3 mL

1. In a saucepan, whisk together sugar and cocoa. Whisk in water and place over medium-high heat. Still whisking, bring to a boil; stir in syrup and salt. Reduce heat and simmer, stirring often, for 5 minutes. Remove from heat.

2. Whisk in chocolate until thoroughly incorporated and smooth. Whisk in vanilla. Strain through sieve (use as fine a mesh as possible to strain out tiny specks of unmelted chocolate). Discard any solids. Set aside to cool.

3. Whisk cooled mixture well and pour into an airtight container. Store, refrigerated, for up to 6 months. Stir or shake well before using.

Milkshake Ice Pops

Makes about
3⅓ cups (825 mL)
10 to 13 ice pops

Quick and easy, these
creamy ice pops are
especially nice to make
during the height of
strawberry season.

Strawberry Milkshake Ice Pops

- Blender

2 cups	halved hulled fresh strawberries or whole frozen strawberries, thawed	500 mL
1⅓ cups	table (18%) cream	325 mL
⅔ cup	sweetened condensed milk	150 mL
1 tsp	vanilla extract	5 mL

1. In blender at medium speed, purée strawberries, cream, condensed milk and vanilla.

2. Pour into molds and freeze until slushy, then insert sticks and freeze until solid, for at least 4 hours. If you are using an ice pop kit, follow the manufacturer's instructions.

Makes about
3 cups (750 mL)
9 to 12 ice pops

This chocolate ice pop
brings back memories
of drugstore, road-
stop and ice cream
parlor milkshakes. Use
commercial chocolate
syrup for convenience,
or make your own
(see page 115).

Chocolate Milkshake Ice Pops

- Blender

2 cups	half-and-half (10%) cream	500 mL
½ cup	sweetened condensed milk	125 mL
⅓ cup + 1 tbsp	chocolate syrup	90 mL
1 tsp	vanilla extract	5 mL

1. In blender at medium-high speed, blend cream, condensed milk, chocolate syrup and vanilla until frothy.

2. Pour into molds and freeze until slushy, then insert sticks and freeze until solid, for at least 4 hours. If you are using an ice pop kit, follow the manufacturer's instructions.

Herbs, Spices and Vegetables

Lemon Honey Mint Ice Pops

Makes about 3½ cups (875 mL) 10 to 14 ice pops	

Soothing and sweet,
**fragrant and tart, this
lemony ice pop is
as refreshing as it is
delicious.**

Tips

Because Meyer lemons
have exceptionally fragrant
zest, they are ideal for these
ice pops.

Use a light honey such as
orange blossom, alfalfa,
clover, wildflower or acacia.

* Fine-mesh sieve

2½ cups	water	625 mL
1 cup	lightly packed fresh mint leaves	250 mL
	Zest of 2 lemons, cut into strips (see Tips, left)	
½ cup	liquid honey (see Tips, left)	125 mL
⅔ cup	freshly squeezed lemon juice	150 mL

1. In a saucepan, bring water to a boil; remove from heat and add mint and lemon zest. Cover and set aside to steep for 10 minutes.

2. Place sieve over a large measuring cup and strain infusion. Discard solids. Stir in honey until fully incorporated. Stir in lemon juice.

3. Pour into molds and freeze until slushy, then insert sticks and freeze until solid, for at least 4 hours. If you are using an ice pop kit, follow the manufacturer's instructions.

Variations

Lemon Balm Honey Ice Pops: Replace the mint with ⅔ cup (150 mL) lightly packed lemon balm leaves.

Lemon Verbena Honey Ice Pops: Replace the mint with ⅔ cup (150 mL) lightly packed lemon verbena leaves.

Rhubarb Mint Ice Pops

**Makes about
2½ cups (625 mL)
7 to 10 ice pops**

**Tart rhubarb and sweet
mint make a smooth
pair in these pretty pink
ice pops. The flavor is
piqued by just a hint of
black pepper.**

Tip

Bruise peppercorns by
pressing down on them and
rolling with the side of a
chef's knife or the bottom of
a heavy saucepan. You want
to crush or crack them a bit,
not grind them into powder.

- Fine-mesh sieve

1 lb	rhubarb, sliced (about 3½ cups/875 mL)	500 g
2 cups	water	500 mL
⅔ cup	granulated sugar	150 mL
4	strips lemon zest, ½ by 2 inches (1 by 5 cm) each	4
4	black peppercorns, bruised (see Tip, left)	4
1 cup	lightly packed fresh mint leaves	250 mL

1. In a saucepan, combine rhubarb, water, sugar, lemon zest and peppercorns. Bring to a boil, reduce heat and simmer, covered, for 15 minutes. Remove from heat and stir in mint. Cover and set aside to steep for 10 minutes.

2. Place sieve over a large measuring cup and strain, pressing down on solids to extract as much juice as possible. Discard solids.

3. Pour into molds and freeze until slushy, then insert sticks and freeze until solid, for at least 4 hours. If you are using an ice pop kit, follow the manufacturer's instructions.

Mint Aryan Ice Pops

**Makes about
2¼ cups (550 mL)
6 to 9 ice pops**

Aryan is a refreshing
savory or slightly
sweetened Turkish
yogurt drink, similar to
Indian lassi and other
yogurt concoctions
enjoyed throughout
the Middle East and
South Asia. With a full,
fresh mint flavor, this
yogurt-drink-turned-ice-
pop has just a touch of
sweetness.

Tip

In many ice pops that
include solid ingredients or
combine liquids of different
viscosities, there is a bit of
layering after freezing, which
is normal. However, if you
want a seamless result, give
the mixture a stir after it has
reached the slushy stage to
ensure that the ingredients
remain integrated.

- Blender
- Fine-mesh sieve

1¾ cups	full-fat or 2% plain yogurt	425 mL
½ cup	packed fresh mint leaves	125 mL
¼ cup	water	60 mL
4 tsp	liquid honey or granulated sugar	20 mL
1 tbsp	freshly squeezed lemon juice	15 mL
Pinch	salt	Pinch

1. In blender, combine yogurt, mint, water, honey,
   lemon juice and a scant pinch of salt. Blend at
   medium-high speed until mixture is frothy and
   mint is finely chopped.

2. Place sieve over a large measuring cup and strain
   mixture, pressing down on solids to get as much
   liquid as possible. Discard solids.

3. Pour into molds and freeze until slushy, then
   insert sticks and freeze until solid, for at least
   4 hours. If you are using an ice pop kit, follow
   the manufacturer's instructions.

Sweet Basil and Citrus Ice Pops

Makes about
2½ cups (625 mL)
7 to 10 ice pops

To make these ice pops really shine, use freshly harvested basil, with all its heady fragrance. Here the basil acts as an undertone to a complex bitter citrus flavor, akin to adding a sprig of mint to a vermouth or Campari aperitif.

Tip

Angostura bitters are available at large grocery stores as well as many liquor stores. It is a famous flavoring produced in Trinidad. The original recipe, which includes gentian and other herbs, was developed in the Venezuelan town of Angostura.

- Fine-mesh sieve

1 cup	water	250 mL
½ cup	granulated sugar	125 mL
2	strips orange zest, ½ by 2 inches (1 x 5 cm) each	2
1	strip grapefruit zest, 1 by 5 inches (2.5 by 12.5 cm)	1
1	strip lemon zest, ½ by 2 inches (1 by 5 cm)	1
½ cup	packed fresh basil leaves, chopped	125 mL
½ cup	freshly squeezed orange juice	125 mL
½ cup	freshly squeezed grapefruit juice	125 ml
¼ cup	freshly squeezed lemon juice	60 mL
Dash	angostura or orange bitters	Dash

1. In a saucepan, combine water, sugar and orange, grapefruit and lemon zests. Bring to a boil, reduce heat and simmer for 4 minutes. Remove from heat and stir in basil. Cover and set aside to steep for 10 minutes. Uncover and set aside to cool.

2. Place sieve over a large measuring cup and strain mixture. Discard solids. Whisk in orange, grapefruit and lemon juices and bitters.

3. Pour into molds and freeze until slushy, then insert sticks and freeze until solid, for at least 4 hours. If you are using an ice pop kit, follow the manufacturer's instructions.

Watermelon Chile Ice Pops

Makes about
3 cups (750 mL)
9 to 12 ice pops

Red-hot peppers flavor the syrup for these unusual ice pops, which, despite the touch of heat, are still very refreshing.

Tip

Although the recipe calls for seedless watermelon for convenience, it is still a good idea to strain the mixture, to remove any soft white immature seeds that dot the flesh.

- Blender
- Fine-mesh sieve

1/3 cup	granulated sugar	75 mL
1/3 cup	water	75 mL
2 tbsp	minced seeded red finger chile peppers	30 mL
Pinch	salt	Pinch
4 cups	chopped seedless (or seeded) watermelon	1 L
2 tbsp	freshly squeezed lemon juice	30 mL

1. In a small saucepan, combine sugar, water, chile peppers and salt. Bring to a boil, reduce heat and simmer for 2 minutes. Remove from heat and set aside to cool.

2. In blender at medium-high speed, blend watermelon and lemon juice until smooth. Place sieve over a large measuring cup and strain mixture, pressing down on solids to extract as much pulp and juice as possible. Discard solids. Return mixture to blender and add reserved chile syrup. Blend until chiles are reduced to tiny specks.

3. Pour into molds and freeze until slushy, then insert sticks and freeze until solid, for at least 4 hours. If you are using an ice pop kit, follow the manufacturer's instructions.

Honeydew Jalapeño Ice Pops

**Makes about
3 cups (750 mL)
9 to 12 ice pops**

Lightly sweet and
slightly hot, these
intriguing ice pops are
very refreshing. Try
serving them between
savory courses at a
barbecue or casual
summer dinner.

Tip

In many ice pops that
include solid ingredients or
combine liquids of different
viscosities, there is a bit of
layering after freezing, which
is normal. However, if you
want a seamless result, give
the mixture a stir after it has
reached the slushy stage
to ensure the ingredients
remain integrated.

- Blender

⅓ cup	granulated sugar	75 mL
⅓ cup	water	75 mL
1	jalapeño pepper, seeded and minced	1
2	strips lime zest, about ½ by 2 inches (1 by 5 cm) each	2
4 cups	chopped honeydew melon	1 L
3 tbsp	freshly squeezed lime juice	45 mL
1 tbsp	chopped fresh cilantro leaves	15 mL
Pinch	salt	Pinch

1. In a small saucepan, combine sugar, water, jalapeño and lime zest. Bring to a boil, reduce heat and simmer for 1 minute. Remove from heat, cover and set aside to steep for 5 minutes. Remove and discard zest.

2. In blender at medium-high speed, purée melon, lime juice, cilantro and a scant pinch salt. Add reserved jalapeño syrup and blend at low speed just until integrated.

3. Pour into molds and freeze until slushy, then insert sticks and freeze until solid, for at least 4 hours. If you are using an ice pop kit, follow the manufacturer's instructions.

Pear and Linden Flower Ice Pops

Makes about 2 cups (500 mL) 6 to 8 ice pops

These ice pops feature the unusual pairing of pears with a traditional European herbal tea (tisane) made from linden tree flowers, as well as honey from the same flowers.

Tips

Linden blossom honey is especially fragrant and flavorful. Look for it in eastern European grocery stores and specialty shops.

Linden tea, properly a tisane or herbal tea, is made from the dried flowers of the linden tree (known as basswood in the US and lime in the UK). The tea sometimes includes the elongated false leaves that are attached to the flower stalks (like the "wings" of maple keys). You can buy linden tea loose or in tea bags.

- Blender

1⅓ cups	boiling water	325 mL
¼ cup	packed linden flowers with attached false leaves or 2 tbsp (30 mL) dried linden flowers only (see Tips, left)	60 mL
12 oz	ripe pears, peeled, cored and chopped (2 cups/500 mL)	375 g
3 tbsp	linden blossom honey or other floral honey, such as orange blossom, clover or acacia (see Tips, left)	45 mL
1½ tbsp	freshly squeezed lemon juice	22 mL

1. Pour boiling water over linden flowers and set aside to steep for 15 minutes. Strain into a small saucepan, discarding solids. Add pears and honey.

2. Bring mixture to a boil, reduce heat and simmer until pears are soft, 10 to 20 minutes, depending on variety and ripeness. Remove from heat and set aside to cool. Transfer to blender and purée at medium-high speed. Stir in lemon juice.

3. Pour into molds and freeze until slushy, then insert sticks and freeze until solid, for at least 4 hours. If you are using an ice pop kit, follow the manufacturer's instructions.

Lavender-Scented Red Grape Ice Pops

Makes about 3 cups (750 mL) 9 to 12 ice pops

Lavender has an incredible, almost iconic aroma reminiscent of sun-baked flowerbeds.

Tips

Although all varieties of lavender are edible and all parts of the plant can be used for flavoring, culinary lavender is usually the dried flower buds of unsprayed English lavender, and that is the kind we use for these ice pops.

Be careful when using lavender in cooking — too much and it becomes overwhelmingly perfumy or even soapy. I prefer just a background hint and use just 1 tsp (5 mL); add more to taste, but don't exceed the maximum amount of 3 tsp (15 mL) or the lavender will overtake all the other flavorings.

- Fine-mesh sieve

1 lb, 6 oz	sweet red grapes (3 cups/ 750 mL)	675 g
½ cup	water	125 mL
⅓ cup	granulated sugar	75 mL
2	strips lemon zest, ½ by 2 inches (1 by 5 cm) each	2
2	sprigs fresh thyme or ¼ tsp (1 mL) dried thyme	2
1 to 3 tsp	dried lavender flowers (see Tips, left)	5 to 15 mL
2 tbsp	freshly squeezed lemon juice	30 mL

1. In a saucepan, combine grapes, water, sugar, lemon zest and dried thyme (if using). Bring to a boil over high heat, reduce heat to medium and simmer, covered, until grapes are falling apart, 15 to 25 minutes.

2. Remove from heat and stir in fresh thyme and lavender. Cover and set aside to steep for 10 minutes.

3. Using a fork or potato masher, mash grapes. Strain through sieve placed over a large measuring cup, pressing down and scraping solids with a rubber spatula to extract as much pulp and juice as possible. Discard solids. Stir in lemon juice and set aside to cool.

4. Pour into molds and freeze until slushy, then insert sticks and freeze until solid, for at least 4 hours. If you are using an ice pop kit, follow the manufacturer's instructions.

Beet and Cucumber Ice Pops

Makes about
2½ cups (625 mL)
7 to 10 ice pops

This ice pop is inspired by an Old World summer favorite — refreshing sweet-and-sour cold beet borscht, served with fresh cucumber slices and a generous dollop of sour cream.

Tips

This recipe was tested using a field cucumber with seeds. If you use a seedless cucumber, the volume and quantity of ice pops will increase.

Cook the beets, whole and unpeeled, with about 1 inch (2.5 cm) of the stems attached, in boiling water to cover until tender, 25 to 45 minutes, depending on size, freshness and variety. Or wrap beets in aluminum foil and bake in preheated 375°F (190°C) oven until tender, 30 to 60 minutes. While they are still warm, cut off the tops and rub off the skins.

- Fine-mesh sieve
- Blender

½ cup	water	125 mL
⅓ cup	granulated sugar	75 mL
	Zest of ½ lemon, cut into strips	
¼ tsp	salt	1 mL
½ cup	fresh dill sprigs	125 mL
3 cups	chopped peeled cucumber	750 mL
1⅓ cups	chopped cooked beets (see Tips, left)	325 mL
⅓ cup	freshly squeezed lemon juice	75 mL
½ cup	light or regular sour cream	125 mL

1. In a small saucepan, combine water, sugar, lemon zest and salt. Bring to a boil, stirring until sugar is dissolved; remove from heat and set aside for 1 minute. Add dill, cover and set aside to steep for 5 minutes. Strain through sieve into blender. Discard solids.

2. Add cucumber, beets and lemon juice to blender and purée at medium-high speed. Strain through sieve placed over a large measuring cup, pressing down on solids to extract as much juice as possible. Discard solids. Whisk in sour cream.

3. Pour into molds and freeze until slushy, then insert sticks and freeze until solid, for at least 4 hours. If you are using an ice pop kit, follow the manufacturer's instructions.

Vegetable Cocktail Ice Pops

**Makes about
4 cups (1 L)
12 to 16 ice pops**

These refreshing and
nutritious vegetable
cocktail ice pops are
lightly sweetened with
either sugar or honey.
Sugar gives a neutral
sweetness, while honey
asserts itself a bit more.
Use whichever suits
your taste.

Tip

A good silicone spatula is
immensely useful, and two
are better. I like to use a
narrow one for scraping the
blender and a wider one for
pressing mixtures through
a sieve or scraping clean
mixing bowls and measuring
cups. The silicone ones are
heatproof and nonstick too,
so they are good for scraping
hot syrup out of saucepans.
If you don't have a silicone
spatula, you can always use
a wooden spoon or soup
ladle for pushing mixtures
through a fine-mesh sieve.

- Blender
- Fine-mesh sieve

1½ lbs	ripe tomatoes, chopped (about 4½ cups/1.125 L)	750 g
1 cup	water	250 mL
¾ cup	chopped carrots	175 mL
½ cup	chopped celery	125 mL
⅓ cup	chopped sweet red pepper	75 mL
¼ cup	chopped sweet green pepper	60 mL
¼ cup	chopped sweet or white onion	60 mL
¼ cup	chopped parsley leaves	60 mL
¼ cup	granulated sugar or 3 tbsp (45 mL) honey	60 mL
¼ tsp	(approx.) freshly ground black pepper	1 mL
¼ tsp	salt	1 mL
2½ tbsp	freshly squeezed lemon juice	37 mL

1. In a large saucepan, stir together tomatoes, water, carrots, celery, red and green peppers, onion, parsley, sugar, pepper and salt. Bring to a boil, reduce heat and simmer, covered, for 20 minutes. Remove from heat, uncover and set aside to cool.

2. Transfer to blender and purée at medium-high speed. Place sieve over a large measuring cup and strain, pressing down and scraping solids with a rubber spatula to extract as much pulp and juice as possible. Discard solids. Stir in lemon juice and a bit of additional black pepper to taste.

3. Pour into molds and freeze until slushy, then insert sticks and freeze until solid, for at least 4 hours. If you are using an ice pop kit, follow the manufacturer's instructions.

Variation

Spiked Vegetable Cocktail Ice Pops: For an
intriguing flavor, stir in ⅓ cup (75 mL) aquavit
with the lemon juice. Or, for just the kick, use
vodka. Freeze overnight, if possible.

Gazpacho Ice Pops

Makes 2⅔ cups
(650 mL)
8 to 10 ice pops

Gazpacho ice pops are fun for picnics and barbecues, or simply as a refreshing savory treat on a hot day. The traditional Spanish cold soup usually incorporates a touch of garlic and loads of fragrant olive oil for flavor and body, but in ice pop form it is better to omit the garlic and use much less oil — just enough to enjoy its fragrance.

Tip

The vodka is used to make the texture a bit less icy; it is barely noticeable, so you can omit it if you prefer.

- Blender
- Fine-mesh sieve

1 lb	very ripe red tomatoes, chopped (about 3 cups/750 mL)	500 g
½ cup	water	125 mL
⅓ cup	chopped peeled cucumber	75 mL
⅓ cup	chopped sweet or white onion	75 mL
¼ cup	chopped green bell pepper	60 mL
2 tbsp	fragrant extra virgin olive oil	30 mL
2 tbsp	vodka, optional (see Tip, left)	30 mL
1 tbsp	sherry vinegar	15 mL
¾ tsp	salt	3 mL
¾ tsp	granulated sugar	3 mL

1. In blender at medium-high speed, blend tomatoes, water, cucumber, onion, green pepper, olive oil, vodka (if using), vinegar, salt and sugar, until smooth.

2. Place sieve over a large measuring cup and strain mixture, pressing down and scraping solids with a rubber spatula to extract as much pulp and juice as possible. Discard solids.

3. Pour into molds and freeze until slushy, then insert sticks and freeze until solid, for at least 4 hours. If you are using an ice pop kit, follow the manufacturer's instructions.

Variation

Yellow Gazpacho Ice Pops: Replace the red tomatoes with yellow tomatoes and the green bell pepper with yellow bell pepper. Increase the vinegar to 4 tsp (20 mL).

Sweet Tomato and Ginger Ice Pops

Makes about 2¼ cups (550 mL) 6 to 9 ice pops

In southern Taiwan I learned to eat the local green-and-red-streaked, unusually sweet tomatoes with a dipping sauce of sugar, ginger and soy sauce. It's strange but good.

Tip

Grape tomatoes are generally the sweetest tomatoes available year-round, but you can use any other cherry or large variety as long as they are fully ripe and sweet.

- Blender
- Fine-mesh sieve

⅓ cup	granulated sugar	75 mL
¼ cup	water	60 mL
1½ tbsp	finely grated gingerroot	22 mL
4 cups	halved grape or cherry tomatoes or chopped large, sweet tomatoes	1 L
1 tbsp	freshly squeezed lemon juice	15 mL
1 tsp	light soy sauce	5 mL

1. In a small saucepan, bring sugar, water and ginger to a boil. Reduce heat and simmer for 2 minutes. Transfer to blender. Add tomatoes, lemon juice and soy sauce and purée at medium-high speed.

2. Place sieve over a large measuring cup and strain mixture, pressing down and scraping solids with a rubber spatula to extract as much pulp and juice as possible. Discard solids.

3. Pour into molds and freeze until slushy, then insert sticks and freeze until solid, for at least 4 hours. If you are using an ice pop kit, follow the manufacturer's instructions.

Carrot, Apple and Ginger Ice Pops

Makes about 2⅔ cups (650 mL) 8 to 10 ice pops

A favorite healthy juice combination makes an excellent ice pop too.

Tip

Because every brand of blender has a different power capacity, speeds vary greatly. Generally, to purée a mixture, start at slow to medium speed and move up to medium-high speed on a powerful blender, or high speed on a less powerful model. If the engine is very strong, too much air may be incorporated into the mixture at high speed.

- Blender
- Fine-mesh sieve

2 cups	chopped carrots	500 mL
2 cups	unsweetened apple juice or apple cider	500 mL
¼ cup	liquid honey	60 mL
4 tsp	minced gingerroot	20 mL

1. In blender at high speed, purée carrots, apple juice, honey and ginger.

2. Place sieve over a large measuring cup and strain mixture, pressing down on solids to extract as much juice as possible. Discard solids.

3. Pour into molds and freeze until slushy, then insert sticks and freeze until solid, for at least 4 hours. If you are using an ice pop kit, follow the manufacturer's instructions.

Creamed Corn Ice Pops

Makes about 2¾ cups (675 mL) 8 to 11 ice pops

Sweet creamed corn ice pops are certainly a pleasant surprise. These are best made with fresh sweet corn, but frozen corn is an acceptable substitute.

Tip

In many ice pops that include solid ingredients or combine liquids of different viscosities, there is a bit of layering after freezing, which is normal. However, if you want a seamless result, give the mixture a stir after it has reached the slushy stage to ensure that the ingredients remain integrated.

- Blender
- Fine-mesh sieve

2 cups	corn kernels (2 to 3 cobs)	500 mL
½ cup	water	125 mL
⅓ cup	packed dark brown sugar	75 mL
2 tbsp	butter	30 mL
	Freshly grated nutmeg	
1 cup	whole milk	250 mL
¼ tsp	vanilla extract	1 mL

1. In a saucepan, combine corn, water, brown sugar, butter and a small scraping of nutmeg. Bring to a boil, reduce heat and simmer until corn is very tender, 10 to 15 minutes for fresh corn or about 5 minutes for frozen kernels. Remove from heat and set aside to cool.

2. In blender at medium-high to high speed, purée corn mixture with milk and vanilla. (Make sure to blend long enough to make as smooth a mixture as you can; it should resemble heavy cream with tiny bits of fibrous matter.)

3. Place sieve over a large measuring cup and strain mixture, pressing down on any solids to extract as much liquid as possible. Discard solids.

4. Pour into molds and freeze until slushy, then insert sticks and freeze until solid, for at least 4 hours. If you are using an ice pop kit, follow the manufacturer's instructions.

Savory Cucumber Aryan Ice Pops

Makes about 2 cups (500 mL) 6 to 8 ice pops

Aryan is a Turkish yogurt drink, similar to Indian lassi, that comes in many versions. This ice pop is a frozen version of the traditional cucumber aryan, which is not sweetened at all. These savory ice pops might not be to everyone's taste, but I particularly enjoy one as a refreshing and healthy between-meal snack on hot summer days.

- Blender

1¼ cups	full-fat or 2% yogurt	300 mL
¼ cup	water	60 mL
1 cup	diced peeled, seeded cucumber	250 mL
¼ tsp	salt	1 mL
Pinch	freshly ground black or cayenne pepper	Pinch

1. In blender at medium-high speed, purée yogurt, water, cucumber, a scant ¼ tsp (0.75 mL) salt, and pepper to taste.

2. Pour into molds and freeze until slushy, then insert sticks and freeze until solid, for at least 4 hours. If you are using an ice pop kit, follow the manufacturer's instructions.

Classic Comfort Desserts

Maple Walnut Ice Pops

**Makes about
2¼ cups (550 mL)
6 to 9 ice pops**

**The classic North
American ice cream
pairing of maple
flavoring with walnuts
also proves irresistible
in ice pop form.**

Tip

In this recipe — and almost
always when cooking with
maple syrup — medium
(amber) or dark maple
syrups are preferable to
the lighter versions, as they
have a more robust and
richer taste that stands up
well to other flavorings.
Medium-grade (amber)
is an all-purpose maple
syrup, while dark is usually
reserved for baking and
commercial preparations.
Light or "fancy" maple syrup
is best used as a table syrup.

- Blender or immersion blender

1 cup	walnut halves	250 mL
1 cup less 2 tbsp	water	220 mL
⅔ cup	maple syrup	150 mL
1 cup	evaporated milk	250 mL

1. In a dry skillet over medium heat, toast walnuts, turning occasionally, until lightly toasted and fragrant, 6 to 8 minutes. Remove from heat and set aside to cool. Chop finely.

2. In a saucepan, combine chopped walnuts, water and maple syrup. Bring to a boil, reduce heat and simmer, uncovered, for 5 minutes. Remove from heat and set aside to cool for 10 minutes. Add evaporated milk. Transfer to blender and blend at medium-high speed until smooth.

3. Pour into molds and freeze until slushy, then insert sticks and freeze until solid, for at least 4 hours. If you are using an ice pop kit, follow the manufacturer's instructions.

Pecan Pie Ice Pops

Makes about
3 cups (750 mL)
9 to 12 ice pops

Who can resist frozen pecan pie? Everything but the pastry is here, and there's no skimping on the nuts.

Tip

Tapioca flour is often called tapioca starch. They are identical products.

- Fine-mesh sieve

¾ cup	pecan halves	175 mL
3 tbsp	butter	45 mL
⅓ cup + 1 tbsp	agave or dark corn syrup	90 mL
5 tsp	fancy molasses	25 mL
Pinch	salt	Pinch
1½ cups	water	375 mL
5 tsp	tapioca flour (see Tip, left)	25 mL
1	egg	1
1	egg yolk	1
⅓ cup + 1 tbsp	heavy or whipping (35%) cream	90 mL
¾ tsp	vanilla extract	3 mL

1. In a dry skillet over medium heat, toast pecans, stirring, until fragrant and lightly toasted, about 6 minutes. Remove from heat and set aside to cool. Chop and set aside.

2. In a saucepan over medium heat, stir together butter, syrup, molasses and salt. When butter has melted, whisk in water and tapioca flour. Bring to a boil over high heat, stirring constantly. Remove from heat.

3. In a bowl, whisk together egg, egg yolk and cream. Whisk ⅓ cup (75 mL) hot mixture into egg mixture, whisking until smooth. Whisk egg mixture into saucepan. Return to stovetop and cook over medium-low heat, stirring (do not boil), until mixture has thickened enough to coat a spoon thickly.

4. Place sieve over a large measuring cup and strain mixture, discarding any solids. Whisk in vanilla and set aside to cool.

5. Stir in reserved chopped pecans. Pour into molds and freeze until slushy, then insert sticks and freeze until solid, for at least 4 hours. If you are using an ice pop kit, follow the manufacturer's instructions.

Apple Crumble Ice Pops

**Makes about
3 cups (750 mL)
9 to 12 ice pops**

**These ice pops taste
just like apple crumble
frozen on a stick.
Delicious!**

⅓ cup	large-flake (old-fashioned) rolled oats	75 mL
⅓ cup	sliced almonds	75 mL
¼ cup	packed dark brown sugar, divided	60 mL
Pinch	salt	Pinch
4 tsp + 1 tbsp	butter, divided	35 mL
¾ cup	finely diced apple	175 mL
1 tbsp	freshly squeezed lemon juice	15 mL
1 tbsp	granulated sugar	15 mL
¼ tsp	cinnamon	1 mL
Pinch	nutmeg	Pinch
Pinch	cloves	Pinch
1½ cups	apple cider or unsweetened apple juice	375 mL

1. In a bowl, toss together oats, almonds, 2 tbsp (30 mL) brown sugar and salt. In a small skillet, melt 4 tsp (20 mL) butter over medium heat; add oat mixture and cook, stirring often, until nuts and oats are well toasted and sugar is lightly caramelized, 7 to 9 minutes. Transfer to a plate and set aside to cool.

2. In a separate bowl, toss apple with lemon juice, remaining 2 tbsp (30 mL) brown sugar, granulated sugar, cinnamon, a generous pinch of nutmeg, and cloves. In a saucepan, melt remaining 1 tbsp (15 mL) butter. Add apple mixture and cook, stirring occasionally, until sugar is melted and begins to bubble up. Stir in cider and bring to a boil. Reduce heat and simmer until apple is soft, 2 to 10 minutes, depending on variety and ripeness. Remove from heat and set aside to cool.

3. Stir apple mixture well and transfer to molds, filling two-thirds full. Freeze until slushy, 1 to 2 hours. Divide oat mixture evenly among molds and stir into apple mixture. Insert sticks and freeze until solid, for at least 4 hours.

Sweet Potato Pie Ice Pops

Makes about
2¾ cups (675 mL)
8 to 11 ice pops

Sweet potato pie is as popular in the southern United States as pumpkin pie is in the northern U.S. and Canada. In these ice pops, which are studded with bits of pecan praline, north and south are united by the delicious addition of maple syrup.

Tip

One large sweet potato will yield more than 1 cup (250 mL) mashed sweet potato. To prepare, prick in a few places with a fork or sharp knife and bake in a 400°F (200°C) oven until tender, 30 to 40 minutes. If you prefer, cook in a microwave oven on High for 8 to 10 minutes, turning once. Or you can cook the (unpricked) sweet potato in boiling water for about 15 minutes. Regardless of which method you use, after cooking, break open the potato to allow steam to escape. Set aside to cool before mashing.

- Fine-mesh sieve

2 tbsp	butter	30 mL
⅓ cup	coarsely chopped pecans	75 mL
1 tbsp	granulated sugar	15 mL
1½ cups	milk	375 mL
⅓ cup	heavy or whipping (35%) cream	75 mL
2 tsp	tapioca flour (see Tips, page 135)	10 mL
1 cup	mashed cooked sweet potato	250 mL
½ cup	maple syrup (see Tip, page 134)	125 mL
1½ tbsp	packed dark brown sugar	22 mL
¼ tsp	nutmeg	1 mL
Pinch	cloves	Pinch
Pinch	salt	Pinch

1. In a small skillet over medium heat, melt butter; add pecans and stir to coat. Sprinkle with granulated sugar and continue cooking and stirring until sugar is melted, no longer granular and lightly caramelized. Scrape onto a plate and set aside to cool.

2. In a saucepan, whisk together milk, cream and tapioca flour. Whisk in sweet potato, maple syrup, brown sugar, a scant ¼ tsp (1 mL) nutmeg, cloves and salt. Stirring constantly, bring to a boil over medium-high heat, then reduce heat and simmer, covered (to prevent spattering) but lifting the lid and stirring often, for 10 minutes.

3. Place sieve over a large measuring cup and strain mixture, discarding solids. Set aside to cool. Stir in reserved pecans.

4. Pour into molds and freeze until slushy, then insert sticks and freeze until solid, for at least 4 hours. If you are using an ice pop kit, follow the manufacturer's instructions.

Lemon Meringue Ice Pops

**Makes about
3⅓ cups (825 mL)
10 to 13 ice pops**

These ice pops
incorporate the flavors
of the diner favorite
lemon meringue pie.
They are made with
an Italian meringue, in
which beaten egg whites
are cooked by whisking
hot syrup into them,
giving the meringue a
thick, silky texture.

Tips

A syrup reaches the hard-ball
(large-ball) stage at 250° to
255°F (121° to 124°C) on a
candy thermometer, or when
the mixture forms a hard ball
when a little is dropped into
cold water.

After scraping the mixture
into the molds, tap them
a few times on your work
surface to remove any air
bubbles.

- Fine-mesh sieve
- Electric mixer

2	eggs, separated	2
	Finely grated zest of 1 lemon	
½ cup	lemon juice, divided	125 mL
1½ cups + 2 tbsp	water, divided	405 mL
2 tsp	tapioca flour (see Tip, page xx)	10 mL
2 tbsp	butter, softened	30 mL
Pinch	cream of tartar	Pinch
⅔ cup	granulated sugar	150 mL

1. In a heatproof bowl, whisk together egg yolks and 2 tbsp (30 mL) lemon juice. Set aside.

2. In a saucepan, whisk together 1½ cups (375 mL) water, lemon zest, remaining lemon juice and tapioca flour. Bring to boil, reduce heat and simmer, whisking constantly, for 3 minutes. Remove from heat.

3. Whisk egg yolk mixture into hot liquid. Place pan over medium-low heat and cook, stirring constantly (do not boil), until it thinly coats a spoon. Remove from heat and whisk in butter, until melted and thoroughly incorporated.

4. Place sieve over a large measuring cup and strain mixture, discarding any solids. Set aside to cool.

5. Beat egg whites and cream of tartar until stiff but not dry. In a small saucepan over high heat, cook sugar and remaining 2 tbsp (30 mL) water to hard-ball stage (see Tips, left). Beating constantly, pour hot syrup in a thin stream into egg whites. Beat at low speed until meringue has cooled 2 to 3 minutes.

6. Stir one-third of egg white mixture into reserved lemon mixture. Fold in remainder until blended but still light and fluffy. Scrape into molds (see Tips left).

7. Freeze until slushy, then insert sticks and freeze until solid, for at least 4 hours. If you are using an ice pop kit, follow the manufacturer's instructions.

Key Lime Pie Ice Pops

Makes about 2⅓ cups (575 mL) 7 to 9 ice pops

These ice pops really taste like the famous pie from southern Florida. Key limes are small, round limes with a vivid fragrance and intense taste. It is worth the effort to find them for their distinctively exuberant flavor.

Tips

Key limes are sold in bags at most supermarkets; they are often imported from Mexico. If Key limes are unavailable, use regular Persian limes.

To juice Key limes properly, you need a handheld squeeze-type citrus juicer. Originally from Mexico, where small limes are used prolifically, these juicers are now available at most cooking supply stores. Besides extracting every last bit of juice while also straining out the seeds, by squeezing halved limes the juicer also extracts essential oils from the zest, which adds flavor to the juice.

2	egg yolks	2
¼ cup	milk	60 mL
½ cup	heavy or whipping (35%) cream	125 mL
1 tsp	finely grated Key lime zest	5 mL
⅔ cup	sweetened condensed milk	150 mL
½ cup	freshly squeezed Key lime juice	125 mL
⅓ cup	water	75 mL

1. In a bowl, beat egg yolks with milk until smooth. Set aside.

2. In a saucepan over medium-high heat, bring cream and lime zest to a boil. Reduce heat and simmer gently for 2 minutes. Remove from heat and whisk in yolk mixture.

3. Place saucepan over low heat and cook, stirring constantly and without returning to a simmer, until mixture is thick enough to coat a spoon, 1 to 2 minutes. Scrape into a large measuring cup. Whisk in condensed milk, lime juice and water. Set aside to cool.

4. Pour into molds and freeze until slushy, then insert sticks and freeze until solid, for at least 4 hours. If you are using an ice pop kit, follow the manufacturer's instructions.

Rum Raisin Ice Pops

**Makes about
3¼ cups (800 mL)
9 to 13 ice pops**

The classic ice cream
flavor makes a new
classic ice pop — sweet,
creamy and rummy,
with a hint of spice.
You can also make these
without the alcohol
(see Tip, below).

Tip

If you don't want to use rum
for these ice pops, you can
imitate the flavor by using
rum extract: add 1 tsp (5 mL)
extract along with the vanilla.
Soak the raisins in orange
juice instead of rum.

½ cup	raisins	125 mL
¼ cup	dark rum	60 mL
⅓ cup	packed dark brown sugar	75 mL
⅓ cup	water	75 mL
½ tsp	finely grated orange zest	2 mL
¼ tsp	cinnamon	1 mL
Pinch	cloves	Pinch
Pinch	nutmeg	Pinch
1	can (12 oz/370 mL) evaporated milk	1
½ cup	heavy or whipping (35%) cream	125 mL
¼ tsp	vanilla extract	1 mL

1. In a small bowl, soak raisins in rum for at least
2 hours or overnight. Drain, reserving rum. Set
raisins and rum aside.

2. In a small saucepan, combine brown sugar,
water, orange zest, cinnamon, cloves, nutmeg and
reserved rum. Bring to a boil, stirring until sugar is
dissolved; reduce heat and simmer for 2 minutes.
Pour into a large measuring cup and set aside to
cool. Whisk in evaporated milk, cream and vanilla.

3. Pour into molds, leaving a little headspace for the
raisins. Freeze until slushy, 1 to 2 hours. Divide
raisins evenly among molds and stir into mixture.
Insert sticks and freeze until solid, for at least
4 hours. If you are using an ice pop kit, follow the
manufacturer's instructions.

Prune and Armagnac Ice Pops

**Makes about
3⅓ cups (825 mL)
10 to 13 ice pops**

It's a little extravagant to
use expensive Armagnac
for an ice pop, but
the traditional French
flavor combination of
Armagnac and prunes
is so appealing that
it is hard to ignore.
You can, if you must,
substitute brandy for
the Armagnac — you
will still have a great ice
pop, just not one that is
truly *magnifique*!

Tip

Try to find all-natural or
organic prunes, without
any added sulfites or
preservatives. They are drier
and will soak up more of
the Armagnac. Chop them
into pieces about the size of
large raisins.

½ cup	prunes, coarsely chopped (see Tip, left)	125 mL
⅓ cup	Armagnac	75 mL
¼ cup	granulated sugar	60 mL
2 tbsp	packed dark brown sugar	30 mL
⅓ cup	water	75 mL
Pinch	ground ginger	Pinch
Pinch	cloves	Pinch
Pinch	nutmeg	Pinch
1	can (12 oz/370 mL) evaporated milk	1
⅔ cup	heavy or whipping (35%) cream	150 mL
¼ tsp	vanilla extract	1 mL

1. In a bowl, soak prunes in Armagnac overnight.
   Drain, reserving Armagnac. Set prunes and
   Armagnac aside.

2. In a small saucepan, combine granulated and
   brown sugars, water, reserved Armagnac and a
   generous pinch each of ginger, cloves and nutmeg.
   Bring to a boil, stirring until sugar is dissolved.
   Reduce heat and simmer, uncovered, for 5 minutes.
   Transfer to a large measuring cup and set aside
   to cool.

3. Whisk in evaporated milk, cream and vanilla.
   Pour into molds, leaving a little headspace for the
   prunes; freeze until slushy, 1 to 2 hours. Divide
   prunes evenly among molds and stir into mixture.
   Insert sticks and freeze until solid, for at least
   4 hours. If you are using an ice pop kit, follow the
   manufacturer's instructions.

Banana Split Ice Pops

Makes about
3½ cups (875 mL)
10 to 14 ice pops

An old-time favorite, banana splits are still a treat.

Tip

You can use commercial chocolate sauce for these ice pops or make your own superb Rich Chocolate Sauce (see page 143).

• Blender

⅓ cup	chopped walnuts	75 mL
3	ripe bananas, sliced	3
⅔ cup	evaporated milk	150 mL
½ cup	water	125 mL
3 tbsp	brown rice, agave or corn syrup	45 mL
¾ tsp	vanilla extract	3 mL
10 to 14	maraschino cherries, halved	10 to 14
⅓ cup	chocolate (fudge) sauce (see Tip, left)	75 mL

1. In a dry skillet over medium heat, toast walnuts until fragrant and lightly toasted, about 6 minutes. Remove from heat and set aside to cool.

2. In blender at medium-high speed, purée bananas, evaporated milk, water, syrup and vanilla. Stir in walnuts.

3. Pour into molds, filling to two-thirds full. Add 2 cherry halves to each mold, pushing down into mixture. Divide chocolate sauce evenly among molds. Using a chopstick or thin-bladed knife, swirl sauce into mixture.

4. Freeze until slushy, then insert sticks and freeze until solid, for at least 4 hours. If you are using an ice pop kit, follow the manufacturer's instructions.

Rich Chocolate Sauce

**Makes about
1¼ cups
(300 mL)**

**I've been making this
classic, rich chocolate
sauce for thirty years.
It is a luxurious
fudge sauce, based
on an old French
recipe, and I still
think it is the best. It
will only be as good
as your chocolate,
though, so make sure
you use the finest.**

Tip

If your sauce is too
thick to pour, heat in
a microwave oven in
10-second bursts, stirring
after each, until pourable
but not warm. Or place
jar or bowl in hot water
and stir until pourable.

4 oz	bittersweet or semisweet chocolate, chopped	125 g
1 oz	milk chocolate, chopped	30 g
⅓ cup	milk	75 mL
5 tsp	butter	25 mL
2 tbsp	granulated sugar	30 mL
2 tbsp	heavy or whipping (35%) cream	30 mL
2 tbsp	brandy, rum or coffee liqueur	30 mL

1. In a small saucepan over medium-low heat,
   stir together bittersweet and milk chocolates,
   milk and butter until melted and smooth.
   Stirring constantly, add sugar and cream and
   bring just barely to a simmer.

2. Remove from heat and whisk in brandy. Store
   in an airtight container at room temperature
   for up to 1 week or refrigerate for up to
   3 months. Bring to room temperature or warm
   before using (see Tip, left).

Peanut Butter Ice Pops

**Makes about
2¼ cups (550 mL)
6 to 9 ice pops**

Fans of peanut butter
and banana sandwiches
will be more than
pleased with this easy-
to-make ice pop.

Tips

You can use natural (peanuts
only) or prepared peanut
butter in these recipes. If
using natural peanut butter
you may want to add salt
and/or sugar to taste.

**Makes about
2⅔ cups (650 mL)
8 to 11 ice pops**

This one is for children
of all ages!

Tips

You can buy plain almond
milk at most supermarkets
or make your own (see
page 105).

Substitute an equal quantity
of any other fruit preserve
or sweetened fruit purée for
the grape jelly.

Peanut Butter and Banana Ice Pops

● Blender

2	ripe bananas, sliced	2
½ cup	smooth peanut butter	125 mL
½ cup	water	125 mL
¼ cup	sweetened condensed milk	60 mL
Pinch	salt	Pinch

1. In blender at medium-high speed, purée bananas, peanut butter, water, condensed milk and salt.

2. Pour into molds and freeze until slushy, then insert sticks and freeze until solid, for at least 4 hours. If you are using an ice pop kit, follow the manufacturer's instructions.

Peanut Butter and Jelly Ice Pops

● Blender

1½ cups	almond milk (see Tips, left) or soy milk	375 mL
½ cup + 1 tbsp	smooth peanut butter	140 mL
1½ tbsp	brown rice, agave or corn syrup	22 mL
⅓ cup + 1 tbsp	grape jelly or jam (see Tips, left)	90 mL

1. In blender at medium-high speed, blend almond milk, peanut butter and syrup until smooth.

2. Transfer to molds, filling three-quarters full, and freeze until slushy. Evenly divide jelly among molds and swirl into peanut butter mixture. Insert sticks and freeze until solid, for at least 4 hours. If you are using an ice pop kit, follow the manufacturer's instructions.

Carrot Cake Ice Pops

**Makes about
3½ cups (875 mL)
10 to 14 ice pops**

Of course these ice pops aren't full of flour, eggs and butter, but they have all the familiar flavors of this well-loved cake, including the sweet cream cheese icing.

Tip

Freshly squeezed juice is always best, but you can also use juice from cartons or from concentrate.

● Blender

2	carrots, finely shredded	2
1 cup	orange juice	250 mL
½ cup	packed dark brown sugar	125 mL
Pinch	nutmeg	Pinch
Pinch	cloves	Pinch
⅓ cup	walnut halves	75 mL
⅓ cup	cream cheese, at room temperature	75 mL
½ tsp	vanilla extract	2 mL
⅔ cup	table (18%) cream	150 mL
¼ cup	milk	60 mL
2 tbsp	sweetened condensed milk	30 mL

1. In a saucepan, combine carrots, orange juice, brown sugar, a generous pinch nutmeg, and cloves. Bring to a boil, stirring until sugar is dissolved, then reduce heat and simmer for 5 minutes. Remove from heat and set aside to cool.

2. In a dry skillet over medium heat, toast walnuts, stirring, until fragrant and lightly toasted, about 6 minutes. Remove from heat and set aside to cool. Chop finely.

3. In blender at medium-high speed, blend cream cheese, vanilla and carrot mixture until smooth. At low speed, blend in cream, milk and condensed milk until thoroughly combined. Stir in chopped walnuts.

4. Pour into molds and freeze until slushy, then insert sticks and freeze until solid, for at least 4 hours. If you are using an ice pop kit, follow the manufacturer's instructions.

Frozen S'mores Ice Pops

**Makes about
2⅔ cups (650 mL)
8 to 10 ice pops**

While freezing this
well-loved campfire
snack might seem
absurd, if not
downright sacrilegious,
the marshmallow,
chocolate and graham
cracker combo makes
a smashingly good
ice pop. Of course it
appeals to children —
and to the nostalgic
child within!

Tip

For the crumbs, simply
break up a couple of graham
crackers by hand. Do not use
packaged graham cracker
crumbs, because they are
too fine.

1	can (12 oz/370 mL) evaporated milk	1
½ cup	water	125 mL
¼ cup	unsweetened cocoa powder	60 mL
2 tsp	tapioca flour (see Tip, page 135)	10 mL
½ cup	miniature marshmallows	125 mL
3 tbsp	mini semisweet chocolate chips	45 mL
¼ cup	coarse graham cracker crumbs (see Tips, left)	60 mL

1. In a saucepan, whisk together evaporated milk, water, cocoa and tapioca flour. Bring to a boil, reduce heat and simmer, stirring often, for 5 minutes. Pour into a large measuring cup and set aside to cool.

2. Stir in marshmallows, coating well with the mixture (they will float to the top). Chill in refrigerator, stirring occasionally, for 1 hour.

3. Pour into molds, filling two-thirds full and evenly distributing marshmallows. Add chocolate chips, dividing evenly among molds, and top each mold with cracker crumbs, dividing equally. Using a chopstick or long spoon, stir lightly, pushing crumbs down into mixture. Freeze until slushy, about 90 minutes. Push any solids that have floated to the top back into the mixture. Insert sticks and freeze until solid, for at least 4 hours. If you are using an ice pop kit, follow the manufacturer's instructions.

Tea and Coffee

Hong Kong Milk Tea Ice Pops

Makes about
3¼ cups (800 mL)
9 to 13 ice pops

3 cups	boiling water	750 mL
3 tbsp	loose Chinese black tea (see Tip, left)	45 mL
¼ cup	sweetened condensed milk	60 mL
⅓ cup	half-and-half (10%) cream	75 mL

Much of Hong Kong starts its day with a cup of "milk tea" — usually sweetened strong black tea made creamy with condensed and/or evaporated milk. Even on swelteringly hot summer days, scalding milk tea is served as a midday refreshment. Some of us might prefer it in the form of a refreshingly cool ice pop.

Tips

Substitute 6 tea bags for the loose tea.

You can also make this ice pop with Indian tea, such as orange pekoe, Darjeeling, or use any of the classic British blends.

1. In a large teapot or heatproof measuring cup, pour water over tea; set aside to steep for 5 minutes. Strain into a large measuring cup. Stir in condensed milk and cream and set aside to cool.

2. Pour into molds and freeze until slushy, then insert sticks and freeze until solid, for at least 4 hours. If you are using an ice pop kit, follow the manufacturer's instructions.

Tapioca Bubbles for Bubble Tea or Coffee Ice Pops

**Makes about
⅓ cup (75 mL)
(enough for about
3 cups/750 mL)
ice pop mixture)**

Since it was exported
from Taiwan some
20 years ago, bubble
tea (made with large
tapioca pearls) has
become quite the rage
all over the world,
especially among
young people. Special
large straws are used
to suck up the tapioca
"bubbles," which
settle at the bottom
of the cup. Now the
bubbles even appear
in ice pops, particularly
in Taiwan. The tapioca
pearls freeze solid but
melt gradually in your
mouth, providing an
appealing textural
contrast. They can
easily be added to any
tea or coffee ice pops;
this recipe makes an
appropriate quantity
for the recipes in this
book.

| 3 cups | water | 750 mL |
| ⅓ cup | large tapioca pearls | 75 mL |

1. In a saucepan, bring water to a boil over high heat, then add tapioca pearls. When water returns to a boil, reduce heat to medium and cook until tender, 5 to 10 minutes, depending on the brand and the age of the pearls. Drain in a colander and rinse under cold water until chilled.

2. Transfer to a bowl and mix in 1 to 2 tbsp (15 to 30 mL) tea or coffee ice pop mixture, to keep them moist and separated until use.

3. Freeze ice pop mixture until slushy, 1 to 2 hours. Divide tapioca bubbles evenly among molds and stir in. Continue with final step of recipe.

Lemon Black Tea Ice Pops

**Makes about
3½ cups (875 mL)
10 to 14 ice pops**

This ice pop is made from a favorite among iced-tea drinkers on a hot day — strong tea with lemon — and it's just as satisfying as the original. It makes a great midday pick-me-up too, any time of the year.

Tips

This recipe uses whole tea leaves. If you want to use broken or ground tea (most Indian or Kenyan tea falls into this category), then use only 2 tbsp (30 mL) or 6 tea bags.

If you like honey in your tea, use a combination of syrup and honey rather than all syrup: ¼ cup (60 mL) syrup + 3 tbsp (45 mL) honey.

3 cups	boiling water	750 mL
3 tbsp	Chinese black tea or orange pekoe tea leaves	45 mL
3	strips (each ½ by 2 inches/1 by 5 cm) lemon zest	3
½ cup	light agave or light corn syrup (see Tips, left)	125 mL
⅓ cup	freshly squeezed lemon juice	75 mL

1. In a large teapot or heatproof measuring cup, pour boiling water over tea leaves and lemon zest. Set aside to steep for 5 minutes. Strain. (You can reuse the tea leaves and zest to make a pot of tea to drink, regular or iced.) Stir in syrup, then stir in lemon juice. Set aside to cool.

2. Pour into molds and freeze until slushy, then insert sticks and freeze until solid, for at least 4 hours. If you are using an ice pop kit, follow the manufacturer's instructions.

Variation

Southern "Hospitalitea" Cocktail Ice Pops: Proceed as above, using all syrup (no honey). Before freezing, stir in ¼ cup (60 mL) Tennessee whiskey or bourbon. Freeze until solid, for at least 4 hours or preferably overnight.

Green Tea and Mint with Lime Ice Pops

Makes about
3 cups (750 mL)
9 to 12 ice pops

Fragrant green tea and fresh mint are a lovely combination. With a touch of lime and sweetening, they combine into a really refreshing ice pop.

Tips

As for all tea ice pops, you must use a stronger and more concentrated tea than you would drink; otherwise it will seem bland when frozen.

The better quality your green tea leaves, the better your ice pop will be.

1 cup	loosely packed mint leaves	250 mL
3 tbsp	whole green tea leaves (or 6 tea bags)	45 mL
3 cups	water	750 mL
⅓ cup	brown rice syrup or ¼ cup (60 mL) agave or corn syrup	75 mL
3 tbsp	freshly squeezed lime juice	45 mL

1. In a large teapot or heatproof measuring cup, combine mint and tea leaves. Bring water to a boil, add a splash (about 2 tbsp/30 mL) of cold water to cool slightly, then pour over leaves. Steep for 8 minutes. Strain. (You can reuse the tea and mint leaves to make a pot for drinking.) Stir in syrup, then lime juice. Set aside to cool.

2. Pour into molds and freeze until slushy, then insert sticks and freeze until solid, for at least 4 hours. If you are using an ice pop kit, follow the manufacturer's instructions.

Indian Chai Ice Pops

Makes about 3 cups (750 mL) 9 to 12 ice pops

Outside of India, when most of us say chai, we really mean masala chai, or spiced tea. But in India *chai* just means "tea." Perhaps not surprisingly, this spiced milk-and-water mixture is perfect for an ice pop.

Tip

After China, India is the most important tea-producing country in the world. In the West we generally drink Assam tea, as a component of the dark, rich and bracing English and Irish breakfast tea blends. Lighter and more fragrant Darjeeling is appreciated as an afternoon tea. Nilgiri and orange pekoe teas from the south of India and Sri Lanka are prized by many Western tea drinkers for their intense yet smooth flavors.

- Fine-mesh sieve

5	thin slices gingerroot	5
3	peppercorns	3
3	cardamom pods	3
2	whole cloves	2
1½ cups	milk	375 mL
1½ cups	water	375 mL
1½ tbsp	loose strong Indian, Sri Lankan or Kenyan tea (see Tip, left)	22 mL
¼ cup	sweetened condensed milk	60 mL

1. In a dry skillet over medium-high heat, toast ginger, turning occasionally, until slightly dry and a bit browned on both sides, 2 to 3 minutes. Place in a mortar with peppercorns, cardamom and cloves and pound until spices are roughly crushed. (You can also do this on a cutting board, crushing each ingredient separately with the side of a knife.)

2. Transfer crushed spices to a saucepan and add milk and water. Bring to a boil. Reduce heat, add tea and simmer for 4 minutes. Remove from heat.

3. Place sieve over a large measuring cup and strain. Discard solids. Stir in condensed milk and set aside to cool.

4. Whisk mixture until frothy. Pour into molds and freeze until slushy, then insert sticks and freeze until solid, for at least 4 hours. If you are using an ice pop kit, follow the manufacturer's instructions.

Chinese Chrysanthemum Tisane Ice Pops

Makes about
3⅓ cups (825 mL)
10 to 13 ice pops

Chrysanthemum tea, with its pleasantly floral and slightly musky flavor, makes a delicious ice pop.

Tips

Dried chrysanthemum blossoms are used to make a favorite tisane in China and Korea, where it is appreciated for its cooling qualities. It is also used medicinally, being thought to be especially good for the eyes and lungs.

Chrysanthemum is often steeped with other flavorings also thought to have beneficial medicinal qualities, such as wolfberries (goji or koji berries) and Chinese red dates (which are actually not dates but dried red jujubes, a fruit with a somewhat apple-like flavor).

⅓ cup	lightly packed Chinese dried chrysanthemum blossoms	75 mL
2 tbsp	wolfberries (goji or koji berries)	30 mL
3½ cups	water	875 mL
12	Chinese red dates (dried jujubes), optional	12
⅓ cup + 2 tbsp	liquid honey	105 mL

1. In a large teapot or heatproof measuring cup, combine chrysanthemums and wolfberries. In a saucepan, bring water and red dates, if using, to a boil; reduce heat and simmer for 3 minutes. Pour into teapot, cover and set aside to steep for 60 to 90 minutes. Strain into a large measuring cup. Stir in honey and set aside to cool completely, if necessary.

2. Whisk mixture. Pour into molds and freeze until slushy, then insert sticks and freeze until solid, for at least 4 hours. If you are using an ice pop kit, follow the manufacturer's instructions.

Variation

Chinese Chrysanthemum Tea Ice Pops: Omit the wolfberries and red dates and add 2 tbsp (30 mL) of your favorite Chinese tea leaves to the pot.

Café au Lait Ice Pops

**Makes about
3 cups (750 mL)
9 to 12 ice pops**

These simple-to-make ice pops are always a welcome refreshment and pick-me-up, any time of the day.

Tips

You can use any coffee you like, from rich and bitter French-roast or dark-roast Kenyan to medium-roast Colombian, Mexican or Ethiopian. If you prefer, you can even make this with a lightly roasted coffee.

Be sure to grind the coffee finely for this recipe.

For a sweet ice pop with a bit less fat, replace the sugar and cream with 3 to 6 tbsp (45 to 90 mL) sweetened condensed milk, to taste.

- Large coffee press or fine-mesh sieve lined with double layer of cheesecloth

1¼ cups	water	300 mL
⅓ cup	freshly ground coffee (see Tips, left)	75 mL
1½ cups	milk	375 mL
3 tbsp	granulated sugar (approx.)	45 mL
¼ cup	heavy or whipping (35%) cream	60 mL

1. In a saucepan over medium heat, bring water to a boil. Add coffee and return to a boil, then add milk. When mixture again returns to a boil, immediately remove from heat (otherwise it will bubble over). When contents have settled, return to heat and again bring to a boil. When mixture bubbles up, remove from heat.

2. Pour into coffee press or cover saucepan and set aside to steep for 5 minutes. Press down plunger of coffee press or strain mixture through prepared sieve placed over a large heatproof measuring cup. Discard solids. Stir in sugar until dissolved, adding more if you prefer a sweet ice pop. Set aside to cool.

3. Whisk in cream until mixture is frothy. Pour into molds and freeze until slushy, then insert sticks and freeze until solid, for at least 4 hours. If you are using an ice pop kit, follow the manufacturer's instructions.

Espresso Ice Pops

**Makes about
2⅓ cups (325 mL)
7 to 9 ice pops**

These ice pops are rather
serious — definitely
for the dedicated coffee
drinker. They are black,
lightly sweetened and
deliver a good caffeine
punch. Use a dark-roast
espresso coffee.

⅓ cup	granulated sugar	75 mL
⅓ cup	water	75 mL
	Zest of 1 lemon, cut into strips	
2 cups	hot espresso or strong black coffee	500 mL

1. In a small saucepan, bring sugar, water and lemon zest to a boil, stirring until sugar is dissolved. Reduce heat and simmer for 2 minutes. Stir into coffee. Remove from heat and set aside to cool.

2. Strain out and discard zest. Pour into molds and freeze until slushy, then insert sticks and freeze until solid, for at least 4 hours. If you are using an ice pop kit, follow the manufacturer's instructions.

Cuban Coffee Ice Pops

**Makes about
2⅔ cups (650 mL)
8 to 10 ice pops**

Cubans love the taste
of coffee brewed with
demerara-style brown
sugar, and it is not
unknown for them to add
a shot of rum to the mix!

Tip

Use an espresso maker to
make the coffee, or drip it
through a filter. Just make sure
it is nice and strong. Since both
syrup and cream are added
to the mixture, weak coffee
will produce insipid ice pops.

⅓ cup	demerara-style brown sugar	75 mL
¼ cup	water	60 mL
2 cups	Cuban or Puerto Rican espresso or strong drip coffee	500 mL
⅓ cup	table (18%) cream	75 mL
2 tbsp	amber or dark rum, optional	30 mL

1. In a small saucepan, bring sugar and water to a boil, stirring until sugar is dissolved; reduce heat and simmer for 2 minutes. Stir in coffee and set aside to cool. Whisk in cream and rum, if using.

2. Pour into molds and freeze until slushy, then insert sticks and freeze until solid, for at least 4 hours. If you are using an ice pop kit, follow the manufacturer's instructions.

Vietnamese Coffee Ice Pops

2 cups	filter/drip-brewed strong Vietnamese coffee (see Tips, left)	500 mL
1/2 cup	sweetened condensed milk	125 mL
1/4 cup	heavy or whipping (35%) cream	60 mL

Makes about 2¾ cups (675 mL) 8 to 11 ice pops

Vietnamese love filtered coffee, which they brew using small metal filters over individual cups or glasses. For making iced coffee, the filter is placed directly over a tall, ice-filled glass holding a generous amount of sweetened condensed milk.

Tips

In Vietnam, coffee is made with a blend of dark-roasted Arabica beans, much like French coffee, and more than often flavored with chocolate or cocoa, but in the North American Vietnamese community, New Orleans–style dark roast blended with roasted chicory has become the coffee of choice.

You can find imported Vietnamese coffee and New Orleans chicory coffee at Asian supermarkets. New Orleans–style chicory coffee is also available at many American supermarkets. Both are available by mail order.

1. In a large heatproof measuring cup, whisk together coffee, condensed milk and cream. Set aside to cool.

2. Pour into molds and freeze until slushy, then insert sticks and freeze until solid, for at least 4 hours. If you are using an ice pop kit, follow the manufacturer's instructions.

Indian Masala Coffee Ice Pops

Makes about
3 cups (750 mL)
9 to 12 ice pops

Masala coffee is spiced coffee brewed with lots of milk. It is very popular in southern India as well as Malaysia, where there is a significant southern Indian population. I'm not a big fan of flavored or spiced coffees and teas, but this preparation is truly delicious. It's a natural for ice pops because it's creamy, spicy and rich — a fantastic and unusual pick-me-up.

Tip

Use a medium-dark or dark-roast coffee, preferably ground just before brewing.

- Large coffee press or fine-mesh sieve lined with double layer of cheesecloth

1	stick (about 2 inches/5 cm) cinnamon	1
5	cardamom pods, crushed	5
4	whole cloves	4
½	whole nutmeg, lightly crushed	½
1 tsp	finely chopped gingerroot	5 mL
1½ cups	water	375 mL
¼ cup	freshly finely ground coffee	60 mL
1½ cups	milk	375 mL
3 tbsp	sweetened condensed milk	45 mL

1. In a saucepan, combine cinnamon, cardamom, cloves, nutmeg and ginger. Lightly toast over medium heat, stirring occasionally, until richly fragrant, about 2 minutes. Add water and coffee, increase heat and bring to a boil. Add milk; when mixture returns to a boil, remove from heat (otherwise it will bubble over). When contents have settled, return to heat and again bring to a boil. When mixture bubbles up, remove from heat.

2. Pour into coffee press or cover saucepan and set aside to steep for 5 minutes. Press down plunger of coffee press or strain mixture through prepared sieve placed over a large heatproof measuring cup. Discard solids. Stir in condensed milk and set aside to cool.

3. Whisk mixture until frothy. Pour into molds and freeze until slushy, then insert sticks and freeze until solid, for at least 4 hours. If you are using an ice pop kit, follow the manufacturer's instructions.

Café Mocha Ice Pops

**Makes about
3¼ cups (800 mL)
10 to 13 ice pops**

**Coffee and chocolate —
no doubt a partnership
made in heaven —
should only make a
positively heavenly
ice pop, and this one
qualifies.**

Tip

Use freshly brewed strong
coffee made to taste from
the finest medium- to dark-
roast coffee you can get,
and make sure you use the
best chocolate.

2½ cups	hot strong black coffee or espresso (see Tip, left)	625 mL
⅓ cup + 1 tbsp	unsweetened cocoa powder	90 mL
½ cup	agave, brown rice or corn syrup	125 mL
¼ tsp	ground cinnamon	1 mL
2 oz	bittersweet or semisweet chocolate, chopped	60 g
1 oz	milk or semisweet chocolate, chopped	30 g
½ cup	heavy or whipping (35%) cream	125 mL
2 tbsp	brandy or dark rum	30 mL

1. In a saucepan, whisk together coffee and cocoa; then whisk in syrup and cinnamon. Whisking, bring mixture to a simmer. Remove from heat and whisk in bittersweet and milk chocolates until thoroughly incorporated and smooth. Whisk in cream. Set aside to cool.

2. Whisk in brandy. Pour into molds and freeze until slushy, then insert sticks and freeze until solid, for at least 4 hours or preferably overnight. If you are using an ice pop kit, follow the manufacturer's instructions.

Latin American Flavors

Strawberry Lime Ice Pops

**Makes about
2²/₃ cups (650 mL)
8 to 10 ice pops**

In Mexico, as in
practically every region
of the world where they
are grown, strawberries
are a favorite fruit
for making sweets,
particularly ice pops.
There, ice pops are
called *paletas*.

Tip

Always use freshly squeezed
lemon juice or lime juice in
your ice pops; bottled just
doesn't compare.

- Blender

³/₄ cup	packed dark brown sugar	175 mL
¹/₂ cup	water	125 mL
	Finely grated zest of 1 lime	
4 cups	halved hulled fresh strawberries or whole frozen strawberries, thawed	1 L
3 tbsp	freshly squeezed lime juice	45 mL

1. In a saucepan, bring sugar, water and lime zest to
   a boil, stirring until sugar is dissolved; reduce heat
   and simmer for 2 minutes. Add strawberries to
   pan, cover and cook over low heat for 2 minutes.
   Remove from heat and transfer to blender. Add
   lime juice and blend until smooth. Set aside to
   cool.

2. Pour into molds and freeze until slushy, then
   insert sticks and freeze until solid, for at least
   4 hours. If you are using an ice pop kit, follow
   the manufacturer's instructions.

Fudge Ice Pops (page 94)

Pomegranate Berry Ice Pops (page 70)

Cranberry Ice Pops (page 61) and
Key Lime Ice Pops (page 139)

Strawberry Ice Pops (page 51) and French Vanilla Ice Pops (page 99)

Sweet Cherry and Currant Ice Pops (page 41),
Jackfruit Ice Pops (page 89) and Melon Cream Ice Pops (page 175)

Margarita Ice Pops (page 236)

Strawberry Lassi Ice Pops (page 200)

Avocado Ice Pops (page 163)

Guava Lime Ice Pops

Makes about
2⅔ cups (650 mL)
8 to 10 ice pops

Guava is one of the world's most aggressively — and pleasantly — fragrant fruits. All it takes is one small basket of ripe guavas to perfume an entire house. Yellow-skinned white- or red-fleshed guavas, as well as the green-skinned ones, can be used for these ice pops. Choose fruit that is nice and ripe, very fragrant and gives a little when pressed lightly.

Tip

Guavas range in size depending upon the type. For this recipe you will need 10 to 16 yellow Mexican guavas, 8 to 14 green pink-fleshed guavas, or 2 to 3 Asian green white-fleshed guavas. If you don't have a kitchen scale, weigh them at the market.

- Blender
- Fine-mesh sieve

1⅔ cups	water, divided	400 mL
⅓ cup	packed dark brown sugar	75 mL
⅓ cup	granulated sugar	75 mL
	Finely grated zest of 1 lime	
Pinch	salt	Pinch
Pinch	cayenne pepper	Pinch
1 lb	ripe guavas (see Tip, left)	500 g
¼ cup	freshly squeezed lime juice	60 mL

1. In a small saucepan, combine ⅔ cup (150 mL) water, brown and granulated sugars, lime zest, salt and cayenne. Bring to a boil, stirring until sugar is dissolved; reduce heat and simmer for 2 minutes. Remove from heat and set aside to cool.

2. Remove dark stem and blossom ends of guavas. Chop guavas. Place in blender with cooled syrup, lime juice and remaining 1 cup (250 mL) water. Blend at medium speed until mixture is smooth and seeds are separated.

3. Place sieve over a large measuring cup and strain mixture, pressing down and scraping solids with a rubber spatula to extract as much pulp and juice as possible. Discard solids.

4. Pour into molds and freeze until slushy, then insert sticks and freeze until solid, for at least 4 hours. If you are using an ice pop kit, follow the manufacturer's instructions.

Soursop Ice Pops

Makes about 2½ cups (625 mL) 7 to 10 ice pops		

¼ cup	granulated sugar	60 mL
1 cup	water, divided	250 mL
2 tbsp	freshly squeezed lime juice	30 mL
1 lb	soursop (see Tips, left)	500 g

Soursop is native to Mexico and neighboring parts of the New World, where it is a popular dessert fruit. It is used extensively in ice creams and iced desserts (as it is in Southeast Asia). It has a distinctive tropical sweet-and-sour taste with a touch of almost citrus-like tartness and wonderful fragrance.

Tip

Soursops range from about 1½ to 5 pounds (750 g to 2.25 kg). This unique fruit is large and irregularly shaped, with a rough green skin that turns brownish when the fruit is fully ripe (it is usually ripened off the tree). The flesh is off-white, soft and juicy, with a slightly granular texture. The fruit should be quite soft, almost mushy, when ripe with a sweet fresh floral smell. Look for it at Mexican, Latin American, Caribbean (especially Jamaican) and Southeast Asian (particularly Filipino) grocery stores.

1. In a small saucepan, bring sugar and ¼ cup (60 mL) water to a boil, stirring until sugar is dissolved. Remove from heat and stir in lime juice. Set aside.

2. Remove and discard peel from soursop; carefully pick out all the seeds from the soft pulp and discard seeds. Place pulp in blender with reserved syrup. Blend at medium-high speed until smooth, adding water as necessary if the mixture is too thick to blend properly. Pour into a large measuring cup. Use remaining water to rinse out blender and then add to soursop mixture; mix well.

3. Pour into molds and freeze until slushy, then insert sticks and freeze until solid, for at least 4 hours. If you are using an ice pop kit, follow the manufacturer's instructions.

Variations

Substitute an equal quantity of tropical sweetsop (sugar apple) or North American pawpaw for the soursop. Both fruits are relatives of soursops.

Avocado Ice Pops

**Makes about
2 cups (500 mL)
6 to 8 ice pops**

In Mexico and other parts of Central America, avocados are sometimes used in sweets. This use certainly won't seem strange to Filipino, Vietnamese and Indonesian people, who primarily enjoy the fruit over shaved ice with sweetened condensed milk or in milkshakes. Native to Central America, avocados are one of many examples — including hot peppers, soursops, potatoes, jicama, squash and many legumes — of how Mexican culinary culture spread to Asia through the important Acapulco–Manila clipper-ship trade route from the mid-16th to early 19th centuries.

- Blender

1 cup	chopped ripe avocado	250 mL
⅓ cup	sweetened condensed milk	75 mL
3 tbsp	freshly squeezed lime juice	45 mL
Pinch	salt	Pinch
⅔ cup	water	150 mL
3 tbsp	extra-fine (fruit) sugar or granulated sugar	45 mL

1. Place avocado, condensed milk, lime juice and a scant pinch of salt in blender. Stir together water and sugar until sugar is dissolved; add to blender. Purée at medium-high speed.

2. Pour into molds, tapping them on work surface to remove any air pockets. Insert sticks and freeze until solid, for at least 4 hours. If you are using an ice pop kit, follow the manufacturer's instructions.

Cucumber Chile Ice Pops

**Makes about
3 cups (750 mL)
9 to 12 ice pops**

A light touch of dried
hot pepper bumps a
refreshing cucumber
and lime ice pop into
a higher realm. This is
a delicious traditional
Mexican treat.

Tip

You can use other mild to
medium-hot dried chile
peppers in these ice pops.
Good medium-hot choices
are New Mexico chiles,
Mexican puyas (which are
slightly hotter than guajillos)
or pasillo chiles. If you prefer
a fruitier, sweeter flavor,
use an ancho or mulatto
chile. However, avoid dried
serrano, arbol and chipotle
peppers, because the smoky
flavor of the chipotle and
the more intense heat of
the other two will not go
well with the light flavor of
cucumber.

- Fine-mesh sieve
- Blender

1	dried guajillo chile pepper	1
¼ cup	granulated sugar	60 mL
½ cup	water, divided	125 mL
2	field cucumbers (peel and seeds included), chopped	2
⅓ cup	freshly squeezed lime juice	75 mL

1. In a small saucepan over medium heat, toast chile pepper, turning occasionally, until lightly darkened and fragrant. Remove from heat and set aside to cool. When chile is cool enough to handle, split it open and remove and discard seeds and inner membranes. Place in a spice grinder or mortar and grind to a fine powder.

2. In saucepan, combine chile powder with sugar and half the water. Bring to boil, stirring until sugar is dissolved. Remove from heat and set aside to cool.

3. In blender at medium speed, blend cucumber, lime juice and remaining water until it resembles thick juice.

Tip

If you don't have a whole dried hot pepper, you can replace it with 1 tsp (5 mL) pure chile powder (ground dried hot red peppers with no other added ingredients). Ancho or New Mexico chile powders are widely available and would be a good choice for this recipe. Toast the powder lightly in the saucepan, until fragrant, before adding the sugar and water.

4. Place sieve over a large measuring cup and strain cucumber mixture, pressing down on solids with a rubber spatula to extract as much juice as possible. Discard solids. Stir in reserved chile syrup.

5. Pour into molds and freeze until slushy, then insert sticks and freeze until solid, for at least 4 hours. If you are using an ice pop kit, follow the manufacturer's instructions.

Variation

Cucumber Chile Cocktail Ice Pops: Stir in 3 tbsp (45 mL) tequila along with the syrup. Gold or reposado tequila will give more flavor, while white tequila will add just a subtle touch of tequila's unique taste.

Pineapple Coconut Ice Pops

**Makes about
3 cups (750 mL)
9 to 12 ice pops**

These ice pops, made
from fresh pineapple
cooked in coconut
milk and flavored with
toasted coconut, are
almost as good as a lazy
day on a Mexican beach.

Tip

In many ice pops that
include solid ingredients or
combine liquids of different
viscosities, there is a bit of
layering after freezing, which
is normal. However, if you
want a seamless result, give
the mixture a stir after it has
reached the slushy stage to
ensure that the ingredients
remain integrated.

- Blender

½ cup	sweetened flaked coconut	125 mL
½	pineapple, peeled, cored and chopped	½
1 cup	coconut milk	250 mL
⅓ cup	light brown (golden yellow) sugar	75 mL
Pinch	salt	Pinch
¼ cup	water	60 mL

1. In a dry skillet over medium-low heat, toast
coconut, stirring often, until golden brown and
fragrant, about 5 minutes. Remove from heat and
set aside.

2. In a saucepan, combine pineapple, coconut milk,
sugar and salt. Bring to a boil, reduce heat and
simmer, covered, for 15 minutes. Remove from
heat, uncover and set aside to cool.

3. Transfer to blender and add water; blend at
medium speed until smooth. Add reserved
toasted coconut and blend at low speed just until
combined.

4. Pour into molds and freeze until slushy, then
insert sticks and freeze until solid, for at least
4 hours. If you are using an ice pop kit, follow
the manufacturer's instructions.

Variation

Piña Colada Ice Pops: Do not toast coconut
(omit Step 1). Replace the water with an equal
quantity of white or amber rum.

Caribbean Fruit Punch Ice Pops

Makes about 3¼ cups (800 mL) 9 to 13 ice pops

A typical Caribbean punch is a spirited mix of fruit and flavorings, often accented with a dash of angostura bitters, which is a Trinidadian trick.

Tip

If you have only whole cardamom in pods rather than ground cardamom, crack about 4 pods to obtain ¼ tsp (1 mL) seeds; grind in a mortar before adding to the recipe.

- Blender

1 cup	coconut milk (see Tips, page 83)	250 mL
⅓ cup	packed dark brown sugar	75 mL
½ tsp	finely grated lime zest	2 mL
¼ tsp	ground cardamom	1 mL
¼ tsp	freshly grated nutmeg	1 mL
1½ cups	chopped ripe mango	375 mL
¾ cup	sliced banana	175 mL
¼ cup	freshly squeezed lime juice	60 mL
½ tsp	rum extract	2 mL
Dash	angostura bitters (see Tip, page 234)	Dash

1. In a saucepan, combine coconut milk, sugar, lime zest, cardamom and a scant ¼ tsp (1 mL) nutmeg. Cook over medium heat until simmering, stirring until sugar is dissolved. Remove from heat and set aside to cool.

2. In blender at medium-high speed, purée mango, banana, lime juice, rum extract, bitters and coconut milk mixture.

3. Pour into molds and freeze until slushy, then insert sticks and freeze until solid, for at least 4 hours. If you are using an ice pop kit, follow the manufacturer's instructions.

Variation

Caribbean Rum Punch Ice Pops: Substitute 2 tbsp (30 mL) dark rum for the rum extract, just for the flavor, or up to ⅓ cup (75 mL) dark or amber rum to add a bit of a kick. Freeze overnight.

Cajeta Ice Pops

Makes about 3 cups (750 mL) 9 to 12 ice pops

Cajeta is thick, dark caramelized goat's milk, and it's one of the most popular sweet ingredients in Mexico. Similar caramelized spreads made from cow's or mixed cow and goat milk are made throughout Latin America and are known as dulce de leche (see Variations, right).

Tip

Sinfully sweet — and addictive to boot — cajeta has a flavor unto itself and is worth searching out at a specialty store. Regular cow's-milk dulce de leche, also a delicious treat, is available in jars at many supermarkets.

2 cups	whole goat's milk	500 mL
½ cup	heavy or whipping (35%) cream	125 mL
2 tbsp	granulated sugar	30 mL
Pinch	salt	Pinch
⅔ cup	cajeta (see Tip, left)	150 mL

1. In a saucepan, combine milk, cream, sugar and a scant pinch of salt. Cook over medium-high heat, stirring, until sugar is dissolved and mixture just reaches a boil. Remove from heat and stir in cajeta. Set aside to cool.

2. Pour into molds and freeze until slushy, then insert sticks and freeze until solid, for at least 4 hours. If you are using an ice pop kit, follow the manufacturer's instructions.

Variations

Dulce de Leche Ice Pops: Replace the goat's milk with cow's milk. Replace the cajeta with dulce de leche. Stir in ½ tsp (2 mL) vanilla extract along with the dulce de leche.

Cinnamon Cajeta or Dulce de Leche Ice Pops: Before adding ingredients to the saucepan, toast 1 stick (about 3 inches/8 cm) Mexican cinnamon over medium-low heat until fragrant, 2 to 3 minutes. Add milk and proceed as for either Cajeta Ice Pops or Dulce de Leche Ice Pops. Remove and discard cinnamon before pouring mixture into molds.

Mexican Chocolate Ice Pops

**Makes about
2½ cups (625 mL)
7 to 10 ice pops**

"Mexican chocolate"
refers to a hot drink
made from cakes or
tablets of grainy native
chocolate flavored with
sugar, cinnamon and
almonds. This is a thick,
egg yolk–enriched
version of that luscious
drink.

Tips

You can buy tablets of
Mexican chocolate at many
large supermarkets or at
Mexican or Central American
grocery stores. Brands vary;
most do not need additional
sugar or almond extract.

If you can't find Mexican
chocolate, substitute with
5 oz (150 g) grated or
finely chopped semisweet
chocolate, 3 tbsp (45 mL)
granulated sugar, 1½ tsp
(7 mL) ground cinnamon
and ¼ tsp (1 mL) almond
extract.

1½ cups	water	375 mL
2	tablets Mexican chocolate (total 6 oz/175 g; see Tips, left)	2
½ cup + 2 tbsp	evaporated milk, divided	155 mL
2	egg yolks	2
	Granulated sugar, optional	
	Almond extract, optional	

1. In a saucepan over medium-high heat, bring water and chocolate to a boil, whisking constantly. Whisk until mixture is smooth and frothy, about 5 minutes. Whisk in ½ cup (125 mL) evaporated milk and return to a boil, then reduce heat to low and simmer.

2. Meanwhile, in a separate bowl, whisk egg yolks with remaining 2 tbsp (30 mL) evaporated milk. Whisk in ¼ cup (60 mL) of the hot chocolate mixture. Whisk egg mixture into chocolate mixture and cook over low heat, stirring constantly and without bringing to a simmer, until mixture is thick enough to coat a spoon, 1 to 2 minutes. Remove from heat. Stir in additional sugar and/ or a few drops of almond extract to taste, if using. Set aside to cool.

3. Whisk mixture until slightly frothy. Pour into molds and freeze until slushy, then insert sticks and freeze until solid, for at least 4 hours. If you are using an ice pop kit, follow the manufacturer's instructions.

Chocolate and Chile Ice Pops

Makes about 3 cups (750 mL) 9 to 12 ice pops

Mildly hot chile peppers are surprisingly good with chocolate. Try these luxurious fruity and rich bittersweet dessert ice pops and you will see what I mean. Mexican dried mulato chile peppers have a fruity, sweet flavor and very mild heat that pair extremely well with dark chocolate. Their fruitiness is further emphasized here by a judicious dose of sweet raisins.

Tip

Mulato chiles (dried mulato peppers) are large and black, similar to ancho chiles (dried poblano peppers). If you can't find them, substitute 3 of the more readily available ancho chiles, which will give the ice pops a hotter bite.

- Blender
- Fine-mesh sieve

2	dried mulato chile peppers (see Tip, left)	2
1/2 cup	raisins	125 mL
2 1/2 cups	boiling water	625 mL
1/4 cup	unsweetened cocoa powder	60 mL
1/4 tsp	ground cinnamon	1 mL
4 oz	bittersweet chocolate, chopped	125 g
1/2 cup	sweetened condensed milk	125 mL

1. Place chiles and raisins in a heatproof bowl. Add boiling water and set aside to soak for 15 minutes. Pour soaking liquid and raisins into blender. Split open chiles and discard seeds and inner membranes. Add to blender and purée at medium-high speed.

2. Place sieve over a saucepan and strain mixture, pushing down and scraping solids to extract as much pulp as possible. Discard solids.

3. Whisk cocoa and cinnamon into chile mixture. Bring to a boil over high heat, reduce heat to low and simmer, covered, lifting the lid and stirring often, for 5 minutes. Remove from heat and whisk in chocolate until thoroughly incorporated and smooth. Whisk in condensed milk and set aside to cool.

4. Whisk mixture. Pour into molds and freeze until slushy, then insert sticks and freeze until solid, for at least 4 hours. If you are using an ice pop kit, follow the manufacturer's instructions.

Mexican Jamaica Ice Pops

**Makes about
4 cups (1 L)
12 to 16 ice pops**

Jamaica (pronounced *hamaica*) is the Spanish name for edible dried red hibiscus flowers. (They are known as sorrel on the Caribbean island of Jamaica; see Jamaican Sorrel Punch Ice Pops, page 172.) In Mexico a fragrant, tart raspberry-red tea is brewed from the dried flowers. It is usually lightly sweetened and served cold with meals or as a refreshing drink over ice, often with an added hint of lime. The tea is also used to make *paletas* (ice pops) such as these.

Tip

Buy Mexican jamaica or Jamaican sorrel at Mexican and Latin American or Caribbean grocery stores.

- Fine-mesh sieve

1¼ cups	dried jamaica flowers (Jamaican sorrel)	300 mL
4 cups	boiling water	1 L
⅓ cup + 2 tbsp	agave or corn syrup	105 mL
⅓ cup	freshly squeezed lime juice	75 mL

1. Place jamaica in a heatproof bowl or pot and add boiling water. Cover and set aside to steep for at least 1 hour or up to 4 hours. Strain through sieve into a large measuring cup. Stir in syrup and lime juice.

2. Pour into molds and freeze until slushy, then insert sticks and freeze until solid, for at least 4 hours. If you are using an ice pop kit, follow the manufacturer's instructions.

Jamaican Sorrel Punch Ice Pops

Makes about
4 cups (1 L)
12 to 16 ice pops

Dried edible red hibiscus flowers are known in Jamaica as sorrel, but they have no relation whatsoever to sorrel greens, the cold-climate leafy herb. However, both share a similarly tart flavor. In Jamaica the dried flowers are used to brew a gingery cold punch that freezes into excellent ice pops.

Tip

Honey keeps almost indefinitely. If your liquid honey crystallizes, just warm it up by heating the uncovered jar in a microwave oven or placing it in hot water. Once it is warmed, give it a stir and it will return to liquid form.

- Fine-mesh sieve

1 cup	dried jamaica flowers (Jamaican sorrel)	250 mL
2 tsp	finely grated gingerroot	10 mL
5	whole allspice	5
4 cups	boiling water	1 L
¼ cup	granulated sugar	60 mL
¼ cup	liquid honey (see Tip, left)	60 mL
3 tbsp	freshly squeezed lemon juice	45 mL

1. Place jamaica flowers, ginger and allspice in a heatproof bowl or pot and add boiling water. Stir in sugar until dissolved. Cover and set aside to steep for at least 2 hours or up to 4 hours. Strain through sieve into a large measuring cup. Stir in honey and lemon juice.

2. Pour into molds and freeze until slushy, then insert sticks and freeze until solid, for at least 4 hours. If you are using an ice pop kit, follow the manufacturer's instructions.

East and Southeast Asian Flavors

Korean Pear and Ginger Ice Pops

**Makes about
3⅓ cups (825 mL)
10 to 13 ice pops**

Pears in Korea — known
as Asian pears in North
America — are often
poached with whole
almonds in ginger-
flavored syrup, which is
the inspiration for these
ice pops.

Tip

Korean pears are large,
heavy, apple-shaped pears
with matte light brown skin.
They range in weight from
about 12 ounces (375 g) to
1½ pounds (750 g) each.
Like many other Asian
varieties, they are often
called simply Asian pears,
or Japanese, Taiwan or
sand pears, so named for
the slightly sandy texture
of their flesh. Korean pears
have a distinctive sweet-and-
sour contrast and firm, crisp
texture, making them ideal
pears for cooking. Don't peel
them too far in advance, as
they tend to oxidize a little
when exposed to air.

- Spice bag or cheesecloth
- Blender

6	slices gingerroot	6
½ tsp	black peppercorns	2 mL
½	stick cinnamon (about 1½ inches/4 cm)	½
2 cups	water	500 mL
⅓ cup	rock (yellow crystal) sugar (see Tips, page 47) or granulated sugar	75 mL
1½ lbs	Korean pears (see Tip, left)	750 g
¼ tsp	almond extract	1 mL

1. Place ginger, peppercorns and cinnamon in spice bag or wrap in cheesecloth. In a saucepan, bring water and sugar to a boil, stirring until sugar is dissolved. Add spice bag, reduce heat and simmer, covered, for 5 minutes.

2. Meanwhile, peel and core pear(s) and cut into large chunks.

3. Add chopped pear to saucepan and bring to a boil. Reduce heat, cover and simmer until very tender, 20 to 25 minutes. Remove from heat and set aside to cool.

4. Remove and discard spice bag. Stir in almond extract. Transfer to blender and purée at medium-high speed.

5. Pour into molds and freeze until slushy, then insert sticks and freeze until solid, for at least 4 hours. If you are using an ice pop kit, follow the manufacturer's instructions.

Melon Cream Ice Pops

Makes about
3 cups (750 mL)
9 to 12 ice pops

These honeydew melon and cream ice pops are one of the most popular frozen sweets in Korea. They are also popular in Japan. You need a ripe and especially juicy melon to ensure that these pops will be really delicious.

Tip

In many ice pops that include solid ingredients or combine liquids of different viscosities, there is a bit of layering after freezing, which is normal. However, if you want a seamless result, give the mixture a stir after it has reached the slushy stage to ensure that the ingredients remain integrated.

- Box grater
- Blender

½	ripe honeydew melon (6 to 7 lbs/ 3 to 3.5 kg whole), seeded and cut into quarters lengthwise	½
⅓ cup	granulated sugar	75 mL
Pinch	salt	Pinch
¼ cup	heavy or whipping (35%) cream	60 mL

1. Using the large holes of box grater set over a large bowl, shred melon. Discard skins.

2. Place a sieve or colander over a large measuring cup and strain shredded melon. Set aside solids. Measure juices and transfer at least 1 cup (250 mL) or up to 1½ cups (375 mL) to a saucepan. (Save any extra for another use.)

3. Add sugar and a tiny pinch of salt to juices. Bring to a boil over high heat, stirring until sugar has dissolved. Boil, stirring occasionally, until reduced to ½ cup (125 mL), about 10 minutes. Remove from heat and set aside to cool.

4. In blender at medium-high speed, purée shredded melon. Stir in reserved melon syrup and cream and blend at low speed until thoroughly incorporated.

5. Pour into molds and freeze until slushy, then insert sticks and freeze until solid, for at least 4 hours. If you are using an ice pop kit, follow the manufacturer's instructions.

Roasted and Malted Barley Ice Pops

Makes about
Makes about
3 cups (750 mL)
9 to 12 ice pops

Roasted barley tea is the most common beverage in Korea. It is served warm and unsweetened year-round and often served chilled in the summer. Barley and other roasted-grain teas are also enjoyed in China, Japan and particularly Taiwan. The barley malt lends depth and sweetness to these ice pops, which are surprisingly light and refreshing.

Tip

Roasted barley is available at all Korean grocery stores, most large Chinese or Asian supermarkets and many Japanese markets, where it might also come in tea bag form. If you can't find it, you can make your own by roasting whole-grain barley (or you can use pot barley) in a dry heavy skillet or wok over medium heat, until the grains turn a rich, dark brown, about 10 minutes.

- Fine-mesh sieve

3 cups	water	750 mL
4 tsp	roasted barley	20 mL
¼ cup	barley malt or regular malt syrup	60 mL
2 tbsp	granulated sugar	30 mL

1. In a saucepan, bring water to a boil. Add roasted barley, cover and boil over medium heat for 5 minutes. Remove from heat and set aside to steep, covered, for 5 minutes.

2. Place sieve over a large measuring cup and strain tea. Discard solids. Stir malt syrup and sugar into liquid, until sugar is thoroughly dissolved. Set aside to cool.

3. Pour into molds and freeze until slushy, then insert sticks and freeze until solid, for at least 4 hours. If you are using an ice pop kit, follow the manufacturer's instructions.

Roasted Barley and Honey Ice Pops

Makes about 3¼ cups (800 mL) 9 to 13 ice pops

Use a dark or full-flavored honey to make these ice pops. The buckwheat fields of Canada and the northern United States provide wonderfully rich buckwheat honey, which I find particularly well suited to the toasty flavor of roasted barley. Another good pairing is chestnut honey, a favorite in Korea as well as in France, Spain and Italy. Or try distinctive manuka honey from New Zealand or dark and creamy avocado honey from California.

- Fine-mesh sieve

3 cups	water	750 mL
2 tbsp	roasted barley (see Tip, page 176)	30 mL
½ cup	buckwheat, chestnut or other full-flavored liquid honey	125 mL

1. In a saucepan, bring water to a boil. Add roasted barley and boil, covered, over medium heat for 5 minutes. Remove from heat and set aside to steep, covered, for 5 minutes.

2. Place sieve over a large measuring cup and strain tea. Discard solids. Stir honey into liquid until thoroughly mixed. Set aside to cool.

3. Pour into molds and freeze until slushy, then insert sticks and freeze until solid, for at least 4 hours. If you are using an ice pop kit, follow the manufacturer's instructions.

Salted Star Fruit Ice Pops

Makes about
2¾ cups (675 mL)
8 to 11 ice pops

These ice pops are made with fresh, ripe star fruit lightly sweetened with honey, which is balanced with lemon juice and just a touch of salt. They truly are among the most refreshing and cooling ice pops ever, perfect for a scorching summer evening.

Tips

In most of subtropical Asia, the star fruit (carambola) is eaten with a touch of salt to bring out its distinctive flavor. In Taiwan, where star fruit is enjoyed more than in any other part of Asia, it is often cured in salt, sugar and licorice root or other flavorings, then used as a base for juice or eaten over shaved ice. It is thought to have medicinal cooling properties.

Make sure you use well-ripened fruit — yellow with just a tinge of green — and honey with a light flavor, such as acacia or alfalfa.

- Blender
- Fine-mesh sieve

2 lbs	ripe star fruits (about 6 large; see Tips, left)	1 kg
1 cup	water	250 mL
¼ cup	liquid honey	60 mL
2 tbsp	freshly squeezed lemon juice	30 mL
½ tsp	salt	2 mL

1. Trim off waxy edges of star fruits. Cut off each rib as close to the pithy central core as possible. Remove any seeds and discard, along with all the pithy parts. Chop roughly and place in blender with water, honey, lemon juice and salt. Purée at medium-high speed.

2. Place sieve over a large measuring cup and strain mixture, using a rubber spatula to scrape and push down solids to extract as much juice and pulp as possible. Discard solids.

3. Pour into molds and freeze until slushy, then insert sticks and freeze until solid, for at least 4 hours. If you are using an ice pop kit, follow the manufacturer's instructions.

Chinese Sour Plum Ice Pops

**Makes about
2¹⁄₂ cups (625 mL)
7 to 10 ice pops**

As a hot or cold drink or as an ice pop, sour plum soup (*suanmeitang*) is popular in China.

Tips

Many kinds of dried sour plums are available at Chinese stores. Read the ingredient lists and choose those that do not have too many added flavorings.

Osmanthus syrup is a sweet syrup flavored with tiny white osmanthus flowers, which have a fragrance reminiscent of apricots and jasmine, with a touch of cinnamon and warm spice. Jars of osmanthus syrup (*guihuajiang*) can be purchased at most large Chinese grocery stores.

If you are not using osmanthus syrup, add 3 tbsp (45 mL) rock or granulated sugar. If you still want a floral note, stir in 1 tsp (5 mL) rose water after the mixture has cooled.

- Fine-mesh sieve

2 oz	dried sour plums (about ³⁄₄ cup/175 mL; see Tips, left)	60 g
3³⁄₄ cups	water, divided	925 mL
¹⁄₄ cup	rock (yellow crystal) sugar (see Tips, page 47) or light brown (golden yellow) sugar	60 mL
3 tbsp	osmanthus syrup (see Tips, left)	45 mL
2 tbsp	tapioca flour (see Tips, page 135)	30 mL

1. In a saucepan, soak plums in 3¹⁄₂ cups (875 mL) water until tender, 30 to 60 minutes. Bring to a boil over high heat. Reduce heat to medium-low, cover and simmer for 10 minutes.

2. Remove from heat and, using a fork, crush plums. Stir in sugar and syrup. Return to stovetop and simmer, covered, over low heat for 5 minutes.

3. Meanwhile, in a small bowl, stir together tapioca flour and remaining ¹⁄₄ cup (60 mL) water until smooth. Stir into plum mixture and simmer for 2 minutes. Remove from heat and set aside to cool for 10 minutes.

4. Place sieve over a large measuring cup and strain mixture, pressing down on solids to extract as much liquid as possible. Discard solids. Set aside to cool.

5. Pour into molds and freeze until slushy, then insert sticks and freeze until solid, for at least 4 hours. If you are using an ice pop kit, follow the manufacturer's instructions.

Sweet Sesame Ice Pops

Makes about
2¾ cups (675 mL)
8 to 11 ice pops

Sesame ice pops made from black sesame seeds are very popular in China. As soon as iced desserts began to become popular there — in the early twentieth century, when electricity became widely available — traditional hot and cold sweet soups were turned into frozen ice pops, or "ice sticks" (*bingbang*, as they are known in Chinese.

Tips

Black sesame seeds are available at all Chinese, Japanese and Korean grocery stores, as well as many supermarkets. For convenience, you can buy already roasted sesame seeds and peanuts and skip Steps 1 and 2 in the recipe. However, if you roast your own seeds and peanuts, the result will be more fragrant.

If you prefer, substitute ¼ cup (60 mL) peanut butter for the peanuts. Skip Step 2 and add along with the water in Step 3.

- Blender

1 cup	raw black sesame seeds (see Tips, left)	250 mL
¼ cup	blanched skinned peanuts (see Tips, left)	60 mL
¾ cup	granulated sugar	175 mL
2 tbsp	sweet rice flour or tapioca flour (see Tips, page 135)	30 mL
2 cups	water	500 mL

1. In a dry skillet or wok over medium heat, cook sesame seeds, stirring constantly, until fragrant and toasted, about 10 minutes. Scrape onto a plate and set aside to cool.

2. In same pan, toast peanuts, stirring often, until golden and fragrant, about 10 minutes. Scrape onto a plate and set aside to cool.

3. In blender, combine sesame seeds, peanuts and sugar; blend at high speed until finely ground. Add rice flour and pulse to combine thoroughly. Add water and blend until smooth.

4. Scrape sesame mixture into a saucepan and bring to a boil over high heat, stirring constantly. Reduce heat to medium and simmer, stirring constantly, for 3 minutes. Remove from heat and set aside to cool.

5. Spoon into molds. Tap molds on work surface to remove any air bubbles. Insert sticks and freeze until solid, for at least 4 hours. If you are using an ice pop kit, follow the manufacturer's instructions.

Sweet Peanut Ice Pops

**Makes about
3¾ cups (925 mL)
11 to 15 ice pops**

Simple hot or cold sweet peanut soups are served as snacks or desserts all over China, as are ice pops based on sweet traditional soups. If you are a fan of boiled peanuts, a delicacy in the American South, you will surely like this ice pop too.

Tips

If you are in a hurry, use the quick-soak method for the peanuts. Place peanuts in a saucepan with 4 cups (1 L) water; bring to a boil and boil over medium-high heat for 4 minutes. Remove from heat, cover and set aside to soak for 1 hour. Drain and rinse.

If you have a pressure cooker, you can use it to cook the peanuts. Boil peanuts and water in pressure cooker under moderate pressure for 45 minutes.

- Blender

6 oz	blanched peeled peanuts, soaked overnight in 4 cups (1 L) water, drained and rinsed (see Tips, left)	175 g
4 cups	water	1 L
¾ cup	light brown (golden yellow) sugar or palm sugar (see Tips, page 82)	175 mL
⅓ cup	evaporated milk or coconut cream, optional	75 mL

1. In a large saucepan, combine soaked peanuts with water and bring to a boil over high heat. Cover, reduce heat to medium and boil, adding additional boiling water if level goes below top of peanuts, until peanuts are completely soft and silky, about 2 to 3 hours (see Tips, left).

2. Stir in sugar and cook, stirring, until dissolved. Remove from heat and set aside to cool.

3. Transfer cooled peanut mixture to blender and purée at medium-high speed. Add evaporated milk, if using, and pulse to blend.

4. Immediately pour into molds and freeze until slushy, then insert sticks and freeze until solid, for at least 4 hours. If you are using an ice pop kit, follow the manufacturer's instructions.

Red Bean Ice Pops

Makes about
3 cups (750 mL)
9 to 12 ice pops

This was one of the first and is still one of the most popular ice pop recipes in Japan and China.

Tip

The cooking time for beans depends upon their freshness and how long they were soaked. Older beans will take longer to cook.

• Food processor

1 cup	dried red adzuki beans	250 mL
	Water	
¾ cup + 2 tbsp	granulated sugar	205 mL
1 cup	milk	250 mL
1 cup	half-and-half (10%) cream	250 mL

1. Cover beans with water by 2 inches (5 cm) and soak for at least 4 hours or overnight. Drain, rinse well and place in a saucepan with 2 cups (500 mL) water. Bring to a boil over high heat. Reduce heat to medium and cook until beans are soft, adding a little more water if level gets below top of beans, 25 to 60 minutes (see Tip, left). Stir in sugar until dissolved and cook, stirring often, until liquid is reduced to about 2 tbsp (30 mL), about 15 minutes. Remove from heat.

2. Scoop out ⅓ cup (75 mL) beans and set aside. Transfer remainder to food processor fitted with the metal blade. Add milk and cream and process until smooth. (You can also do this in a blender, or by hand with a potato masher.) Set aside to cool. Stir in reserved whole beans.

3. Pour into molds and freeze until slushy, then insert sticks and freeze until solid, for at least 4 hours. If you are using an ice pop kit, follow the manufacturer's instructions.

Variations

Red Bean and Coconut Ice Pops: These dairy-free ice pops are popular in the Philippines and Taiwan. Replace the milk and cream with 2 cups (500 mL) scalded coconut milk (see Tip, page 188).

Brown Sugar Red Bean Ice Pops: Replace the granulated sugar with packed brown sugar (demerara, light brown/golden yellow and dark brown are all fine) and 2 tbsp (30 mL) light (fancy) molasses.

Split Mung Bean Ice Pops

**Makes about
2¾ cups (675 mL)
8 to 11 ice pops**

Sweet mung bean soup, served hot or cold, is a well-loved treat in China. Mung bean ice pops appeared as soon as ice pops started becoming popular in China and Southeast Asia, before the Second World War.

Tip

Split peeled mung beans, which are pale yellow, are available at Chinese, Korean and South Asian markets.

1 cup	split peeled mung beans	250 mL
	Water	
½ cup + 1 tbsp	rock (yellow crystal) sugar or granulated sugar (see Tips, page 47)	140 mL

1. Cover beans in water by 1 inch (2.5 cm) and soak for 2 to 4 hours. Drain and rinse well.

2. In a saucepan, combine beans with 3 cups (750 mL) water. Bring to a boil and boil gently over medium heat until soft, 20 to 30 minutes. Stir in sugar and cook, stirring occasionally, until beans have broken apart, 15 to 20 minutes. Pour beans and liquid into a large measuring cup; if necessary, add water to make 2¾ cups (675 mL). Set aside to cool.

3. With a fork, whisk mixture well. Pour into molds and freeze until slushy, then insert sticks and freeze until solid, for at least 4 hours. If you are using an ice pop kit, follow the manufacturer's instructions.

Filipino Mung Bean Ice Pops

Makes about 3¼ cups (800 mL) 9 to 13 ice pops

In the Philippines, small green whole mung beans are the most popular of all legumes, for desserts as well as hot savory dishes. Here is a much-loved ice pop version. Whole mung beans, which are deep green, are available at most large supermarkets and bulk stores.

Tip

Raw cane sugar is sugar that has been solidified in large chunks from unrefined sugar cane juice; it contains all the molasses flavor and minerals from pressed sugar cane. Don't confuse it with refined light brown "evaporated cane sugar," although that is often labeled "raw cane sugar" too. *Jaggery* is the Indian name for raw cane sugar (and just to confuse things further, in India it can also refer to cakes of palm sugar). Raw cane sugar is also available in Latin American markets, where it is known as *piloncillo*.

1 cup	mung beans	250 mL
	Water	
½ cup + 1 tbsp	raw cane sugar, palm sugar or brown sugar (see Tip, left)	140 mL
½ cup	evaporated milk	125 mL

1. Cover beans with water by 1 inch (2.5 cm) and soak for 4 to 6 hours. Drain and rinse well.

2. In a saucepan, combine beans with 4 cups (1 L) water. Bring to a boil and simmer over low heat until tender, about 45 minutes. Stir in sugar and cook, stirring often, adding a little more water if mixture is sticking or drying out, until beans have broken apart, 20 to 30 minutes. Pour beans and liquid into a large measuring cup; if necessary, add water to make 2¾ cups (675 mL). Set aside to cool. Whisk in evaporated milk until thoroughly incorporated.

3. Pour into molds and freeze until slushy, then insert sticks and freeze until solid, for at least 4 hours. If you are using an ice pop kit, follow the manufacturer's instructions.

Taro Ice Pops

**Makes about
3⅓ cups (825 mL)
10 to 13 ice pops**

Starchy taro root
is used in both
savories and sweets
throughout South
and Southeast Asia,
southern China and
Oceania. It is especially
popular for sweets
in the Philippines,
Taiwan, the north-
eastern Guangdong
and southern Fujian
provinces of China,
Thailand and Guam,
among other places.
Ices, ice creams,
puddings, cakes and
cookies all use taro as
their base.

Tip

Taro has an unusual,
somewhat sticky texture
when cooked and requires
some patience to achieve
the right consistency in
Step 2.

- Immersion blender

3 cups	diced peeled taro root (about 1 lb/500 g)	750 mL
2 cups	(approx.) water, divided	500 mL
Pinch	salt	Pinch
½ cup	granulated sugar	125 mL
⅓ cup + 1 tbsp	packed dark brown sugar	90 mL
¾ cup	half-and-half (10%) cream	175 mL

1. In a saucepan, combine taro, 1¾ cups (425 mL) water and salt. Bring to a boil over high heat. Reduce heat to medium, cover and cook until taro is very soft, 20 to 25 minutes.

2. Stir in granulated and brown sugars and cook, stirring continuously, until taro has broken down into a purée, 10 to 15 minutes, adding a little water if mixture is sticking or becomes too thick to stir easily.

3. Remove from heat and stir in cream. Using an immersion blender (you can also do this in a blender at low speed), blend until mixture is completely smooth but not frothy, adding up to ½ cup (125 mL) water to make mixture the consistency of porridge (it should be thick but just pourable). Set aside to cool.

4. Pour into molds and freeze until slushy, then insert sticks and freeze until solid, for at least 4 hours. If you are using an ice pop kit, follow the manufacturer's instructions.

Jackfruit Coconut Ice Pops

Makes about
1¾ cups (425 mL)
5 to 7 ice pops

You can use canned,
frozen or, of course,
fresh ripe jackfruit for
these sweet, almost
candy-like Filipino-style
ice pops.

Tips

You can use drained canned,
thawed frozen or fresh
jackfruit in this recipe. One
standard can of jackfruit
yields 8 ounces (250 g) fruit.
The recipe uses that amount
and thus makes only a few
ice pops, but it is easily
doubled.

Raw cane sugar is sugar that
has been solidified in large
chunks from unrefined sugar
cane juice; it contains all the
molasses flavor and minerals
from pressed sugar cane.
Don't confuse it with refined
light brown "evaporated
cane sugar," although that
is often labeled "raw cane
sugar" too. *Jaggery* is the
Indian name for raw cane
sugar (and just to confuse
things further, in India it can
also refer to cakes of palm
sugar).

- Blender

1 cup	coconut milk	250 mL
½ cup	raw cane sugar (see Tips, left) or palm sugar	125 mL
8 oz	seeded ripe jackfruit (see Tips, left)	250 g

1. In a saucepan over medium-high heat, bring coconut milk and sugar to a boil, stirring until sugar is dissolved. Continue boiling until thick and syrupy and reduced to about 1 cup (250 mL), about 10 minutes. Remove from heat and set aside to cool.

2. Transfer to blender and add jackfruit. Purée at medium-high speed.

3. Pour into molds and freeze until slushy, then insert sticks and freeze until solid, for at least 4 hours. If you are using an ice pop kit, follow the manufacturer's instructions.

Tamarind Ice Pops

**Makes about
2½ cups (625 mL)
7 to 14 ice pops**

The sweet-and-sour
pulpy fruit surrounding
the seeds in the pods of
the tropical tamarind
tree is a favorite for
sweet and savory
cooking worldwide.
In Asia, particularly
in the Philippines
and throughout most
of India, it is usually
sweetened with raw
cane sugar. In the rest of
Southeast Asia and in
some regions of India,
palm sugar is used. Each
type of sugar adds its
own character to these
ice pops.

Tip

If you prefer, substitute
2 tbsp (30 mL) tamarind
concentrate for the pulp. It
comes in a jar rather than a
block. Cook it with the sugar
and water for 2 minutes.
There is no need to strain.

- Fine-mesh sieve

2½ cups	water	625 mL
1 cup	raw cane sugar (see Tips, page 186), palm sugar (see Tips, page 82) or brown sugar	250 mL
⅓ cup	tamarind pulp (with seeds)	75 mL
4 tsp	freshly squeezed lime juice	20 mL

1. In a saucepan, bring water, sugar and tamarind pulp to a boil, stirring until sugar is dissolved. Reduce heat and simmer until seeds loosen and tamarind is falling apart, about 2 minutes.

2. Place sieve over a large measuring cup and strain mixture, using a rubber spatula to scrape and push down solids to extract as much juice and pulp as possible. Discard solids. Stir in lime juice and set aside to cool.

3. Pour into molds and freeze until slushy, then insert sticks and freeze until solid, for at least 4 hours. If you are using an ice pop kit, follow the manufacturer's instructions.

Cashew Ice Pops

Makes about
2½ cups (625 mL)
8 to 10 ice pops

Rich, creamy cashew
nuts are a favorite
ingredient for sweets in
tropical Asia, and they
shine in these delicious
ice pops.

Tips

For scalded coconut milk,
bring coconut milk to a full
boil, remove from heat and
set aside to cool.

Each different sugar will
provide a unique flavor in
these ice pops. Look for raw
cane sugar in Asian and Latin
American markets, where it
is known as *piloncillo*. Palm
sugar, which is produced
from the sweet sap of
various palm trees, is sold in
cakes; it should be chopped
before measuring.

- Blender

2 cups	whole raw cashew nuts (8½ oz/265 g)	500 mL
¾ cup	palm sugar, raw cane sugar or light brown (golden yellow) sugar (see Tips, left)	175 mL
¼ cup	water	60 mL
1 cup	evaporated milk or cooled scalded coconut milk (see Tips, left)	250 mL

1. In a dry, heavy-bottomed skillet over low heat, toast cashews, stirring frequently, until golden, 15 to 18 minutes. Remove from heat and set aside to cool. Chop ⅓ cup (75 mL) and transfer to a small bowl. Set aside.

2. In a small saucepan over medium heat, heat sugar and water until sugar dissolves. Remove from heat and set aside to cool.

3. In blender at medium-high speed, purée whole cashews, sugar syrup and evaporated milk until smooth.

4. Pour cashew mixture into molds, leaving a scant ½ inch (1 cm) headspace. Divide reserved chopped cashews evenly among molds, stirring to distribute evenly. Freeze until slushy, then insert sticks and freeze until solid, for at least 4 hours. If you are using an ice pop kit, follow the manufacturer's instructions.

Purple Sweet Potato and Coconut Ice Pops

**Makes about
2⅔ cups (650 mL)
8 to 10 ice pops**

In the Philippines,
purple sweet potatoes
or purple yams (*ube*) are
used to make purple
cakes, cookies, candies,
ice creams and ice pops.

Tips

Tropical pandan (pandanus)
leaves are long, spear-
like green leaves used for
flavoring in Southeast Asian
cooking. They are available
frozen and occasionally fresh
at Asian markets specializing
in Southeast Asian
ingredients, where you may
also find pandan leaf extract.
To cook the leaf with the
sweet potato, double it over
lengthwise and tie into a
simple knot.

Substitute a small star anise
for the pandan leaf (adding
in Step 1) or ½ tsp (2 mL)
vanilla extract, adding it to
the blender in Step 2.

- Blender or food processor

1½ cups	coconut milk	375 mL
⅓ cup	granulated sugar	75 mL
8 oz	purple sweet potato, peeled and cut into chunks	250 g
1	pandan (pandanus) leaf (see Tips, left) or ½ tsp (2 mL) pandan extract	1

1. In a saucepan, bring coconut milk and sugar to a boil, stirring until sugar is dissolved. Add sweet potato and pandan leaf; simmer, with lid slightly ajar and stirring occasionally, until sweet potato is soft and beginning to fall apart, 15 to 20 minutes. Remove from heat and set aside to cool.

2. Remove pandan leaf and transfer mixture to blender or food processor. (If using pandan extract or vanilla extract, add before puréeing.) Purée.

3. Pour into molds and freeze until slushy, then insert sticks and freeze until solid, for at least 4 hours. If you are using an ice pop kit, follow the manufacturer's instructions.

Thai Pumpkin Ice Pops

**Makes about
3 cups (750 mL)
9 to 12 ice pops**

A well-loved traditional Thai dessert, *sangkaya fak-thong*, is coconut custard steamed inside a seeded small pumpkin. It is served cool and cut into wedges. This ice pop incorporates the flavors of that dessert.

Tips

Use a ripe pie pumpkin or calabaza, kabocha, butternut or other full-flavored orange-fleshed squash. Canned pumpkin purée is acceptable.

To make pumpkin or squash purée: Cut vegetable in half lengthwise and remove seeds. Place halves, cut side down, on a rimmed baking sheet. Bake in 425°F (220°C) oven until very tender, 30 to 60 minutes. Remove from oven and set aside to cool. Scoop out flesh and mash well or purée in a food processor.

● Fine-mesh sieve

2 cups	coconut milk	500 mL
½ cup	palm sugar	125 mL
1¼ cups	puréed cooked pumpkin or squash (see Tips, left)	300 mL
2	egg yolks	2
¼ tsp	pandan (pandanus leaf) extract, rose water or vanilla extract	1 mL

1. In a saucepan, bring coconut milk and sugar to a boil, stirring until sugar is dissolved. Stir in pumpkin purée. Reduce heat to medium-low and simmer, with lid slightly ajar and stirring occasionally, for 10 minutes. Reduce heat to low.

2. In a heatproof bowl, beat egg yolks until smooth. Beat in ½ cup (125 ml) hot pumpkin mixture. Whisk mixture into pan and cook, stirring, until thick enough to coat a spoon, 1 to 2 minutes (do not let it come to a boil). Remove from heat and set aside to cool.

3. Place sieve over a large measuring cup and strain. Discard any solids. Stir in pandan extract.

4. Pour into molds and freeze until slushy, then insert sticks and freeze until solid, for at least 4 hours. If you are using an ice pop kit, follow the manufacturer's instructions.

Indian-Style Ice Pops

Traditional Kulfi Ice Pops

Makes about
3⅓ cups (825 mL)
10 to 13 ice pops

This is the traditional way to make kulfi, India's version of ice cream pops: from concentrated milk that has been cooked down to about a third of its volume. As boiling down the milk is a bit time-consuming, most Indian home cooks don't make these ice pops. But they are better than any commercial ones I've tried, so I think they are well worth the effort.

Tip

I like to fortify the milk with a little 10% cream to boost the milk-fat content just a touch, to approximate rich natural milk.

7 cups	whole milk	1.75 L
1 cup	half-and-half (10%) cream (see Tip, left)	250 mL
8	cardamom pods, crushed	8
3	whole cloves	3
½ cup	granulated sugar	125 mL
2 tbsp	chopped blanched almonds	30 mL
2 tbsp	chopped natural pistachios (skins rubbed off) or blanched almonds	30 mL

1. In a large, wide, heavy-bottomed saucepan or Dutch oven, combine milk, cream, cardamom and cloves. Bring to a boil over high heat, reduce heat to medium and boil gently, stirring often (at least every 5 minutes) and stirring in any skin that forms, until liquid is reduced to 3 cups (750 mL), about 80 to 100 minutes.

2. Place a sieve over a large measuring cup and strain. Discard solids. Return mixture to saucepan. Stir in sugar, almonds and pistachios; simmer over low heat, stirring, for 5 minutes. Remove from heat and set aside to cool.

3. Transfer mixture to a bowl. Place in freezer and chill, stirring a few times, until slushy, about 1½ to 2 hours. Whisk until smooth and thick. Spoon into molds, tapping them on work surface to remove any air pockets. Insert sticks and freeze until solid, at least 3 more hours.

Variation

Saffron and Pistachio Kulfi Ice Pops:
Reduce cardamom to 6 pods. Omit almonds and increase pistachios to ⅓ cup (75 mL). In a small bowl, using the back of a spoon, coarsely grind a pinch of saffron threads with 1 tsp (5 mL) of the sugar. Stir into kulfi at the very end of cooking. While kulfi mixture is cooling, stir it 2 or 3 times.

Quick Nut Kulfi Ice Pops

Makes about
2⅓ cups (575 mL)
7 to 9 ice pops

Not everyone has the time and patience to make kulfi at home in the traditional manner, but there are several good ways to approximate its rich reduced-milk flavor and texture. Canned evaporated milk and sweetened condensed milk come to the rescue for cooks with less time.

Tip

When buying cardamom, look for fresh-looking green pods (they fade with time); white pods are bleached and should be avoided. (Black cardamom is from a different plant species and is not used in sweet dishes.) When using them whole or to extract the seeds, crack cardamom pods with the side of a chef's knife.

1	can (12 oz/370 mL) evaporated milk	1
1 cup	whole or 2% milk	250 mL
½ cup	half-and-half (10%) cream	125 mL
8	cardamom pods, crushed	8
2	whole cloves	2
2 tbsp	chopped blanched almonds	30 mL
2 tbsp	chopped natural pistachios (skins rubbed off) or blanched almonds	30 mL
⅓ cup + 1 tbsp	sweetened condensed milk	90 mL

1. In a large, wide, heavy-bottomed saucepan, combine evaporated milk, whole milk, cream, cardamom and cloves. Bring to a boil over high heat, reduce heat to medium-high and boil, stirring every few minutes and stirring in any skin that forms, until mixture is reduced by about one-quarter, 10 to 15 minutes. (Lower heat a little if mixture threatens to overflow.)

2. Place a sieve over a large measuring cup and strain. Discard solids. Return mixture to saucepan. Stir in almonds and pistachios; simmer over low heat, stirring often, for 5 minutes. Stir in condensed milk. Remove from heat and set aside to cool.

3. Pour into molds and freeze until slushy, then insert sticks and freeze until solid, for at least 4 hours. If you are using an ice pop kit, follow the manufacturer's instructions.

Mango Kulfi Ice Pops

Makes about
2⅓ cups (575 mL)
7 to 9 ice pops

This recipe uses an even quicker method of making kulfi than the "quick method" used in Quick Nut Kulfi Ice Pops (page 193), so it's easy to put together whenever mangoes are ripe and sweet. These ice pops are nice with or without the nuts, so feel free to leave them out if you wish (making the second simmering unnecessary).

● Blender

1	can (12 oz/370 mL) evaporated milk	1
6	cardamom pods, crushed	6
3 tbsp	chopped natural pistachios (skins rubbed off) or blanched almonds, optional	45 mL
⅔ cup	sweetened condensed milk	150 mL
2 cups	chopped ripe mango	500 mL

1. In a saucepan, bring evaporated milk and cardamom to a boil over medium-high heat. Reduce heat to low and simmer for 5 minutes. Remove from heat and set aside for 10 minutes.

2. Place a strainer over a large measuring cup and strain. Discard solids. If using nuts, return liquid to saucepan, stir in pistachios and simmer over low heat, stirring often, for 5 minutes. Stir in condensed milk and set aside to cool.

3. In blender at medium-high speed, purée mango. Stir into milk mixture until thoroughly combined.

4. Pour into molds and freeze until slushy, then insert sticks and freeze until solid, for at least 4 hours. If you are using an ice pop kit, follow the manufacturer's instructions.

Variations

Peach, Nectarine or Apricot Kulfi Ice Pops: Sweet, fully ripe peaches, nectarines or apricots make lovely kulfi ice pops. Substitute an equal quantity of peeled, pitted and chopped peaches, nectarines or apricots for the mango. Purée in blender with 1 tbsp (15 mL) lemon or lime juice.

Spiced Almond Ice Pops

**Makes about
2 cups (500 mL)
6 to 8 ice pops**

Sweetened with raw
cane sugar and spiced
with cardamom, these
rich, fragrant and
unusual ice pops really
taste like a frozen
Indian sweet.

Tips

Make sure your ground
almonds are fresh. They
should have a light, sweet
fragrance, without any hint
of rancidity.

You can use commercial
almond milk or make your
own (page 105).

Ground cardamom has a
much shorter shelf life than
whole cardamom pods,
and the seeds are easy to
extract. Crack the pods with
the side of a chef's knife.
About 8 pods will yield
$1/2$ tsp (2 mL) seeds, which
are easily ground in a mortar
or can be crushed with the
side of a knife.

1 cup	ground almonds (see Tips, left)	250 mL
$3/4$ cup	raw cane sugar (see Tips, page 186) or light brown (golden yellow) sugar	175 mL
1 tsp	ground cardamom (see Tips, left)	5 mL
2 cups	almond milk (see Tips, left)	500 mL
2 tsp	rose water	10 mL

1. In a saucepan over medium heat, toast almonds, stirring almost constantly, until slightly darkened and fully fragrant, 8 to 10 minutes. Stir in sugar and cardamom and cook, stirring, for 1 minute. Whisk in almond milk and bring to a boil. Reduce heat to medium-low and simmer, stirring often, for 10 minutes. Remove from heat and set aside to cool.

2. Whisk in rose water. Pour into molds and freeze until slushy, then insert sticks and freeze until solid, for at least 4 hours. If you are using an ice pop kit, follow the manufacturer's instructions.

Indian Fruit Punch Ice Pops

Makes about
2½ cups (625 mL)
7 to 10 ice pops

This fruit "punch" is inspired by Indian fruit salads sprinkled with a fragrant spice mix called chat masala. It is used for all kinds of dishes. For these ice pops it is definitely in the background, but still lends a unique flavor.

Tip

You can buy chat masala, often labeled "chunk [or chunky] chat masala" or "chaat masala" at many large supermarkets, in the Indian food aisle, or at Asian grocery shops. Or you can make your own (see page 197).

● Blender

1 cup	chopped ripe mango	250 mL
1 cup	orange juice	250 mL
½ cup	sliced banana	125 mL
½ cup	freshly squeezed lime juice	125 mL
3 tbsp	liquid honey	45 mL
½ tsp	chat masala (see Tip, left)	2 mL

1. In blender at medium-high speed, purée mango, orange juice, banana, lime juice, honey and chat masala.

2. Pour into molds and freeze until slushy, then insert sticks and freeze until solid, for at least 4 hours. If you are using an ice pop kit, follow the manufacturer's instructions.

Chat Masala

**Makes about
1/3 cup (75 mL)**

Chat masala is a
wonderfully tart and
savory combination
of black salt, dried
green mango,
pomegranate seeds,
spice and chile.

Tip

Sprinkle chat (also called
chaat) masala over
sliced fresh fruit, fried or
roasted nuts, vegetable
salads or grilled
vegetables.

2 tbsp	coriander seeds	30 mL
2 tbsp	cumin seeds	30 mL
1 tsp	ajwain (carom) or fennel seeds	5 mL
1/2 tsp	caraway seeds	2 mL
2 tsp	dried pomegranate seeds	10 mL
4 tsp	black salt	20 mL
1 tbsp	amchur (green mango powder)	15 mL
1 1/2 tsp	garam masala	7 mL
1 tsp	cayenne pepper	5 mL
1/2 tsp	asafetida powder (hing)	2 mL
1/4 tsp	ground ginger	1 mL

1. In a dry skillet over medium-low heat, separately toast coriander, cumin, ajwain and caraway seeds until each is fragrant and slightly darkened, 1 to 4 minutes a batch.

2. Transfer toasted seeds to a mortar or spice grinder. Add pomegranate seeds and grind to a fine powder.

3. Transfer to a small bowl. Add black salt, amchur, garam masala, cayenne, asafetida and a generous 1/4 tsp (1 mL) ginger. Combine well. Store in an airtight container for up to 3 months.

Pomegranate Rose Ice Pops

**Makes about
2¾ cups (675 mL)
8 to 11 ice pops**

**Two favorite ingredients
of Indian cuisine,
pomegranate and yogurt,
come together beautifully
in these pretty pink ice
pops, enhanced by the
fragrance of sweet rose
water.**

Tip

In many ice pops that
include solid ingredients or
combine liquids of different
viscosities, there is a bit of
layering after freezing, which
is normal. However, if you
want a seamless result, give
the mixture a stir after it has
reached the slushy stage to
ensure that the ingredients
remain integrated.

3 cups	unsweetened pomegranate juice	750 mL
⅓ cup	granulated sugar	75 mL
1¾ cups	Greek-style, Balkan-style or drained plain yogurt	425 mL
2 tbsp	liquid honey	30 mL
1 tbsp	rose water	15 mL

1. In a saucepan over high heat, boil pomegranate
juice and sugar until reduced by half, 15 to
20 minutes. Remove from heat and set aside
to cool.

2. Whisk in yogurt, honey and rose water.

3. Pour into molds and freeze until slushy, then
insert sticks and freeze until solid, for at least
4 hours. If you are using an ice pop kit, follow
the manufacturer's instructions.

Mango Lassi Ice Pops

**Makes about
3 cups (750 mL)
9 to 12 ice pops**

With just a few
manipulations, mango
lassi, the popular Indian
mango and yogurt
drink, transforms into
wonderfully delicious
and rich ice pops.

Tip

Use at least 2% yogurt or
yogurt with a higher fat
content for this ice pop.
Greek-style or drained
(thickened) yogurt also
produces a good result.
Non-fat or 1% yogurt can be
used but will produce an icy
rather than creamy result.

- Fine-mesh sieve
- Blender

½ cup	milk	125 mL
8	cardamom pods, crushed, or scant ½ tsp (2 mL) ground cardamom (see Tips, page 195)	8
2 tbsp	brown rice, agave or corn syrup or liquid honey	30 mL
1⅔ cups	chopped ripe mango	400 mL
¾ cup	plain yogurt (see Tip, left)	175 mL
Pinch	salt, optional	Pinch

1. In a small saucepan, heat milk and cardamom just until boiling. Remove from heat, cover and set aside to steep for 5 minutes.

2. Place sieve over a bowl and strain milk, discarding solids. Stir in syrup. Set aside to cool.

3. In blender at medium-high speed, purée mango, yogurt, a scant pinch of salt (if using) and milk mixture.

4. Pour into molds and freeze until slushy, then insert sticks and freeze until solid, for at least 4 hours. If you are using an ice pop kit, follow the manufacturer's instructions.

Strawberry Lassi Ice Pops

**Makes about
2²⁄₃ cups (650 mL)
8 to 10 ice pops**

**Honey and a touch of
black pepper flavor
these lassi-inspired
ice pops.**

Tips

It is preferable to use at
least 2% yogurt or yogurt
with a higher fat content for
this ice pop. Greek-style or
drained (thickened) yogurt
also produces a good result.
Non-fat or 1% yogurt can be
used but will produce an icy
rather than creamy result.

Use a light-flavored floral
honey such as wildflower,
orange blossom, acacia or
clover.

- Blender

2 cups	halved hulled strawberries or frozen whole strawberries, thawed	500 mL
1 cup	plain yogurt (see Tips, left)	250 mL
⅓ cup	milk	75 mL
¼ cup	liquid honey (see Tips, left)	60 mL
Pinch	freshly ground black pepper	Pinch

1. In blender at medium speed, purée strawberries, yogurt, milk, honey and pepper.

2. Pour into molds and freeze until slushy, then insert sticks and freeze until solid, for at least 4 hours. If you are using an ice pop kit, follow the manufacturer's instructions.

Sweet Carrot Raita Ice Pops

**Makes about
2½ cups (625 mL)
7 to 10 ice pops**

In South Asian cooking, raita is a side dish traditionally served with spicy main dishes to cool and refresh the palate. It comprises yogurt mixed with a vegetable or fruit (such as cucumber, carrot, onion, pineapple or banana) and spices and/or herbs (often cumin, black pepper, mustard seeds, coriander or mint). Raitas are usually unsweetened or only lightly sweetened, but for an ice pop, additional sweetening is necessary to bring out the flavors and make it palatable. These ice pops are an interesting and fun way to enjoy a cooling carrot raita.

Tip

Shred carrots using the small holes of a box grater or a fine rasp grater.

½ tsp	cumin seeds	2 mL
¼ tsp	black peppercorns	1 mL
1½ cups	finely shredded carrots (see Tip, left)	375 mL
¼ cup	granulated sugar	60 mL
¼ cup	water	60 mL
2 tbsp	liquid honey	30 mL
1⅓ cups	plain yogurt	325 mL
⅔ cup	table (18%) cream or ⅓ cup (75 mL) each milk and heavy or whipping (35%) cream	150 mL

1. In a small, dry skillet over medium-low heat, lightly toast cumin and peppercorns until fragrant, 2 to 3 minutes. Transfer to a spice grinder or mortar and grind to a coarse powder. Set aside.

2. In a saucepan, stir together carrots, sugar, water and toasted spice mixture. Bring to a boil over medium-high heat and cook, stirring often, for 5 minutes. Remove from heat and stir in honey. Set aside to cool.

3. In a large measuring cup, whisk together yogurt and cream until smooth and silky. Whisk in carrot mixture.

4. Pour into molds and freeze until slushy, then insert sticks and freeze until solid, for at least 4 hours. If you are using an ice pop kit, follow the manufacturer's instructions.

Salty Lime Soda Ice Pops

Makes about
3 cups (750 mL)
9 to 12 ice pops

A touch of celery salt
complements the
traditional roasted cumin
in these East-meets-
West ice pop versions of
Indian-style lime soda,
which is lightly salted
and barely sweetened.
As the ice pop freezes,
some of the spice will
settle to the bottom of
the mold (the top of the
ice pop), which mimics
the cumin sprinkled on
top of the drink in India.
This ice pop is one of
my all-time favorites
for the middle of a hot
day when I don't feel
like something sweet.
It also works as a palate
cleanser after lunch or
dinner.

Tip

To make ground roasted
cumin, toast whole cumin
seeds in a dry skillet over
medium-low heat until
slightly dark and fragrant,
about 3 minutes. Transfer
to a spice grinder or mortar
and grind. Set aside to cool.
Store in an airtight jar for up
to one month.

2 cups	water	500 mL
½ cup	freshly squeezed lime juice	125 mL
3 tbsp	agave, brown rice or corn syrup	45 mL
1½ tbsp	liquid honey	22 mL
⅜ tsp	celery salt	1.5 mL
Pinch	ground roasted cumin (see Tip, left)	Pinch
Pinch	salt	Pinch

1. In a large measuring cup, whisk together water, lime juice, syrup, honey, celery salt, a generous pinch of cumin, and salt.

2. Pour into molds and freeze until slushy, then insert sticks and freeze until solid, for at least 4 hours. If you are using an ice pop kit, follow the manufacturer's instructions.

Less-Drip Ice Pops for Kids

Orange Carrot Less-Drip Ice Pops

**Makes about
3 cups (750 mL)
9 to 12 ice pops**

Unless your kids are carrot lovers, just call these orange ice pops — they'll never know the difference. The pops are bright orange, sweet and a good healthy treat, especially on a hot day.

Tip

Freshly squeezed juice is always best, but you can also use juice in cartons or from concentrate.

- Blender
- Fine-mesh sieve

1½ tbsp	unsweetened gelatin powder	22 mL
2 cups	orange juice, divided	500 mL
¾ cup	chopped carrots	175 mL
1 cup	water	250 mL
3 tbsp	granulated sugar	45 mL
2 tbsp	honey	30 mL

1. In a large measuring cup, sprinkle gelatin over ½ cup (125 mL) orange juice. Set aside until gelatin is softened, about 3 minutes.

2. In blender, purée carrots, ½ cup (125 mL) orange juice and water. Transfer to a saucepan and stir in sugar and honey. Bring to a boil, reduce heat and simmer for 3 minutes.

3. Place sieve over gelatin mixture and strain carrot mixture into it, pressing out as much juice and pulp as possible. Discard solids. Whisk until gelatin is thoroughly dissolved, about 1 minute. Whisk in remaining 1 cup (250 mL) orange juice. Set aside to cool.

4. Give mixture a quick stir. Pour into molds and freeze until slushy, then insert sticks and freeze until solid, for at least 4 hours. If you are using an ice pop kit, follow the manufacturer's instructions.

Cherry Less-Drip Ice Pops

**Makes about
3⅓ cups (825 mL)
10 to 13 ice pops**

**Fresh cherries, apple
juice and a touch of
honey make delicious
and healthy cherry ice
pops for kids — which
is not to say parents
won't like them too!**

Tip

If you are using agar-agar
(see page 209) rather than
gelatin to make these pops,
cook it in ½ cup (125 mL)
of the apple juice.

- Blender
- Fine-mesh sieve

2 cups	unsweetened apple juice, divided	500 mL
1½ tbsp	unsweetened gelatin powder	22 mL
1 lb	ripe sweet cherries, pitted (about 3 cups/750 mL)	500 g
3 tbsp	honey	45 mL

1. Pour ½ cup (125 mL) apple juice into a large measuring cup. Sprinkle gelatin overtop and set aside until gelatin is softened, about 3 minutes.

2. In a saucepan, combine remaining 1½ cups (375 mL) apple juice, cherries and honey. Bring to a boil, reduce heat to medium, cover and simmer for 10 minutes.

3. Pour about half the hot liquid into gelatin mixture and whisk until gelatin is thoroughly dissolved, about 1 minute. Transfer remaining liquid and cherries to blender and purée at medium-high speed.

4. Place sieve over gelatin mixture and strain cherry purée into it, pushing down on solids to extract as much juice as possible. Discard solids. Thoroughly whisk together gelatin and cherry mixtures. Set aside to cool.

5. Give mixture a quick stir. Pour into molds and freeze until slushy, then insert sticks and freeze until solid, for at least 4 hours. If you are using an ice pop kit, follow the manufacturer's instructions.

Red Apple Berry Less-Drip Ice Pops

> **Makes about
> 3 cups (750 mL)
> 9 to 12 ice pops**

Bright red and appealingly sweet and fruity, these ice pops are easy to make with just a few simple ingredients.

Tip

If you are using agar-agar (see page 209) rather than gelatin to make these pops, cook it in ½ cup (125 mL) of the apple juice.

- Blender
- Fine-mesh sieve

1½ tbsp	unsweetened gelatin powder	22 mL
2¾ cups	unsweetened apple juice, divided	675 mL
3 tbsp	maple syrup or packed dark brown sugar	45 mL
1 cup	fresh or frozen raspberries	250 mL

1. In a heatproof bowl, sprinkle gelatin over ½ cup (125 mL) apple juice. Set aside until gelatin is softened, about 3 minutes.

2. In a saucepan, bring 1½ cups (375 mL) of the remaining juice and syrup to a boil. (If using brown sugar, stir until sugar is thoroughly dissolved.) Pour into gelatin mixture and whisk until gelatin is thoroughly dissolved, about 1 minute.

3. In blender at low speed, blend raspberries and remaining ¾ cup (175 mL) apple juice into a thin paste. Whisk into gelatin mixture.

4. Place sieve over a large measuring cup and strain, pushing down on solids to extract as much juice as possible. Discard solids. Set aside to cool.

5. Give mixture a quick stir. Pour into molds and freeze until slushy, then insert sticks and freeze until solid, for at least 4 hours. If you are using an ice pop kit, follow the manufacturer's instructions.

> ## Variation
>
> *Purple Apple Berry Less-Drip Ice Pops:*
> Replace the raspberries with blueberries or blackberries.

Green Grape Less-Drip Ice Pops

Makes about
3 cups (750 mL)
9 to 12 ice pops

Kids love green grapes, so why not make delicious, almost dripless green grape ice pops for them as a treat?

- Blender
- Fine-mesh sieve

1½ tbsp	unsweetened gelatin powder	22 mL
1⅓ cups	unsweetened apple juice, divided	325 mL
3 cups	seedless green grapes, stemmed	750 mL
3 tbsp	agave syrup or liquid honey or ¼ cup (60 mL) brown rice syrup	45 mL

1. In a heatproof bowl, sprinkle gelatin over ⅓ cup (75 mL) apple juice. Set aside until gelatin is softened, about 3 minutes.

2. In blender at medium-high speed, blend remaining 1 cup (250 mL) apple juice and grapes until smooth. Transfer to a saucepan, add syrup and bring to a boil. Pour into gelatin mixture and whisk until gelatin is thoroughly dissolved, about 1 minute.

3. Place sieve over a large measuring cup and strain mixture, pushing down on solids to extract as much juice as possible. Discard solids. Set aside to cool.

4. Give mixture a quick stir. Pour into molds and freeze until slushy, then insert sticks and freeze until solid, for at least 4 hours. If you are using an ice pop kit, follow the manufacturer's instructions.

Vanilla Pudding Less-Drip Ice Pops

Makes about 3 cups (750 mL) 9 to 12 ice pops

Creamy, sweet pudding appeals to many children, and adults too. Because the gelatin prevents the ice pop from dripping excessively, this nutritious ice pop is good for slow-eating toddlers on a hot day.

Tip

If using agar-agar instead of gelatin, soften and cook it in ½ cup (125 mL) of the milk, adding remaining 2 cups (500 mL) to the saucepan with the condensed milk.

- Fine-mesh sieve

1 tbsp	unsweetened gelatin powder	30 mL
2½ cups	whole milk, divided	625 mL
2	egg yolks	2
½ cup	sweetened condensed milk	125 mL
1½ tsp	vanilla extract	7 mL

1. In a heatproof bowl, sprinkle gelatin over ¼ cup (60 mL) milk. Set aside until gelatin is softened, about 3 minutes.

2. In a bowl, whisk egg yolks until fluffy. Set aside.

3. In a saucepan, whisk together remaining 2¼ cups (550 mL) milk and condensed milk. Bring to a boil. Add to gelatin mixture and whisk until gelatin is thoroughly dissolved, about 1 minute.

4. Whisk about ½ cup (125 mL) hot milk mixture into reserved egg yolks, then whisk yolk mixture into remaining milk mixture and return to saucepan. Cook over medium heat, stirring constantly, until mixture is hot and coats a spoon (do not allow to simmer; see Tip, page 209).

Tip

When heating mixtures enriched with eggs or egg yolks, you must make the mixture hot enough to properly cook the eggs and thicken the mixture, but not so hot that it will cause the eggs to curdle. Even a low simmer will curdle the eggs, so always watch your pot, stirring constantly, and remove it from the heat as soon as the mixture reaches the desired thickness and is steaming hot. If you leave the mixture in the hot saucepan (not recommended), you must continue to stir, even off the heat, until it is cool enough to ensure that the cooking process has stopped, usually 1 to 2 minutes.

5. Place sieve over a large measuring cup and strain mixture. Do not push solids through, but shake sieve to strain out as much smooth mixture as possible. Discard any solids. Whisk in vanilla. Cover with plastic wrap, placing it directly on the surface, and set aside to cool.

6. Give mixture a quick stir. Pour into molds and freeze until slushy, then insert sticks and freeze until solid, for at least 12 hours. If you are using an ice pop kit, follow the manufacturer's instructions.

Agar-Agar

These "less-drip" ice pops rely on gelatin powder to thicken and stabilize the mixture to be frozen. Vegetarians, however, will want to use seaweed-based agar-agar rather than gelatin powder, which is animal based. Agar-agar powder is more convenient than the flake form, but either can be used. Substitute 2 tsp (10 mL) agar-agar powder or 2 tbsp (30 mL) flakes for each 1 tbsp (15 mL) gelatin powder called for. Proceed as with the gelatin powder, but put the liquid over which the gelatin is sprinkled in a small saucepan. Let the agar-agar sit until softened, then transfer to the stovetop and simmer, stirring occasionally, for 5 minutes (powder) or 10 minutes (flakes). Proceed with the recipe.

Strawberry Pudding Less-Drip Ice Pops

Makes about 3¼ cups (800 mL) 9 to 13 ice pops

You can use fresh, in-season strawberries or frozen ones for these ice pops, giving you a relatively easy less-drip option for kids any time of the year.

Tip

If using agar-agar instead of gelatin (see page 209), soften and cook it in ½ cup (125 mL) of the milk, adding remaining ¾ cup (175 mL) to the saucepan with the condensed milk.

- Blender
- Fine-mesh sieve

1 tbsp	unsweetened gelatin powder	15 mL
1¼ cups	milk, divided	300 mL
2	egg yolks	2
⅔ cup	sweetened condensed milk	150 mL
1¾ cups	halved hulled fresh strawberries or whole frozen strawberries, thawed	425 mL
1 tsp	vanilla extract	5 mL

1. In a heatproof bowl, sprinkle gelatin over ¼ cup (60 mL) milk. Set aside until gelatin is softened, about 3 minutes.

2. In a bowl, whisk egg yolks until fluffy. Set aside.

3. In a saucepan, whisk together remaining 1 cup (250 mL) milk and condensed milk. Bring to a boil, then stir into gelatin mixture and whisk until gelatin is thoroughly dissolved, about 1 minute.

4. Whisk about ½ cup (125 mL) hot milk mixture into egg yolks. Whisk yolk mixture into remaining milk mixture and return to saucepan. Cook over medium heat, stirring constantly, until mixture is hot and coats a spoon (do not allow to simmer).

5. Place sieve over blender and strain mixture. Do not push solids through, but shake sieve to strain out as much smooth mixture as possible. Discard any solids. Add strawberries and vanilla to blender and purée at medium speed. Set aside to cool.

6. Give mixture a quick stir. Pour into molds and freeze until slushy, then insert sticks and freeze until solid, for at least 12 hours. If you are using an ice pop kit, follow the manufacturer's instructions.

Milk Chocolate Less-Drip Ice Pops

**Makes about
3 cups (750 mL)
9 to 12 ice pops**

Kids love milk chocolate for its dairy goodness and rich, sweet taste.

Tip

If using agar-agar instead of gelatin (see page 209), soften and cook it in ⅔ cup (150 mL) of the milk. Add remaining 2 cups (500 mL) to the saucepan with the condensed milk.

- Fine-mesh sieve

1 tbsp	unsweetened gelatin powder	15 mL
2⅔ cups	whole milk, divided	650 mL
⅓ cup + 1 tbsp	sweetened condensed milk	90 mL
3 tbsp	unsweetened cocoa powder	45 mL
3 oz	milk chocolate, chopped	90 g
1 tsp	vanilla extract	5 mL

1. In a heatproof bowl, sprinkle gelatin over ⅓ cup (75 mL) milk. Set aside until gelatin is softened, about 3 minutes.

2. In a saucepan, whisk together remaining 2⅓ cups (575 mL) milk, condensed milk and cocoa. Bring to a boil. Stir into gelatin mixture and whisk until gelatin is thoroughly dissolved, about 1 minute.

3. Transfer milk mixture to saucepan and cook over medium heat, stirring, until mixture returns to a boil. Remove from heat. Whisk in chocolate until chocolate is thoroughly melted and mixture is smooth. Whisk in vanilla. Pour into a large measuring cup. Cover with plastic wrap, placing it directly on the surface. Set aside to cool.

4. Give mixture a quick stir. Pour into molds and freeze until slushy, then insert sticks and freeze until solid, for at least 12 hours. If you are using an ice pop kit, follow the manufacturer's instructions.

Banana Maple Less-Drip Ice Pops

Makes about
3 cups (750 mL)
9 to 12 ice pops

Soy milk is especially good with bananas, but you can, of course, use regular milk for these kid-friendly ice pops too.

Tip

Substitute an equal quantity of any nut milk or rice milk for the soy milk.

● Blender

1 tbsp	unsweetened gelatin powder	15 mL
2 cups	soy milk or dairy milk, divided	500 mL
⅓ cup	maple syrup	75 mL
2	ripe bananas, sliced (about 1½ cups/375 mL)	2

1. In a heatproof bowl, sprinkle gelatin over ¼ cup (60 mL) soy milk. Set aside until gelatin is softened, about 3 minutes.

2. In a saucepan, bring remaining 1¾ cups (425 mL) soy milk to a boil. Stir into gelatin mixture and whisk until gelatin is thoroughly dissolved, about 1 minute. Stir in maple syrup. Transfer to blender, add bananas and purée at medium-high speed. Set aside to cool.

3. Give mixture a quick stir. Pour into molds and freeze until slushy, then insert sticks and freeze until solid, for at least 4 hours. If you are using an ice pop kit, follow the manufacturer's instructions.

Holiday Ice Pops

Green, White and Orange Layered Honey Ice Pops

**Makes about
3 cups (750 mL)
9 to 12 ice pops**

Choose this national
flag–inspired ice pop
to celebrate Irish St.
Patrick's Day or India's
Republic Day, or any
other holiday on which
green, white and orange
flags might be flown.

Tips

Use a light-colored honey for
visual appeal.

Rose water (and orange
flower water) are traditional
Middle Eastern and southern
Mediterranean flavorings.
Look for them in well-
stocked supermarkets or
specialty stores.

- Blender
- Fine-mesh sieve

3	green-fleshed kiwifruit, peeled, cored and chopped	3
½ cup + 1 tbsp	liquid honey, divided	140 mL
1 tbsp	freshly squeezed lemon juice	15 mL
1 tbsp	water	15 mL
2 tsp	rose water, divided	10 mL
Pinch	saffron threads	Pinch
1 tsp	granulated sugar	5 mL
½ tsp	finely grated orange zest	2 mL
2 tbsp	boiling water	30 mL
1¾ cups	Greek- or Balkan-style or drained plain yogurt	425 mL

1. In blender at medium speed, purée kiwis with
   3 tbsp (45 mL) honey, lemon juice, water and
   1 tsp (5 mL) rose water.

2. Place sieve over a large measuring cup and strain
   mixture, pushing down on solids with a rubber
   spatula to extract as much pulp and juice as
   possible. Discard solids. Set mixture aside.

3. In a small bowl, using the back of a spoon, grind
   saffron with sugar and orange zest. Add boiling
   water, stirring until sugar is dissolved. Set aside
   to cool.

4. Whisk yogurt with remaining honey and rose water. Divide into two equal portions and whisk saffron mixture into one half.

5. Total the volume of plain and saffron-infused yogurt mixtures and kiwi mixture combined and determine the number of ice pop molds you will need to accommodate the amount.

6. Pour saffron-infused mixture into molds to form first layer, then freeze. (Keep remaining mixtures in refrigerator until ready to use.) When frozen, pour in plain yogurt mixture. Freeze until slushy, then insert sticks and freeze until solid. After plain layer is frozen, pour in green kiwi mixture. Freeze until solid, for at least 4 hours. If you are using an ice pop kit, follow the manufacturer's instructions.

Valentine's Day Pink and White Layered Ice Pops

**Makes about
3 cups (750 mL)
9 to 12 ice pops**

White chocolate and
mint are traditional
ingredients in
Valentine candies,
and strawberries have
always been associated
with lovers. Hence the
white and pink layers
in these ice pops.

Tips

Look for natural peppermint
essence or flavoring made
from peppermint oil for
these rich, creamy layered
ice pops.

If you have the time and
patience, these ice pops
look especially attractive
with several alternating pink
and white layers. For ice
pops with four layers, pour
only half of each mixture at
a time into the molds and
freeze each layer separately.
For eight layers, work with
a quarter of each mixture
at a time. Insert sticks into
second layer, when it is still
slushy but frozen enough to
hold up sticks.

- Blender
- 2 large measuring cups

1½ cups	halved hulled strawberries or whole frozen strawberries, thawed	375 mL
1 tbsp	granulated sugar	15 mL
½ tsp	vanilla extract	2 mL
1½ cups	milk	375 mL
⅔ cup	heavy or whipping (35%) cream	150 mL
½ cup	sweetened condensed milk	125 mL
¾ tsp	finely grated orange zest	3 mL
2 oz	white chocolate, chopped	60 g
1 tsp	peppermint essence	5 mL

1. In blender at medium speed, purée strawberries, sugar and vanilla. Set aside.

2. In a saucepan, whisk together milk, cream, condensed milk and orange zest. Bring to a boil and remove from heat. Pour 1¾ cups (425 mL) into a large measuring cup. Whisk in white chocolate until thoroughly incorporated and smooth, then whisk in peppermint essence. Set aside to cool.

3. Pour remaining milk mixture into another large measuring cup. Whisk in strawberry mixture. Set aside to cool.

4. Total the volume of white and pink mixtures combined and determine the number of ice pop molds you will need to accommodate the amount. For two-layer ice pops, pour one mixture into molds, dividing equally; this will be your first layer. (Place second mixture in refrigerator until ready to use it.) Freeze first layer until slushy, then insert sticks and freeze until solid, for at least 4 hours. Add second mixture and freeze until solid, for at least 4 hours. If you are using an ice pop kit, follow the manufacturer's instructions.

Red and White Maple Ice Pops

**Makes about
3 cups (750 mL)
9 to 12 pops**

Celebrate Canada
Day with these
patriotic ice pops. Or,
notwithstanding the
maple symbolism,
use them to represent
the red and white flag
of Austria, Denmark,
Indonesia, Latvia,
Poland or Switzerland,
among others, on their
national holidays.

Tip

In this recipe — and almost
always when cooking with
maple syrup — medium
(amber) or dark maple
syrups are preferable to
the lighter versions, as they
have a more robust and
richer flavor that stands up
well to other flavorings.
Medium-grade (amber)
is an all-purpose maple
syrup, while dark is usually
reserved for baking and
commercial preparations.
Light or "fancy" maple syrup
is best used as a table syrup.

- Fine-mesh sieve
- Blender

2 cups	fresh or frozen raspberries	500 mL
1 cup	unsweetened apple juice	250 mL
½ cup	maple syrup, divided	125 mL
1 cup	Greek, or Balkan-style or drained plain yogurt	250 mL

1. Combine raspberries, apple juice and half the
   maple syrup in a saucepan. Simmer over low heat
   until fruit is very soft, 2 to 5 minutes.

2. Place sieve over a large measuring cup and strain,
   pressing down and scraping solids with a rubber
   spatula to extract as much pulp and juice as
   possible. Discard solids. Set mixture aside to cool.

3. In a bowl, whisk together yogurt and remaining
   maple syrup.

4. Total the volume of red raspberry and white yogurt
   mixtures combined and determine the number of
   ice pop molds you will need to accommodate the
   amount.

5. Pour half of the raspberry mixture into molds to
   form the first layer. (Place remaining raspberry
   and yogurt mixtures in refrigerator until ready to
   use.) Freeze until slushy, then insert sticks and
   freeze until solid. When frozen, pour in white
   yogurt mixture. After yogurt layer is frozen, pour
   in remaining red raspberry mixture. Freeze until
   solid, for at least 4 hours. If you are using an ice
   pop kit, follow the manufacturer's instructions.

Red, White and Blue Ice Pops

**Makes about
3 cups (750 mL)
9 to 12 ice pops**

It is quite impossible to get a true blue natural food based ice pop color. Without using food coloring, a bluish purple is the best that can be achieved — a little closer to Union Jack blue than that of the Star-Spangled Banner.

Tips

Always use freshly squeezed lemon juice or lime juice in your ice pops; bottled just doesn't compare.

Grenadine syrup is a clear red syrup originally made from pomegranates (*grenades* in French) and now often from a combination of red fruit flavorings. Look for it in well-stocked supermarkets or liquor stores.

- 3 large measuring cups
- Blender
- Fine-mesh sieve

1⅓ cups	water, divided	325 mL
⅓ cup	granulated sugar	75 mL
½ tsp	finely grated lemon zest	2 mL
½ cup + 2 tsp	freshly squeezed lemon juice, divided	155 mL
1 cup	raspberries	250 mL
1 tbsp	grenadine syrup	15 mL
1 cup	blueberries (preferably wild)	250 mL
1 cup	vanilla-flavored yogurt	250 mL
¼ cup	liquid honey	60 mL

1. In a small saucepan, bring ⅓ cup (75 mL) water, sugar and lemon zest to a boil; reduce heat and simmer for 3 minutes. Whisk in ½ cup (125 ml) lemon juice. Transfer to each of the three measuring cups, dividing equally.

2. In blender at medium speed, purée raspberries with ½ cup (125 mL) water and grenadine syrup. Place sieve over one of the measuring cups and strain mixture, pushing down to extract as much juice as possible. Discard solids and rinse out sieve. Whisk mixture and set aside.

3. Rinse out blender. Add blueberries and remaining ½ cup (125 mL) water; purée at medium speed. Place sieve over second measuring cup and strain mixture, pushing down to extract as much juice as possible. Discard solids. Whisk mixture.

Tip

Use a light-flavored and light-colored honey, such as acacia or clover, to sweeten the yogurt mixture.

4. In third measuring cup, whisk together yogurt, honey and remaining 2 tsp (10 mL) lemon juice.

5. Total the volume of blueberry, white yogurt and red raspberry mixtures combined and determine the number of ice pop molds you will need to accommodate the amount.

6. Pour blueberry mixture into molds to form first layer. (Keep remaining mixtures in refrigerator until ready to use.) Add sticks when slushy, then freeze until solid. When frozen, pour in white yogurt mixture. After yogurt layer is frozen, pour in red raspberry mixture. Freeze until solid, for at least 4 hours. If you are using an ice pop kit, follow the manufacturer's instructions.

Candy Corn Ice Pops

Makes about
3 cups (750 mL)
9 to 12 ice pops

It's ideal to have cone-
or pyramid-shaped
molds for these fanciful
autumn ice pops, which
are ideal for Halloween
parties or other fall
gatherings.

Tips

These pops are time-
consuming to put together
because you need to cook
the layers separately, but
you can prepare the second
and third layers while the
first one is freezing. If
you chill each mixture in
the refrigerator while the
previous layer is freezing,
it will help to speed up the
process.

Tapioca flour is often called
tapioca starch. They are
identical products.

- Blender
- Fine-mesh sieve

White Layer

½ cup	whole milk	125 mL
1 tsp	tapioca flour (see Tips, left)	5 mL
1 oz	white chocolate, chopped	30 g
2 tbsp	sweetened condensed milk	30 mL
¼ tsp	vanilla extract	1 mL

Orange Layer

½ tsp	finely grated orange zest	2 mL
⅔ cup	orange juice	150 mL
⅓ cup	chopped carrots	75 mL
⅓ cup	water	75 mL
3 tbsp	granulated sugar	45 mL
2 tbsp	sweetened condensed milk	30 mL
¼ tsp	vanilla extract	1 mL

Brown Layer

1¼ cups	whole milk	300 mL
1½ tsp	tapioca flour	7 mL
¼ cup	unsweetened cocoa powder	60 mL
¼ cup	sweetened condensed milk	60 mL
1 tbsp	molasses	15 mL
¼ tsp	vanilla extract	1 mL

1. *White Layer:* In a small saucepan, whisk together milk and tapioca flour. Bring to a boil, reduce heat and simmer, stirring, for 30 seconds. Remove from heat and stir in white chocolate until thoroughly melted. Stir in condensed milk and vanilla and set aside to cool.

2. *Orange Layer:* In blender at medium-high speed, blend orange zest and juice and carrots until smooth. Transfer to a small saucepan. Stir in water and sugar and bring to a boil; reduce heat and simmer for 3 minutes. Strain through sieve into a measuring cup. Stir in condensed milk and vanilla and set aside to cool.

Freshly squeezed juice is always best, but you can also use juice in cartons or from concentrate. In this recipe, if you do not have enough after juicing the orange, top off the quantity with prepared juice.

3. *Brown Layer:* In a small saucepan, whisk together milk and tapioca flour; then whisk in cocoa. Bring to a boil, reduce heat and simmer, stirring often, for 5 minutes. Pour into a second measuring cup and stir in condensed milk, molasses and vanilla. Set aside to cool.

4. Total the volume of white, orange and brown mixtures combined and determine the number of ice pop molds you will need to accommodate the amount.

5. Pour white mixture into molds to form first layer. Freeze until slushy and insert sticks, then freeze until solid. When frozen, pour in orange mixture. When orange layer is frozen, pour in brown mixture. Freeze until solid, for at least 4 hours. If you are using an ice pop kit, follow the manufacturer's instructions.

Thanksgiving Pumpkin Pie Ice Pops

**Makes about
3 cups (750 mL)
9 to 12 ice pops**

A well-spiced sweet pumpkin pie really summons up images of autumn. These ice pops capture the delectable flavors of that traditional Thanksgiving treat.

Tips

If you prefer, substitute an equal quantity of table (18%) cream, half-and-half (10%) cream or milk for the heavy or whipping (35%) cream.

To make pumpkin or squash purée: Cut vegetable in half lengthwise and remove seeds. Place halves, cut side down, on a rimmed baking sheet. Bake in 425°F (220°C) oven until very tender, 30 to 60 minutes. Remove from oven and set aside to cool. Scoop out flesh and mash well or purée in a food processor.

- Fine-mesh sieve

1	can (12 oz/170 mL) evaporated milk	1
1 tsp	tapioca flour (see Tips, page 220)	5 mL
1½ cups	pumpkin or squash purée (see Tips, left)	375 mL
⅓ cup + 2 tbsp	granulated sugar	105 mL
3 tbsp	light (fancy) molasses or maple syrup	45 mL
½ tsp	ground ginger	2 mL
¼ tsp	cinnamon	1 mL
Pinch	nutmeg	Pinch
Pinch	cloves	Pinch
Pinch	white pepper	Pinch
Pinch	salt	Pinch
2	egg yolks	2
3 tbsp	heavy or whipping (35%) cream	45 mL

1. In a saucepan, whisk together evaporated milk and tapioca flour. Whisk in pumpkin purée, sugar, molasses, ginger, cinnamon, a generous pinch of nutmeg, cloves, white pepper and salt. Bring to a boil, stirring constantly. Reduce heat, cover and simmer, stirring often, for 10 minutes. Remove from heat.

2. In a bowl, whisk egg yolks with cream. Add ¼ cup (60 mL) hot pumpkin mixture and whisk until blended. Whisk into pumpkin mixture in saucepan and place over low heat. Cook, without simmering, and stirring constantly, until steaming hot, 1 to 2 minutes (see Tip, page 223).

Tip

When heating mixtures enriched with eggs or egg yolks, you must make the mixture hot enough to properly cook the eggs and thicken the mixture, but not so hot that it will cause the eggs to curdle. Even a low simmer will curdle the eggs, so always watch your pot, stirring constantly, and remove it from the heat as soon as the mixture reaches the desired thickness and is steaming hot. If you leave the mixture in the hot saucepan (not recommended), you must continue to stir, even off the heat, until it is cool enough to ensure that the cooking process has stopped, usually 1 to 2 minutes.

3. Place sieve over a large measuring cup and strain mixture, shaking the sieve to strain out as much smooth mixture as possible without pushing down on solids. Discard any solids. Set mixture aside to cool.

4. Pour into molds and freeze until slushy, then insert sticks and freeze until solid, for at least 4 hours. If you are using an ice pop kit, follow the manufacturer's instructions.

Christmas Brandied Fruitcake Ice Pops

**Makes about
3¼ cups (800 mL)
9 to 13 ice pops**

**Frozen fruitcake on
a stick is great for
Christmas holiday
times in Australia or
New Zealand, where it's
the middle of their hot
summer, and for those
of us from the northern
hemisphere who crave
Christmas treats —
and eat frozen treats —
year-round. These are
the ultimate sweet, rich
Christmas ice pops.**

¼ cup	chopped walnuts or pecans	60 mL
2 tbsp	chopped candied citron or mixed peel	30 mL
2 tbsp	chopped candied cherries	30 mL
2 tbsp	dark raisins	30 mL
2 tbsp	golden raisins or sultanas	30 mL
¼ cup	brandy or dark rum	60 mL
½ cup	water	125 mL
⅓ cup	packed dark brown sugar	75 mL
1½ tbsp	light (fancy) molasses	22 mL
½ tsp	ground ginger	2 mL
¼ tsp	cinnamon	1 mL
Pinch	cloves	Pinch
Pinch	nutmeg	Pinch
1	can (12 oz/370 mL) evaporated milk	1
⅔ cup	heavy or whipping (35%) cream	150 mL
¼ tsp	vanilla extract	1 mL

1. In a bowl at room temperature, soak nuts, candied citron, cherries and dark and golden raisins in brandy for at least 2 hours or overnight. Drain, reserving liquid and solids separately. Set both aside.

2. In a small saucepan, combine water, reserved soaking liquid, sugar, molasses, ginger, cinnamon, and a generous pinch each of cloves and nutmeg. Bring to a boil, reduce heat and simmer for 3 minutes. Pour into a large measuring cup and set aside to cool. Whisk in evaporated milk, cream and vanilla.

3. Pour into molds, leaving 1½ inches (4 cm) headspace for fruit and nut mixture; freeze until slushy. Divide fruit and nut mixture among molds and stir in. Insert sticks and freeze until solid, for at least 4 hours.

Cocktail Hour

Negroni Ice Pops

**Makes about 2 cups (500 mL)
6 to 8 ice pops**

Like most cocktails, my favorite Italian aperitif, the classic Negroni, is too boozy to freeze. Because it is usually garnished with an orange slice, I figured we could incorporate all the flavors of the cocktail with its garnish, in a sophisticated frozen orange "aperitif pop."

Tip

Freshly squeezed orange juice is always best, but you can also use juice from cartons or from concentrate.

¼ cup	sugar	60 mL
3 tbsp	water	45 mL
1 tsp	finely grated orange zest	5 mL
1¾ cups	orange juice (see Tip, left)	425 mL
1 tbsp	gin	15 mL
1 tbsp	Campari	15 mL
1 tbsp	red vermouth	15 mL

1. In a small saucepan, bring sugar, water and orange zest to a boil, stirring until sugar is dissolved. Pour into a measuring cup and set aside to cool. Stir in orange juice, gin, Campari and vermouth.

2. Pour into molds and freeze until slushy, then insert sticks and freeze until solid, for at least 4 hours or preferably overnight. If you are using an ice pop kit, follow the manufacturer's instructions.

Minty Campari Sunset Ice Pops

Makes about
2 cups (500 mL)
6 to 8 ice pops

As in Negroni Ice Pops, the bitter and sweet flavors of Campari pair nicely with orange juice. Here I've added a cool accent of fresh mint. For an English garden-party version, use the Pimm's.

¼ cup	fresh mint leaves	60 mL
1 tbsp	granulated sugar	15 mL
1¾ cups	orange juice	425 mL
⅓ cup	freshly squeezed lime juice	75 mL
½ cup	Campari or Pimm's No. 1 Cup	125 mL

1. Chop or tear mint leaves into 3 or 4 pieces each, place in a measuring cup and sprinkle with sugar. With a muddler, pestle or the back of a wooden spoon, crush mint and sugar until leaves are well bruised and broken up. Stir in orange and lime juices.

2. Pour Campari evenly into each mold, using either six ⅓-cup (75 mL) molds or eight ¼-cup (60 mL) molds. Pour juice mixture gently into molds. Freeze until slushy, then insert sticks and freeze until solid, for at least 4 hours or preferably overnight. If you are using an ice pop kit, follow the manufacturer's instructions.

Bloody Mary Ice Pops

Makes about 2⅓ cups (575 mL) 7 to 9 ice pops

Fresh and spirited, Bloody Marys are justifiably the favorite brunch and hair-of-the-dog drink in the United States, like Bloody Caesars in Canada (see Variations, page 229). The ice pop versions are equal to both of their models, for sure. And no Shakespeare fan will want to miss out on another variation: Queen Gertrude's Bloody Ice Pops!

- Blender
- Fine-mesh sieve

¼ cup	water	60 mL
2 tbsp	granulated sugar	30 mL
¼ tsp	freshly ground black pepper	1 mL
¼ tsp	celery salt	1 mL
¼ tsp	finely grated lemon zest	1 mL
1½ cups	chopped celery	375 mL
1¾ cups + 2 tbsp	tomato juice	455 mL
¼ cup	vodka	60 mL
2 tbsp	freshly squeezed lemon juice	30 mL
2 tsp	freshly grated or prepared horseradish, optional	10 mL
½ tsp	Worcestershire sauce (approx.)	2 mL
¼ tsp	hot pepper sauce, such as Tabasco	1 mL

1. In a small saucepan, combine water, sugar, pepper, celery salt and lemon zest. Bring to a boil, add celery and return to boiling for 30 seconds. Transfer to blender and add tomato juice. Blend at medium-high speed until smooth.

2. Place sieve over a large measuring cup and strain mixture, pushing down on solids to extract as much juice and smooth pulp as possible. Discard solids. Stir in vodka, lemon juice, horseradish (if using), Worcestershire sauce and hot pepper sauce.

Tip

In many ice pops that include solid ingredients or combine liquids of different viscosities, there is a bit of layering after freezing, which is normal. However, if you want a seamless result, give the mixture a stir after it has reached the slushy stage to ensure that the ingredients remain integrated.

3. Pour into molds and freeze until slushy, then insert sticks and freeze until solid, for at least 4 hours or preferably overnight. If you are using an ice pop kit, follow the manufacturer's instructions.

Variations

Frozen Caesar Ice Pops: Substitute tomato-clam juice for the tomato juice, lime zest for the lemon zest and 3 tbsp (45 mL) lime juice for the lemon juice.

Queen Gertrude's Bloody Ice Pops: To honor the mother of Hamlet, the troubled Danish prince, and to further boost the flavor with a little Scandinavian kick, replace the vodka with aquavit.

Sweet Screwdriver Ice Pops

**Makes about
2 cups (500 mL)
6 to 8 ice pops**

A lightly sweetened
treatment of the popular
cocktail suits its ice pop
form. In many ways
this is an adult version
of that old standby, the
classic orange ice pop.

Tip

Freshly squeezed orange
juice is always best, but
you can also use juice from
cartons or from concentrate.
In this recipe, if you do not
have enough after juicing the
zested orange, top off the
quantity with prepared juice.

● Fine-mesh sieve

¼ cup	granulated sugar	60 mL
¼ cup	water	60 mL
	Grated zest of 1 orange	
1⅔ cups	orange juice	400 mL
2 tbsp	vodka	30 mL
2 tbsp	orange liqueur, such as	30 mL
	Cointreau or Triple Sec	

1. In a small saucepan, bring sugar, water and
orange zest to a boil. Reduce heat and simmer for
1 minute. Remove from heat and set aside to cool.

2. Place sieve over a large measuring cup and strain
mixture. Stir in orange juice, vodka and liqueur.

3. Pour into molds and freeze until slushy, then insert
sticks and freeze until solid, for at least 4 hours or
preferably overnight. If you are using an ice pop
kit, follow the manufacturer's instructions.

Strawberry Daiquiri Ice Pops

**Makes about
2 cups (500 mL)
6 to 8 ice pops**

**Frozen daiquiris
transform quite naturally
into ice pops.**

● Blender

¼ cup	water	60 mL
¼ cup	granulated sugar	60 mL
¼ tsp	finely grated lime zest	1 mL
3 cups	halved hulled fresh strawberries or whole frozen strawberries, thawed	750 mL
3 tbsp	white rum	45 mL
3 tbsp	freshly squeezed lime juice	45 mL

1. In a small saucepan, bring water, sugar and lime zest to a boil, stirring until sugar is dissolved. Simmer for 1 minute, then set aside to cool.

2. In blender at medium speed, purée strawberries, rum, lime juice and reserved sugar syrup.

3. Pour into molds and freeze until slushy, then insert sticks and freeze until solid, for at least 4 hours or preferably overnight. If you are using an ice pop kit, follow the manufacturer's instructions.

Peach Daiquiri Ice Pops

**Makes about
2 cups (500 mL)
6 to 8 ice pops**

The beautiful summer flavor of sweet ripe peaches, emphasized with a splash of peach schnapps, makes a fine and unusual daiquiri ice pop.

Tips

You can also use thawed frozen peaches or drained canned peaches for this recipe. If using canned peaches, replace the water and sugar with ⅓ cup (75 mL) syrup from the can.

To peel fresh peaches with tight skin, plunge into boiling water for 10 to 15 seconds to loosen skins. If the peaches are perfectly ripe, they can often be peeled easily without any preparation.

● Blender

3 tbsp	water	45 mL
3 tbsp	granulated sugar	45 mL
¼ tsp	finely grated lime zest	1 mL
2½ cups	chopped peeled ripe peaches (see Tips, left)	625 mL
3 tbsp	amber or white rum	45 mL
¼ cup	freshly squeezed lime juice	60 mL
2 tbsp	peach schnapps	30 mL

1. In a small saucepan, bring water, sugar and lime zest to a boil, stirring until sugar is dissolved. Simmer for 1 minute. Remove from heat and set aside to cool.

2. In blender at medium-high speed, purée peaches, rum, lime juice, schnapps and reserved sugar syrup.

3. Pour into molds and freeze until slushy, then insert sticks and freeze until solid, for at least 4 hours or preferably overnight. If you are using an ice pop kit, follow the manufacturer's instructions.

Coconut Daiquiri Ice Pops

**Makes about
2 cups (500 mL)
6 to 8 ice pops**

Coconut milk makes a
really pleasant summer
cocktail ice pop.

1½ cups	coconut milk	375 mL
¼ cup	palm sugar or light brown (golden yellow) sugar	60 mL
3 tbsp	coconut rum, amber rum or white rum	45 mL
¼ cup	freshly squeezed lime juice	60 mL

1. In a small saucepan, bring coconut milk and sugar to a boil, stirring until sugar is dissolved. Pour into a measuring cup and set aside to cool. Whisk in rum and lime juice.

2. Pour into molds and freeze until slushy, then insert sticks and freeze until solid, for at least 4 hours or preferably overnight. If you are using an ice pop kit, follow the manufacturer's instructions.

Spiced Banana Cocktail Ice Pops

**Makes about
2 cups (500 mL)
6 to 8 ice pops**

This is a sweet and
slightly tart ice pop
with an intriguing hint
of spice, like a banana
punch.

• Blender

2	ripe bananas, sliced	2
⅓ cup	water	75 mL
3 tbsp	liquid honey	45 mL
2 tbsp	freshly squeezed lemon juice	30 mL
2 tbsp	brandy	30 mL
1½ tbsp	amber or white rum	22 mL
Pinch	cinnamon	Pinch
Pinch	nutmeg	Pinch

1. In blender, purée bananas, water, honey, lemon juice, brandy, rum, cinnamon and nutmeg.

2. Pour into molds and freeze until slushy, then insert sticks and freeze until solid, for at least 4 hours or preferably overnight. If you are using an ice pop kit, follow the manufacturer's instructions.

Fruity Rum Punch Ice Pops

**Makes about
2½ cups (625 mL)
7 to 10 ice pops**

Citrus, pineapple and
strawberries make an
unusual but vibrant
punch base for these
ice pops.

Tips

Grenadine syrup is a
clear red syrup originally
made from pomegranates
(*grenades* in French)
and now often from a
combination of red fruit
flavorings. Look for it in
well-stocked supermarkets
or liquor stores.

Angostura bitters are
available at large grocery
stores as well as many
liquor stores. It is a famous
flavoring produced in
Trinidad. The original recipe,
which includes gentian and
other herbs, was developed
in the Venezuelan town of
Angostura.

- Blender

⅓ cup	water	75 mL
3 tbsp	granulated sugar	45 mL
½ tsp	finely grated orange zest	2 mL
¼ tsp	finely grated lime zest	1 mL
1 cup	orange juice	250 mL
1 cup	chopped pineapple	250 mL
1 cup	halved hulled fresh strawberries or whole frozen strawberries, thawed	250 mL
3 tbsp	freshly squeezed lime juice	45 mL
¼ cup	amber rum	60 mL
2 tbsp	grenadine syrup (see Tips, left)	30 mL
Dash	angostura bitters (see Tips, left)	Dash

1. In a small saucepan, combine water, sugar and
   orange and lime zest. Bring to a boil, stirring
   until sugar is dissolved. Reduce heat and simmer
   for 2 minutes. Remove from heat and set aside
   to cool.

2. In blender, purée orange juice, pineapple,
   strawberries and lime juice. Stir in rum, grenadine,
   cooled sugar syrup and bitters.

3. Pour into molds and freeze until slushy, then insert
   sticks and freeze until solid, for at least 4 hours or
   preferably overnight. If you are using an ice pop
   kit, follow the manufacturer's instructions.

Watermelon Citrus Cooler Ice Pops

**Makes about
2 cups (500 mL)
6 to 8 ice pops**

**Fresh, citrusy and not
too sweet, this cocktail
ice pop can be enjoyed
any time of day.**

Tips

If your watermelon has
soft white immature seeds
embedded in the flesh, then
strain mixture through a fine
sieve before pouring into
molds.

In many ice pops that
include solid ingredients or
combine liquids of different
viscosities, there is a bit of
layering after freezing, which
is normal. However, if you
want a seamless result, give
the mixture a stir after it has
reached the slushy stage
to ensure the ingredients
remain integrated.

- Blender

3 cups	chopped seedless or seeded watermelon (see Tips, left)	750 mL
½ cup	water	125 mL
¼ cup	vodka, white rum or white tequila	60 mL
¼ cup	orange juice concentrate	60 mL
3 tbsp	freshly squeezed lemon juice	45 mL
2 tbsp	freshly squeezed lime juice	30 mL

1. In blender, purée watermelon, water, vodka, orange juice concentrate, lemon juice and lime juice.

2. Pour into molds and freeze until slushy, then insert sticks and freeze until solid, for at least 4 hours or preferably overnight. If you are using an ice pop kit, follow the manufacturer's instructions.

Margarita Ice Pops

Makes about
2¼ cups (550 mL)
6 to 9 ice pops

This frozen Margarita is a true classic.

Tip

Always use freshly squeezed lemon juice or lime juice in your ice pops; bottled just doesn't compare.

1⅓ cups	water	325 mL
¼ cup	granulated sugar	60 mL
2	strips (each ½ by 2 inches/ 1 by 5 cm) lime zest	2
Pinch	salt	Pinch
⅔ cup	freshly squeezed lime juice	150 mL
3 tbsp	gold or white tequila	45 mL
1½ tbsp	orange liqueur, such as Cointreau or Triple Sec	22 mL

1. In a small saucepan, combine water, sugar, lime zest and salt. Bring to a boil, reduce heat and simmer for 2 minutes. Pour into a measuring cup and set aside to cool. Discard lime zest. Stir in lime juice, tequila and liqueur.

2. Pour into molds and freeze until slushy, then insert sticks and freeze until solid, for at least 4 hours or preferably overnight. If you are using an ice pop kit, follow the manufacturer's instructions.

Tequila Sunrise Ice Pops

**Makes about
2¼ cups (550 mL)
6 to 9 ice pops**

**Grenadine syrup
mimics the red flash of
emerging sunlight in
these delicious ice pops.**

Tip

Grenadine syrup is a
clear red syrup originally
made from pomegranates
(*grenades* in French)
and now often from a
combination of red fruit
flavorings. Look for it in
well-stocked supermarkets
or liquor stores.

½ tsp	finely grated lime zest	2 mL
3 tbsp	granulated sugar	45 mL
3 tbsp	water	45 mL
1½ cups	orange juice	375 mL
3 tbsp	freshly squeezed lime juice	45 mL
3 tbsp	gold or white tequila	45 mL
2 tbsp	grenadine syrup (approx.)	30 mL

1. In a small saucepan, bring lime zest, sugar and water to a boil. Reduce heat and simmer for 2 minutes. Pour into a large measuring cup and set aside to cool. Whisk in orange juice, lime juice and tequila.

2. Pour about 1 tsp (5 mL) grenadine into each ice pop mold. Very slowly and gently, pour orange mixture down the side into molds. Freeze until slushy, then insert sticks and freeze until solid, for at least 4 hours or preferably overnight. If you are using an ice pop kit, follow the manufacturer's instructions.

Paloma Ice Pops

Makes about 2¼ cups (550 mL) 6 to 9 ice pops

Mexico's second-favorite tequila cocktail freezes with amazing success.

1 cup	water	250 mL
¼ cup	granulated sugar	60 mL
2	strips (each ½ by 2 inches/ 1 by 5 cm) lime zest	2
Pinch	salt	Pinch
1 cup	grapefruit juice	250 mL
2 tbsp	freshly squeezed lime juice	30 mL
¼ cup	white or gold tequila	60 mL

1. In a small saucepan, combine water, sugar, lime zest and salt. Bring to a boil, reduce heat and simmer for 2 minutes. Pour into a measuring cup and set aside to cool. Discard lime zest. Stir in grapefruit juice, lime juice and tequila.

2. Pour into molds and freeze until slushy, then insert sticks and freeze until solid, for at least 4 hours or preferably overnight. If you are using an ice pop kit, follow the manufacturer's instructions.

Mint Julep Ice Pops

Makes about 2¼ cups (550 mL) 6 to 9 ice pops

As a nod to tradition, you could replace the usual wooden sticks with silver spoons for these sweet frozen versions of the classic Kentucky cocktail, which is customarily served in a silver cup.

2 cups	water	500 mL
¾ cup	granulated sugar	175 mL
1 cup	lightly packed mint leaves (preferably spearmint)	250 mL
¼ cup	bourbon	60 mL
2 tbsp	freshly squeezed lemon juice	30 mL

1. In a saucepan, bring water and sugar to a boil, stirring until sugar is dissolved. Add mint and remove from heat. Cover and set aside to steep for 10 minutes.

2. Strain into a large measuring cup and set aside to cool. Stir in bourbon and lemon juice.

3. Pour into molds and freeze until slushy, then insert sticks and freeze until solid, for at least 4 hours or preferably overnight. If you are using an ice pop kit, follow the manufacturer's instructions.

Whiskey Sweet-and-Sour Ice Pops

Makes about
2¼ cups (550 mL)
6 to 9 ice pops

Another classic American cocktail, the Whiskey Sour is a natural base for an ice pop. It just needed to be sweetened up a bit.

Tips

Freshly squeezed orange juice is always best, but you can also use juice from cartons or from concentrate. In this recipe, if you do not have enough after juicing the zested orange, top off the quantity with prepared juice.

Always use freshly squeezed lemon juice or lime juice in your ice pops; bottled just doesn't compare.

● Fine-mesh sieve

¼ cup	granulated sugar	60 mL
1 tsp	finely grated lemon zest	5 mL
¼ cup	boiling water	60 mL
1 cup	orange juice (see Tips, left)	250 mL
⅔ cup	freshly squeezed lemon juice (see Tips, left)	150 mL
¼ cup	Canadian or American whiskey or bourbon	60 mL
6 to 9	maraschino cherries, stems removed	6 to 9

1. In a small bowl, mix together sugar and lemon zest, rubbing together with the back of a spoon to muddle. Add water, stirring until sugar is dissolved.

2. Place sieve over a large measuring cup and strain. Stir in orange juice, lemon juice and whiskey of choice.

3. Drop one cherry into each ice pop mold. Pour whiskey mixture into molds and freeze until slushy, then insert sticks and freeze until solid, for at least 4 hours or preferably overnight. If you are using an ice pop kit, follow the manufacturer's instructions.

Ginger Rye Ice Pops

**Makes about
2¼ cups (550 mL)
6 to 9 ice pops**

Rye whisky and ginger
ale is a Canadian
favorite. This "ginger
and rye" cocktail
version in ice pop form
has a bit more ginger
bite.

- Fine-mesh sieve

2 cups	water	500 mL
½ cup	granulated sugar	125 mL
2 tbsp	finely grated gingerroot	30 mL
½ tsp	finely grated lime zest	2 mL
¼ cup	Canadian or American rye whiskey	60 mL
2 tbsp	freshly squeezed lime juice	30 mL

1. In a saucepan, combine water, sugar, ginger and lime zest. Bring to a boil, reduce heat and simmer for 3 minutes. Strain through sieve placed over a large measuring cup and set aside to cool. Stir in whiskey and lime juice.

2. Pour into molds and freeze until slushy, then insert sticks and freeze until solid, for at least 4 hours or preferably overnight. If you are using an ice pop kit, follow the manufacturer's instructions.

Red Greyhound Ice Pops

**Makes about
2 cups (500 mL)
6 to 8 ice pops**

Vodka and grapefruit
juice make a classic
Florida cocktail known
as the Greyhound. Here
I've used gin instead
of vodka and added
a blush of red with
grenadine and sweet
vermouth.

1¾ cups	red grapefruit juice	425 mL
3 tbsp	gin	45 mL
2 tbsp	red (sweet) vermouth	30 mL
1½ tbsp	grenadine syrup	22 mL

1. In a measuring cup, stir together grapefruit juice, gin, vermouth and grenadine.

2. Pour into molds and freeze until slushy, then insert sticks and freeze until solid, for at least 4 hours or preferably overnight. If you are using an ice pop kit, follow the manufacturer's instructions.

Pink Gin Lemonade Ice Pops

Makes about 2¼ cups (550 mL) 6 to 9 ice pops

In my mind, Pink Gin brings up the image of an old (British) gentleman seated in a leather chair sipping a warm cocktail. Here is a much-needed update.

Tip

Always use freshly squeezed lemon juice or lime juice in your ice pops; bottled just doesn't compare.

1½ cups	water, divided	375 mL
¼ cup	granulated sugar	60 mL
½ tsp	finely grated lemon zest	2 mL
⅓ cup	freshly squeezed lemon juice	75 mL
3 tbsp	gin	45 mL
1½ tbsp	grenadine syrup	22 ml
¼ tsp	angostura bitters (approx.)	1 mL

1. In a small saucepan, combine ¼ cup (60 mL) water, sugar and lemon zest. Bring to a boil, stirring until sugar is dissolved. Reduce heat and simmer for 2 minutes. Pour into a large measuring cup and set aside to cool.

2. Add remaining 1¼ cups (300 mL) water, gin, grenadine and a generous ¼ tsp (1 mL) bitters to reserved syrup. Stir well.

3. Pour into molds and freeze until slushy, then insert sticks and freeze until solid, for at least 4 hours or preferably overnight. If you are using an ice pop kit, follow the manufacturer's instructions.

White Russian Ice Pops

**Makes about
2 cups (500 mL)
6 to 8 ice pops**

The coffee in this ice pop is a wake-me-up, while the vodka and brandy make a settle-me-down combination.

1¼ cups	milk	300 mL
⅓ cup	sweetened condensed milk	75 mL
⅓ cup	espresso or strong coffee	75 mL
2 tbsp	vodka	30 mL
1 tbsp	brandy or amber rum	15 mL
½ tsp	vanilla extract	2 mL

1. In a large measuring cup, whisk together milk, condensed milk, espresso, vodka, brandy and vanilla.

2. Pour into molds and freeze until slushy, then insert sticks and freeze until solid, for at least 4 hours or preferably overnight. If you are using an ice pop kit, follow the manufacturer's instructions.

Brandy Alexander Ice Pops

**Makes about
2 cups (500 mL)
6 to 9 ice pops**

These extremely rich ice pops are decidedly for after-dinner entertaining.

Tip

These ice pops have slightly more of a kick than most of the others in this chapter, which means they will freeze a little less solidly. Don't let them stay out of the freezer for too long before serving.

1½ cups	table (18%) or half-and-half (10%) cream	375 mL
¼ tsp	nutmeg	1 mL
1½ oz	semisweet chocolate, chopped	45 g
⅓ cup	sweetened condensed milk	75 mL
3 tbsp	brandy	45 mL

1. In a saucepan, bring cream and nutmeg just to a boil. Remove from heat and whisk in chocolate until thoroughly incorporated. Transfer to a measuring cup and set aside to cool. Whisk in condensed milk and brandy.

2. Pour into molds and freeze until slushy, then insert sticks and freeze until solid, for at least 4 hours or preferably overnight. If you are using an ice pop kit, follow the manufacturer's instructions.

Strawberry Sangria Ice Pops

Makes about
3 cups (750 mL)
9 to 12 ice pops

This bright, summery take on sangria makes a lovely ice pop.

Tip

In many ice pops that include solid ingredients or combine liquids of different viscosities, there is a bit of layering after freezing, which is normal. However, if you want a seamless result, give the mixture a stir after it has reached the slushy stage to ensure that the ingredients remain integrated.

- Blender

½ cup	water	125 mL
⅓ cup	granulated sugar	75 mL
3	strips (each ½ by 2 inches/ 1 by 5 cm) lemon zest	3
2 cups	halved hulled strawberries	500 mL
1 cup	rosé wine	250 mL
3 tbsp	freshly squeezed lemon juice	45 mL
2 tbsp	brandy	30 mL

1. In a small saucepan, bring water, sugar and lemon zest to a boil, stirring until sugar is dissolved. Reduce heat and simmer for 3 minutes. Remove from heat and set aside to cool. Discard zest.

2. In blender, purée strawberries, wine, lemon juice and brandy. Stir in reserved sugar syrup.

3. Pour into molds and freeze until slushy, then insert sticks and freeze until solid, for at least 4 hours or preferably overnight. If you are using an ice pop kit, follow the manufacturer's instructions.

Sangria Ice Pops

**Makes about
3 cups (750 mL)
9 to 12 ice pops**

Sangria, with its
abundant fruit flavors,
makes a natural ice pop.

Tip

Use a red wine that is
unoaked (not aged in
wooden barrels) or, at the
most, only lightly oak-aged.
The tannins from oak would
be too strong with all the
other flavorings.

⅓ cup	granulated sugar	75 mL
⅓ cup	unsweetened apple juice	75 mL
3	strips (each ½ by 2 inches/ 1 by 5 cm) orange zest	3
2	strips (each ½ by 2 inches/ 1 by 5 cm) lemon zest	2
2 cups	red wine (see Tip, left)	500 mL
½ cup	orange juice	125 mL
3 tbsp	freshly squeezed lemon juice	45 mL
2 tbsp	orange liqueur, such as Cointreau or Triple Sec	30 mL

1. In a small saucepan, combine sugar, apple juice and orange and lemon zest. Bring to a boil, stirring until sugar is dissolved. Reduce heat and simmer for 3 minutes. Pour into a large measuring cup and set aside to cool.

2. Discard zest. Stir in wine, orange juice, lemon juice and liqueur.

3. Pour into molds and freeze until slushy, then insert sticks and freeze until solid, for at least 4 hours or preferably overnight. If you are using an ice pop kit, follow the manufacturer's instructions.

Frozen Glühwein Ice Pops

**Makes about
3 cups (750 mL)
9 to 12 ice pops**

**This frozen version
of a holiday mulled
wine punch would
perhaps best be
served at a "down-
under" (summertime)
Christmas party.**

Tip

Freshly squeezed orange
juice is always best, but
you can also use juice from
cartons or from concentrate.
In this recipe, if you do not
have enough after juicing the
orange, top off the quantity
with prepared juice.

2 cups	dry red wine	500 mL
⅔ cup	granulated sugar	150 mL
½ cup	water	125 mL
	Zest of 1 orange, cut into strips	
8	whole cloves	8
6	whole allspice	6
1	cinnamon stick, broken into a few pieces	1
1	whole star anise	1
½ cup	orange juice (see Tip, left)	125 mL
¼ tsp	almond extract	1 mL

1. In a saucepan, stir together wine, sugar and water until sugar is dissolved. Add cloves, allspice, cinnamon and star anise. Bring just to a simmer over medium-high heat, reduce heat to low and keep to just under a simmer for 15 minutes. Remove from heat, cover and set aside to steep for 1 hour.

2. Strain into a large measuring cup, discarding solids. Stir in orange juice and almond extract.

3. Pour into molds and freeze until slushy, then insert sticks and freeze until solid, for at least 4 hours or preferably overnight. If you are using an ice pop kit, follow the manufacturer's instructions.

Mulled Apple Cider Punch Ice Pops

**Makes about
3 cups (750 mL)
9 to 12 ice pops**

**Another frozen version
of a warm winter treat!**

3 cups	apple cider (non-alcoholic)	750 mL
3 tbsp	packed brown sugar	45 mL
1	small orange, thinly sliced	1
1	small lemon, thinly sliced	1
8	whole cloves	8
4	cardamom pods, crushed	4
1	cinnamon stick, crushed	1
¼ cup	amber or dark rum	60 mL

1. In a saucepan, combine cider, sugar, orange, lemon, cloves, cardamom and cinnamon. Bring just to a boil, stirring until sugar is dissolved. Reduce heat and simmer for 15 minutes. Remove from heat, cover and set aside to steep for 1 hour.

2. Uncover and set aside to cool completely. Strain, discarding solids. Stir in rum.

3. Pour into molds and freeze until slushy, then insert sticks and freeze until solid, for at least 4 hours or preferably overnight. If you are using an ice pop kit, follow the manufacturer's instructions.

Library and Archives Canada Cataloguing in Publication

Chase, Andrew
   200 best ice pop recipes / Andrew Chase.

Includes index.
ISBN 978-0-7788-0441-3

   1. Ice pops. 2. Cookbooks. I. Title. II. Title: Two hundred best ice pop recipes.

TX795.C43 2013   641.86'3   C2012-907497-7

Index